Language Hub

ADVANCED
Student's Book B

JEREMY DAY
GRAHAM SKERRITT

macmillan education

C1

Contents

Irregular Verbs

Infinitive	Past simple	Past participle
be	was/were	been
become	became	become
begin	began	begun
break	broke	broken
bring	brought	brought
build	built	built
buy	bought	bought
can	could	(been able to)
catch	caught	caught
choose	chose	chosen
come	came	come
cost	cost	cost
cut	cut	cut
drink	drank	drunk
eat	ate	eaten
fall	fell	fallen
feel	felt	felt
find	found	found
forget	forgot	forgotten
get	got	got
give	gave	given
go	went	gone/been
grow	grew	grown
have	had	had
hear	heard	heard
hit	hit	hit
hold	held	held
hurt	hurt	hurt
keep	kept	kept
know	knew	known
leave	left	left
lend	lent	lent
let	let	let

Infinitive	Past simple	Past participle
lose	lost	lost
make	made	made
mean	meant	meant
meet	met	met
must	had to	(had to)
pay	paid	paid
put	put	put
read	read **/red/**	read **/red/**
ride	rode	ridden
run	ran	run
say	said	said
see	saw	seen
sell	sold	sold
send	sent	sent
set	set	set
shut	shut	shut
sing	sang	sung
sit	sat	sat
sleep	slept	slept
speak	spoke	spoken
spell	spelt/spelled	spelt/spelled
spend	spent	spent
stand	stood	stood
steal	stole	stolen
take	took	taken
teach	taught	taught
tell	told	told
think	thought	thought
throw	threw	thrown
understand	understood	understood
wear	wore	worn
win	won	won
write	wrote	written

PHONETIC SYMBOLS											
Single vowels			Diphthongs			Consonants					
/ɪ/	f**i**sh	/fɪʃ/	/ɪə/	**ear**	/ɪə/	/p/	**p**en	/pen/	/s/	**s**nake	/sneɪk/
/iː/	b**ea**n	/biːn/	/eɪ/	f**a**ce	/feɪs/	/b/	**b**ag	/bæg/	/z/	**z**oo	/zuː/
/ʊ/	f**oo**t	/fʊt/	/ʊə/	t**ou**rist	/'tʊərɪst/	/t/	**t**ea	/tiː/	/ʃ/	**sh**op	/ʃɒp/
/uː/	sh**oe**	/ʃuː/	/ɔɪ/	b**oy**	/bɔɪ/	/d/	**d**og	/dɒg/	/ʒ/	televi**si**on	/'telɪvɪʒən/
/e/	**e**gg	/eg/	/əʊ/	n**o**se	/nəʊz/	/ʧ/	**ch**ip	/ʧɪp/	/m/	**m**ap	/mæp/
/ə/	moth**er**	/'mʌðə/	/eə/	h**air**	/heə/	/ʤ/	**j**azz	/ʤæz/	/n/	**n**ame	/neɪm/
/ɜː/	w**or**d	/wɜːd/	/aɪ/	**eye**	/aɪ/	/k/	**c**ake	/keɪk/	/ŋ/	ri**ng**	/rɪŋ/
/ɔː/	t**al**k	/tɔːk/	/aʊ/	m**ou**th	/maʊθ/	/g/	**g**irl	/gɜːl/	/h/	**h**ouse	/haʊs/
/æ/	b**a**ck	/bæk/				/f/	**f**ilm	/fɪlm/	/l/	**l**eg	/leg/
/ʌ/	b**u**s	/bʌs/				/v/	**v**erb	/vɜːb/	/r/	**r**oad	/rəʊd/
/ɑː/	**ar**m	/ɑːm/				/θ/	**th**ing	/θɪŋ/	/w/	**w**ant	/wɒnt/
/ɒ/	t**o**p	/tɒp/				/ð/	**th**ese	/ðiːz/	/j/	**y**es	/jes/

6 DISCOVERIES

Unearthing the past in Huara Rajada, Northern Peru.

> The real voyage of discovery consists not in seeking new landscapes, but in having new eyes.
>
> Marcel Proust

OBJECTIVES

- speculate and make deductions about the past
- plan an amazing journey
- discuss rewarding jobs
- give a presentation about someone you admire
- plan and perform an interview
- write an expository essay

Work with a partner. Discuss the questions.

1 Look at the picture. What do discoveries like this tell us? Are they important? Why/Why not?

2 Read the quote. What does Proust mean? Do you agree?

3 What do you think has been the greatest discovery ever? Give reasons for your answer.

6.1 Challenging journeys

- Speculate and make deductions about the past
- Plan an amazing journey

V – journeys and adventures; three-part phrasal verbs
P – showing your attitude
G – past modals of speculation and deduction
S – prediction strategies for reading

READING

A SPEAK Work in pairs. Do you know any famous explorers? What did they do?

B PREDICT Look at the title and the pictures in the article. Read the information in the box and answer questions a and b.

Prediction strategies for reading

Use the prediction cycle to help you predict the content of a text:

- Make predictions about the content of the text.
  - **a** What information will be included?
  - **b** What questions will it answer?
- Read part of the text to find out if your predictions were correct or not.
  - **c** Were your predictions correct?
  - **d** What information supported or challenged your predictions?

C SKIM Read *The disappearance of Percy Fawcett*. Answer questions c and d in the box in Exercise B.

D READ FOR DETAIL Complete the table with evidence for and against each theory in the article.

	For
1	
2	
3	
	Against
1	
2	
3	

E SPEAK Work in groups. Which theory do you think is the most likely explanation for what happened? Why?

THE DISAPPEARANCE OF PERCY FAWCETT

In the age of **long-haul** flights and travel **off the beaten track**, many now consider themselves seasoned **globetrotters**. However, there was a time when travelling to the far corners of the world was both dangerous and rare.

This was true in January 1925 when accomplished British explorer Percy Fawcett **embarked on** his latest expedition, hoping to find an ancient city in the jungle, the Lost City of Z.

Despite previous failed attempts to find it, he was still convinced that a large city that was 'more ancient than the oldest Egyptian discoveries' lay **at the heart of** the Amazon. On 20th April, his group departed from the Brazilian city of Cuiabá and headed for the jungle.

On 29th May, Fawcett sent a letter to his wife telling her that they were about to enter **uncharted territory**. They were never heard from again.

So what happened to Fawcett and his party? This remains one of the world's greatest unsolved mysteries and has inspired a lot of speculation. Here are three possible explanations.

1 THEY WERE KILLED BY INDIGENOUS PEOPLE

Some people believe that Fawcett and his companions must have been killed by an indigenous tribe. While journalist David Grann was retracing Fawcett's journey in 2005, he met with a tribe called the Kalapalo. They told him that they had heard stories from their grandparents about explorers coming to their territory and ignoring warnings not to walk through territory belonging to another tribe because this tribe were hostile to intruders. The Kalapalo tribe believe that it is highly likely Fawcett and his companions were killed by this other tribe. However, no bones have ever been found.

2 THEY DIED OF NATURAL CAUSES: EXHAUSTION, STARVATION OR ILLNESS

According to Henry Costin, a man who accompanied Fawcett on several of his previous expeditions, Fawcett was always friendly and respectful towards the tribes he met, so he can't have been killed by them.

Costin believed that there was a distinct possibility, given the scale of the expedition and the **impenetrable** terrain, that Fawcett and his companions died from exhaustion, or lack of food when their **provisions** ran out. Alternatively, given that several explorers at the time died from tropical diseases, they may well have succumbed to illness in the jungle.

3 THEY STAYED IN THE JUNGLE

After studying Fawcett's private papers, television director Misha Williams came up with an alternative theory. She believed that Fawcett had become disillusioned with life in Europe and may have decided to establish a commune in the jungle and live a simpler life.

However, many people point out that this theory doesn't make a lot of sense, because Fawcett had a wife and two children, so he couldn't have deliberately abandoned them. Similarly, he could have found the Lost City of Z and decided to stay. In recent years, archaeological discoveries have shown that Fawcett might have been right after all.

Researchers have found the ruins of huge cities in the Amazon that may well have been home to thousands of people. Did he finally find what he was looking for?

Glossary

disillusioned (adj) disappointed because you have discovered that someone or something is not as good as you had believed

starvation (n) a situation in which a person or animal suffers or dies because they do not have enough to eat

succumb (v) to become very sick or to die from a disease

intruder (n) someone who enters a place where they are not allowed to go

retrace (v) to go along the same path or route that someone else has gone along previously

seasoned (adj) experienced in a particular activity or job

VOCABULARY

Journeys and adventures

A Scan the article again. Complete the definitions with the words in bold.

1 ________________ (n) supply of food, drink, equipment, etc for a journey
2 ________________ (adj) impossible to move through or enter
3 ________________ (v) begin
4 ________________ (n phr) places not covered by maps
5 ________________ (n) middle of
6 ________________ (n) frequent international travellers
7 ________________ (adj) long distance
8 ________________ (phr) away from frequently visited places

B Go to the Vocabulary Hub on page XVI.

C SPEAK Work in pairs. Tell your partner about an adventurous journey you've been on or heard about.

GRAMMAR

Past modals of speculation and deduction

A Look at the underlined sentences in the article. Complete the rules with the words in the box.

adjective adverb can't/couldn't could/might/may may well must

Past modals of speculation and deduction

1 We use ________________ + *have* + past participle for things we believe logically happened.
2 We use ________________ + *have* + past participle for things we think are likely to have happened.
3 We use ________________ + *have* + past participle for things we think possibly happened.
4 We use ________________ + *have* + past participle to say something was not logically possible.
5 We can use phrases that start with *There's a/an* + ________________ + noun + (*that*) … to speculate.
6 We can use phrases that start with *It's* + ________________ + adjective (*that*) … to speculate.

B Go to the Grammar Hub on page VI.

C SPEAK Work in pairs. Discuss these theories about Percy Fawcett's disappearance.

1 They were attacked by wild animals.
2 Rival explorers killed them.
3 They were killed by a natural disaster.
4 They decided to join one of the tribes.

SPEAKING

A DISCUSS Work in small groups. Group A – go to the Communication Hub on page XXI. Group B – go to the Communication Hub on page XXIII.

B PRESENT Work with someone from the other group. Tell them about the historical mystery you read about.

VOCABULARY

Three-part phrasal verbs

A Work in pairs. Read *Seven reasons to go travelling*. Discuss which you think is the best reason to go travelling.

B Find nine three-part phrasal verbs in the article. Use the information in the box to help you.

1 ________________
2 ________________
3 ________________
4 ________________
5 ________________
6 ________________
7 ________________
8 ________________
9 ________________

Three-part phrasal verbs

Phrasal verbs are common in informal English.

Most phrasal verbs only have two parts (for example, *sit down*, *turn up*). However, there are also three-part phrasal verbs which contain a verb + a particle + a preposition (for example, *look up to*).

C Choose the correct options to complete the rules. Use the examples in Exercise B to help you decide.

1 Most three-part phrasal verbs are ***separable / inseparable***.
2 The particle and the preposition ***can / can't*** be separated.
3 Some three-part phrasal verbs can take an object after the ***verb / particle***.

D Complete the sentences with a three-part phrasal verb from Exercise B. Use the hint in brackets to help you.

1 It's important to ________________ (*research*) a place before you visit it.
2 If you ________________ (*experience*) problems on a trip, it makes it more of an adventure.
3 ________________ (*moving away from*) the crowds is more interesting than going sightseeing.
4 I don't think I ________________ (*be interested in*) travelling to another country by myself.
5 I ________________ (*remember*) my childhood holidays with fondness.
6 Travel is a great way to help people to ________________ (*stop thinking about*) work or study.
7 You should always ________________ (*review and practise*) your language skills before a trip.
8 You should always pack in advance rather than only ________________ (*eventually do*) it the night before you leave.

E Work in pairs. Discuss whether you agree or disagree with the sentences in Exercise D.

F SPEAK Work in small groups. Which reasons from the article do you think are the most worthwhile? Why? Think of three more reasons to go travelling.

Seven reasons TO GO TRAVELLING

1 Because you are up for an adventure. Challenge yourself with something that pushes you outside your comfort zone. See how you react when you come up against obstacles.

2 Because you want to find out about the world. You can read about different countries and cultures, but nothing compares to being there and seeing it for yourself.

3 Because you want to learn the language. If you really want to brush up on your language skills, you need to travel to where the language is spoken.

4 Because you want to learn about yourself. Getting away from home and work means you have time to reflect on your life and decide if you want to make any changes.

5 Because you need to recharge your batteries. If you find it hard to keep yourself away from work, travelling can help you unplug from all the things you need to do and get some well-earned rest.

6 Because you want to celebrate a special occasion with friends or family. Travel can create precious memories that you can look back on together.

7 Because you always wanted to. Don't keep putting it off or you'll never get round to it!

LISTENING

A PREDICT Work in pairs. You are going to listen to a discussion about travel challenges on a radio programme. What do you think a travel challenge is?

6.1 **B LISTEN FOR GIST** Listen to the radio programme. Answer the following questions.

1 What is a travel challenge?

____

2 How many examples of travel challenges does Kyle give?

____

3 What reasons other than to be different does Kyle give for people doing these challenges?

____

4 What does the presenter think you need to do a trip like Adam Leyton's?

____

5 What does Kyle admire about Daniel Tunnard?

____

6 What is Kyle's most vital piece of advice for someone doing a travel challenge?

____

6.1 **C LISTEN FOR DETAIL** Listen again. What is the significance of the following numbers?

1 24	______	5 41	______
2 12	______	6 140	______
3 22	______	7 14	______
4 900	______	8 55	______

D SPEAK Work in pairs. Discuss the questions.

1 Do you agree that these kinds of travel challenges are becoming more popular?
2 Which of the three travel challenges sounds the most interesting to you?
3 Would you donate money to help someone pay for their trip?
4 Would you rather go on a normal holiday or try a travel challenge?

PRONUNCIATION
Showing your attitude

6.2 **A** Listen to these extracts from the radio programme. Match each extract (1–4) with the speaker's attitudes to what they say (a–d).

a certain that what they say is true ___
b believes what they say is a generalisation or approximation ___
c believes that what they say is an important point ___
d unsure that something is true ___

6.3 **B** Work in pairs. Draw arrows to predict whether the intonation rises (↗), falls (↘) or fall-rises (↘↗) on the underlined attitude words. Then listen to check.

1 Allegedly, (___) you need to be very careful backpacking in some areas of that country.
2 On the whole, (___) I think it's better to travel alone than with a group of friends.
3 The question is, (___) have you got the luxury of taking time out from work.
4 Surely, (___) it can't be that much fun visiting a lot of countries in a short space of time.

C SPEAK Work in pairs. Discuss the questions using words, phrases and intonation to show your attitude.

1 Which countries would you like to visit and why?
2 Should people travel more within their own countries before they go abroad?
3 Do you think taking time out to go travelling can help your career?

SPEAKING HUB

A PREPARE Work in small groups. You have entered a competition to win sponsorship for a trip abroad. To win, you must come up with an original travel challenge. Think of an idea to enter into the competition and prepare to present this idea to your class. Think about:

- how you will travel.
- where you will travel.
- what your goal will be.
- what the budget will be.
- how you will publicise the trip.

B PRESENT Present your idea to the class. Listen to the other groups' ideas.

C DISCUSS Vote on the most interesting idea.

- Speculate and make deductions about the past
- Plan an amazing journey

6.2 Inquisitive minds

- Discuss rewarding jobs
- Give a presentation about someone you admire

G – *-ing* and infinitive forms
V – binomial expressions
P – pauses and pitch in presentations
S – taking notes while listening

READING

A SPEAK Work in pairs. Rank the following qualities in order of how important they are in journalism. Give reasons for your answer.

___ passion
___ courage
___ curiosity
___ determination
___ integrity

B READ FOR MAIN IDEA Read *Chase down your story*. What is the purpose of the article?

1 To give advice to journalism students.
2 To share life lessons which the writer has learnt from journalism.
3 To evaluate the importance of journalism in the 21st century.

C READ FOR DETAIL Read the article again. Match the questions (1–6) with the sections (a–d). Sections may be chosen more than once.

Which section of the article …

1 acknowledges a misconception the writer had? ___
2 highlights the difference between news in the past compared to now? ___
3 mentions an event which changed the writer's approach to learning? ___
4 describes a characteristic which the writer admires? ___
5 emphasises the importance of personal experience? ___
6 mentions discovering lessons by accident when looking for help? ___

D SPEAK Work in pairs. Discuss the questions.

1 Which do you think is the most useful piece of advice? Which do you think is the least useful? Why?
2 Have you ever learnt anything from work or study that you could apply to your personal life?

Chase down your story

a Finding stories

Ever wondered how journalists find the stories worth telling? Over my first year at a bona fide national newspaper, I learnt the hard way that getting the 'scoop' – being the first to report an exciting or important newsworthy story – was easier said than done. So I asked some of my more experienced colleagues to pass on their tricks of the trade. But what I soon discovered was that their advice could be applied not only to my job, but also to my personal life.

b Be curious

As journalists, we're paid to be curious. The number one suggestion I got was to have an inquisitive mind: figure out what matters, and which stories will inspire, move or make us laugh. It is not enough to report facts these days. But if something sparks your curiosity, the chances are other people will be interested, too.

There was the time I met a woman who mentioned she was thinking about moving to a remote Pacific island for a year. A whole year away from family, friends … the internet! I had so many questions – and it was no surprise it made a great story, too.

In every conversation I have now, I think about what I can ask and what I can learn. Everybody has something they can teach you. It also helps to ask yourself questions about your own life: Why am I doing what I'm doing? What do I hope to achieve?

c Local is global

Writers have a great imagination. But, as I learnt from my colleagues, that can sometimes have a downside. It can keep us looking towards the horizon, craving uncharted territory. Fresh out of university, I pictured myself jetting off to parts unknown to break the next big story. While there is much to be said for this, articles don't need to be exotic or even big news to catch a reader's attention. More often than not, we find that we write best when we write what we know. This second lesson is perhaps one of the hardest to learn as a new writer.

GRAMMAR

-ing and infinitive forms

A Choose the correct form of the verbs to complete the sentences.

1. She was thinking about ***moving*** / ***to move*** to a remote Pacific island for a year.
2. It is time to acknowledge how vital it is ***staying*** / ***to stay*** on course.
3. It's all too easy for details ***slipping*** / ***to slip*** through the cracks.
4. Articles don't need to be exotic ***catching*** / ***to catch*** a reader's attention.
5. It is not enough ***reporting*** / ***to report*** facts these days.
6. Ever wondered how journalists find the stories worth ***telling*** / ***to tell***?

B Scan the article again and check your answers to Exercise A.

Most of the greatest reporters have cut their teeth reporting on local news, whether that's uncovering home-grown corruption and injustice or just telling human-interest stories. What I've come to realise is that these stories often have a global reach because we have the same emotions, interests and concerns the world over. This has led me to believe – that whilst we must not be inward looking – appreciating what is right in front of us can be just as rewarding as looking further afield.

d *Follow up*

We are living in a world that is always on, where consumers can access massive amounts of content and expect instant gratification. In comparison to only five or ten years ago, we are so concerned with the beginning of the story that the middle and end have fallen by the wayside. It's all too easy for details to slip through the cracks and for stories, which should be huge, to be all but forgotten by the next news cycle.

And here lies the last tip, get to the conclusion of your story. Don't get distracted. Many of the finest journalists in history were renowned for their tenacity – their innate ability to chase down the facts in the face of seemingly indomitable odds.

This is a quality to aspire to in life. It is time to acknowledge how vital it is to stay on course, not to allow yourself to be side-tracked by modern distractions and the illusion of endless choice. See things through to their conclusion: whether that's the project you're working on or the sport you're learning. And it applies to people too – valuing and caring for the friends and networks you have is as important as growing them.

Glossary

cut your teeth on sth (phr) to get your first experience in a particular job by doing something

tenacity (n) the behaviour of being very determined and unwilling to stop when trying to achieve something

C Match the examples in Exercise A to the rules in the box.

-ing and infinitive forms

We use the *-ing* form:

- **a** after prepositions ______
- **b** after expressions such as *it's no good …*, *it's not worth …*, *there's no point in …*, *have a good time/difficulty/fun/problems …* ______

We use *to* + infinitive:

- **c** after adjectives ______
- **d** after nouns ______
- **e** after quantifiers ______
- **f** after the word *time* ______

D Go to the Grammar Hub on page VI.

SPEAKING

Work in pairs. Look at the pictures of people with different jobs below.

Student A: Compare the two pictures. Say what qualities and skills people need for these jobs and why people choose to do these jobs.

Student B: Which job would you most like to do and why?

LISTENING

A PREDICT Work in pairs. Look at the infographic of events in a famous inventor's life. Can you guess who it is?

B Read the information in the box and look at the notes table.

Taking notes while listening

When you need to take effective notes, you can use the Cornell system. It involves the following five stages:

Stage 1 Notes: Write notes in the note-taking column. Focus on main ideas. Use bullet points and abbreviations.

Stage 2 Questions: Write questions about your notes in the column on the left. (e.g. *Is this still true today?, What does inhalation mean?*)

Stage 3 Summarise: Read your notes and questions. Then write a summary of what you learnt.

Stage 4 Reflect: Think about what you have written. (e.g. *Overall, do you agree with the speaker?*)

Stage 5 Review and recall: Review your notes. Cover the second column and answer the questions in the first.

6.4 **C LISTEN TO MAKE NOTES** Listen to a presentation about an inventor. Follow the method in Stage 1 in the box. Make notes in the table as you listen.

Questions	Notes
Summary	

D REFLECT Read your notes. Follow Stage 2 in the box. Write questions in the table.

E SUMMARISE Follow Stage 3 from the box. Write a summary of your notes in the table. Use the questions in the box to help you.

F REVIEW Compare your notes and questions with your partner. Are they similar? Can your partner answer any of your questions?

G SPEAK Work in pairs. If you were an inventor what type of invention would you focus on?

- inventions that save lives
- everyday products that fix common problems
- niche products for rich people

AN INVENTIVE LIFE

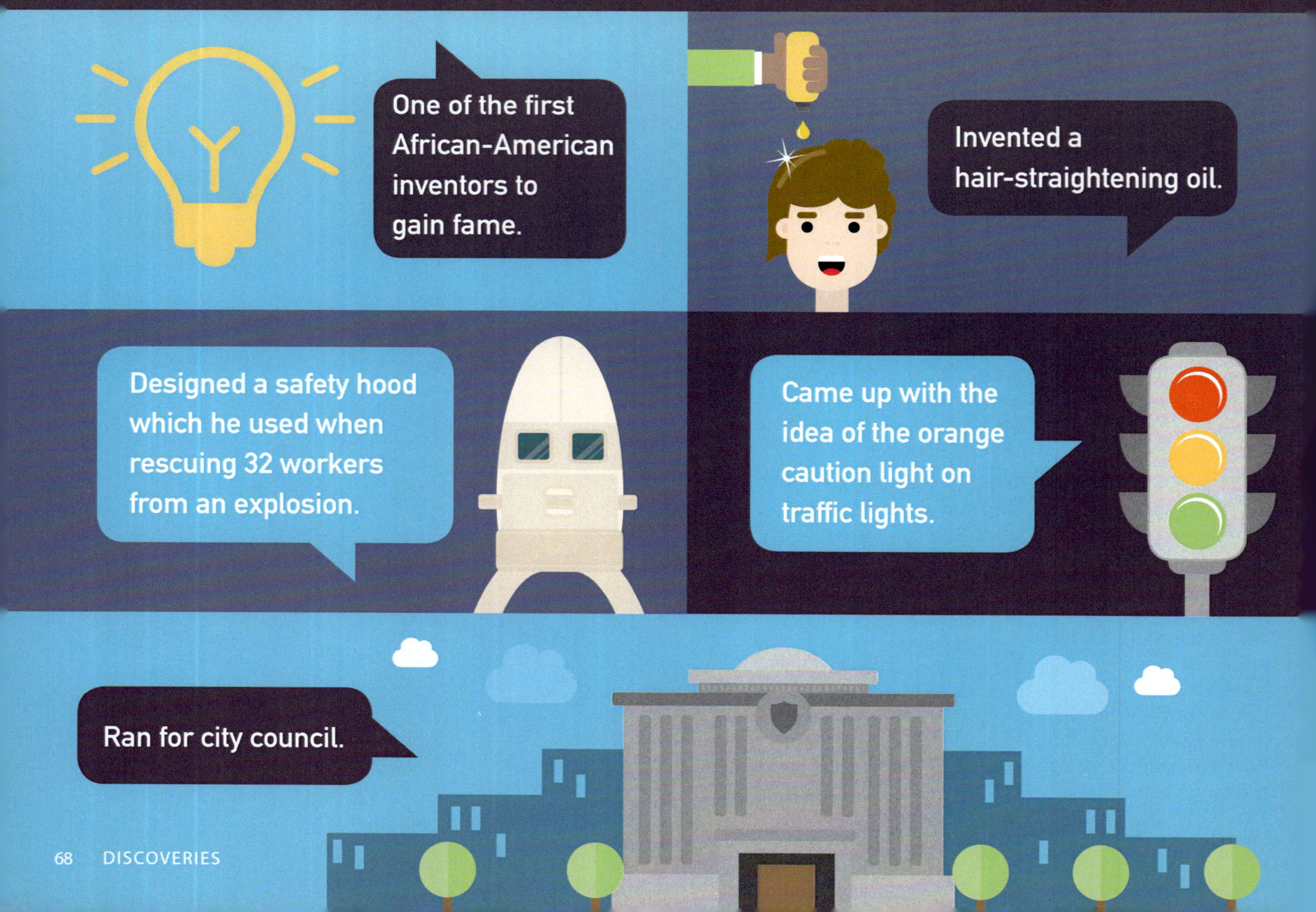

VOCABULARY
Binomial expressions

A **Match the binomials in bold (1–10) with their definitions (a–j). Use the information in the box to help you.**

Binomial expressions

A binomial expression is two words (nouns, verbs, adjectives or adverbs) joined by words like *and*, *or*, *but*, *by* and *to*.

The two words can:

- be antonyms (*give and take*)
- be synonyms (*peace and quiet*)
- use the same word twice (*back to back*)
- use words that start with the same sound (*black and blue*)
- use words that sound similar (*here and there*).

When a binomial expression is a compound adjective used before a noun it is generally hyphenated (a *happy-go-lucky* person).

1 In my opinion, he's **far and away** one of America's greatest inventors.
2 He was soon selling it **far and wide**.
3 It was truly a **life-or-death** situation.
4 Morgan and his brother Frank raced to the scene and went in **side by side**.
5 They soon re-emerged **safe and sound** with survivors.
6 Morgan's fame began to spread **slowly but surely**.
7 **By and large**, in the early 1920s, American roads were dangerous places.
8 **Time after time** there were stories of injuries and fatalities in traffic accidents.
9 But he also put his **heart and soul** into the community.
10 While his life was a classic **rags-to-riches** story.

a generally
b all of one's energy and passion
c repeatedly
d by a very large amount
e next to each other
f from poor to wealthy
g unharmed and not in danger
h in many different places
i potentially fatal
j gradually

B **Go to the Vocabulary Hub on page XVI.**

C SPEAK **Work in pairs. Complete the sentences with your own ideas. Then share your ideas with your partner.**

1 ______________ is **far and away** the greatest invention.
2 I always put my **heart and soul** into ______________.
3 When I was younger, I couldn't ______________. Then **slowly but surely**, I learnt how.

PRONUNCIATION
Pauses and pitch in presentations

6.5 **A** **Listen to the first part of the presentation again and mark any pauses with (/).**

Today, I'd like to talk about someone who I particularly admire. In my opinion, he's far and away one of America's greatest inventors. His innovations have fixed everyday problems but also probably saved thousands of lives. In addition, he was one of the first African-American inventors to gain public recognition for his work. His name was Garrett Morgan and he was a prolific inventor and entrepreneur who lived between 1877 and 1963. And while you may not all know his name, you're likely to have experienced his innovations.

One of Morgan's early successes was actually an accident. He was repairing a sewing machine in his shop when he noticed that some oil he was using had straightened the hairs on a cloth.

B **Work in pairs. Turn to the audioscript on page XXIX and practise reading the presentation about Garrett Morgan. Focus on pauses and pitch.**

SPEAKING HUB

A THINK **You are going to give a presentation about someone you admire. Choose someone who made a big difference to the world by:**

- leading social change
- challenging the status quo
- inventing or discovering something important.

B PREPARE **Write a short presentation to tell your classmates about this person. Focus on:**

- the life of the person you are talking about
- the main achievements of the person you are talking about
- a big problem the person solved.

C PRESENT **Give your presentation.**

D DISCUSS **Listen to your classmates' presentations. Which of the people do you want to learn more about? Why?**

Discuss rewarding jobs
Give a presentation about someone you admire

Café Hub

6.3 World of knowledge

Ⓐ engaging listeners Ⓢ conducting an interview

Connecting with nature

a

b

c

A Work in pairs. Look at the pictures (a–c) and discuss these questions.

1 What are they?

2 How might they be connected?

B ▶ Watch the video. Check your answers to Exercise A.

Glossary

assemble (v) to build something by joining parts together
countless (adj) very many
tangled (adj) twisted into an untidy mass
vaporise (v) to turn from a solid or liquid state into gas

C ▶ Watch the video again. Are the sentences true (T) or false (F) according to the video? Correct the false sentences.

1 An oak tree is made up of only carbon, nitrogen, oxygen and hydrogen. *T / F*

2 The carbon atom in the acorn was created inside a star billions of years ago. *T / F*

3 The carbon atom in the acorn has formed part of the earth for two billion years. *T / F*

4 The carbon atom in the acorn got into some ancient oak tree through the action of photosynthesis. *T / F*

5 In billions of years, when the sun dies and the earth is vaporised, all atoms will die. *T / F*

D ▶ Watch the video again. Complete the sentences.

1 When atoms react and ________________ they make up everything in the Universe.

2 Many different types of plants, trees and animals make up the ________________ of a woodland.

3 When you understand that everything is made of atoms, a woodland doesn't seem such a ________________ place.

4 An atom in an acorn has spent many years in ________________.

5 Life is only a ________________ home of the atoms that make up the universe.

AUTHENTIC ENGLISH

A Work in pairs. Read the sentence from the video and the information in the box. Which device has been used to engage listeners?

So life is just a temporary home for the immortal elements that build up the universe.

Engaging listeners

Brian Cox is a very engaging speaker. He uses a number of strategies to engage listeners.

- Summarising information, for example, *So, when you look at it like that it's really not that complicated at all.*
- Repetition of certain words such as *billions* to emphasise a point.
- Dynamic words such as *thrown back out* and *vaporise*.

B Go to the transcript on page XXII. Underline examples of the strategies from the box that Brian Cox uses to engage listeners.

C Write a short speech on a topic that you're passionate about. Use strategies to engage your listeners.

D Work in pairs. Read your speech to your partner. Try to be as engaging and passionate as possible.

SAM MALCOLM AMANDA HARRY EMILY

Getting answers

A Work in pairs. Discuss the questions.

1 Do you ever watch documentaries about science? Why/Why not?
2 Should we try to make science more accessible than it is now?
3 Are there any cons to simplifying science for a wider audience?
4 What is Malcolm doing?

B ▶ Watch the video. Were any of the things you discussed in Exercise A mentioned?

C ▶ Watch the video again. Complete the sentences with one to three words.

1 Amanda is interviewing Veronica about ______________.
2 Malcolm tells Sam that Veronica is one of the country's ______________.
3 Veronica says she saw Brian Cox ______________.
4 Since being inspired by Brian Cox, Veronica has been ______________.
5 Malcolm comments that Veronica's book is at the top of the ______________.

SPEAKING SKILL

A Work in pairs. Complete the line from the video. Why has Amanda asked her question in this way?

Professor Matos, ______________ respond to accusations that your book is under-researched?

B Look at the information in the box. Match the questions (1–5) with the types (a–e).

Conducting an interview

a **Direct questions** are asked in order to make a point about a situation or to point out something for consideration. For example, ___
b **Indirect questions** are used when we want to be more polite. We use an introductory phrase followed by the question itself in a positive sentence structure. For example, ___
c **Negative questions** can ask for confirmation of our opinions or make invitations or suggestions. For example, ___
d **Tag questions** can either be 'real' questions where we want to know the answer or simply ask for agreement when we already know the answer. For example, ___
e **Rhetorical questions** are often statements given in question format in order to make a point about a situation. For example, ___

1 Why don't you go over and introduce yourself?
2 It builds on some of the theories set out by Professor Brian Cox, doesn't it?
3 I hope you don't mind me asking, why did you decide to write a book?
4 Can I quote you on that?
5 Did I dumb down the science a bit for the masses?

C Work in pairs. Think of one more example for each of the question types (1–5) in Exercise B.

SPEAKING HUB

A PLAN Work in pairs. Student A: Imagine you are a journalist for a website. Look at the bullet points and prepare a list of questions to ask Veronica Matos.

Student B: Imagine you are Veronica Matos. You are going to be interviewed. Plan what you are going to say using the bullet points.

- when you first became interested in science
- your book
- your future career plans
- advice to young people

B DISCUSS Work in pairs. Perform your roleplay.

A: What advice would you give to teenagers who want a career in science?
B: Decide early which area of science you want to work in. There are hundreds and hundreds of different career paths.

Plan and perform an interview

➤ Turn to page XXIV to learn how to write an expository essay about space exploration.

Unit 6 Review

VOCABULARY

A Choose the correct words to complete the sentences.

1 Airlines keep introducing new long-haul flights to tempt today's *globetrotters* / *distance travellers*.

2 You *embargo* / *embark* from Santiago, Chile, to fly direct to Easter Island.

3 Fourteen of the world's highest *summits* / *culminations* are in the Himalayas.

4 It takes several hours of trekking through *ragged terraces* / *impenetrable terrain* to reach Waimea.

5 Manaus is the closest city to the *heart* / *heat* of the Amazon.

6 Siberia still has a lot of *unchartered* / *uncharted* territory.

7 You can quickly get off the beaten *track* / *road* in the outback in Australia.

B Complete the three-part phrasal verbs with the correct preposition.

1 I use language learning apps to **brush up** ________ my vocabulary.

2 I'd like to **find out** ________ volunteering.

3 Playing video games helps me **switch off** ________ the stress of the day.

4 I often **look back** ________ the holidays I took with my parents as a child.

5 I keep meaning to visit my grandparents, but I never **get round** ________ it.

6 I **am up** ________ a camping trip.

7 Whenever I suggest somewhere to go, my family **come up** ________ objections.

8 I don't like staycations. I want to **get away** ________ the area where I live for a holiday.

C Match numbers (1–10) to letters (a–j) to form full sentences.

1 I looked far and

2 She amazes me time after

3 Slowly but

4 She's far and

5 He always puts his heart and

6 They always work side by

7 It was a matter of life

8 It's a real rags-to-

9 By and

10 She returned safe and

a surely he taught himself how to do it.

b riches story, because he was born into a very poor family.

c soul into everything he does.

d wide, but I couldn't find it.

e large, I don't read biographies, but his story was fascinating.

f time with her ideas.

g away the most important scientist working today.

h side, which is really sweet.

i sound from her adventures.

j or death at one point, but he survived.

GRAMMAR

A Complete the text using *can't have, could have, couldn't have, may/might well have, might have, must have* and the verbs in brackets.

In 1900, three men mysteriously disappeared from the lighthouse where they were working on a remote island in Scotland. Initially, newspapers contained implausible explanations such as that they [1] ________________ (*kill*) by ghosts or they [2] ________________ (*capture*) by foreign spies. However, a later investigation concluded that they [3] ________________ (*not abduct*), because there were no signs of a struggle.

The investigation found a lot of damage had been done to one of the landing stages and that the kind of damage indicated that this [4] ________________ (*cause*) by large waves during a storm. Therefore, it's possible that the men were securing boxes on the landing stage in bad weather and the investigators believed that they [5] ________________ (*sweep*) into the sea by strong waves. Normally, one man should have stayed behind to man the lighthouse, but he [6] ________________ (*go*) to the landing stage to warn his colleagues of the approaching waves.

B Choose the correct words to complete the sentences. Then decide if you agree or disagree with each sentence.

1 In my country, schools have problems *encouraging* / *to encourage* children to study science.

2 It's not worth *studying* / *to study* the arts at school because it's not useful for work.

3 It's impossible *making* / *to make* history interesting for school children.

4 It's time *introducing* / *to introduce* more practical subjects into the school curriculum.

5 Schools need to teach computer programming *helping* / *to help* students get jobs in the future.

7 EXTREMES

Courage is resistance to fear, mastery of fear – not absence of fear.

Mark Twain

Stepping over the abyss in Mondsee, Austria.

OBJECTIVES

- describe reactions to extreme experiences
- describe extreme situations and achievements
- discuss extreme jobs
- deal with difficult interview questions
- tell a story about an exciting journey
- write a cover letter

Work with a partner. Discuss the questions.

1 Look at the picture. Why do people put themselves in extreme situations? When do you think this is a positive thing? When is it negative?

2 Look at the quote. How can we resist fear? Is it possible to master fear? Think of examples.

3 Do you prefer extreme experiences or safe/predictable ones? Why? What does it depend on?

7.1 Beyond the limits

- Describe reactions to extreme experiences
- Describe extreme situations and achievements

G – *it* clefting V – feelings P – intonation in question tags S – identifying causation

READING

A PREDICT **Work in pairs. Look at the picture. Discuss the questions.**

1 What do you think the story is going to be about?

2 Have you ever been somewhere like this? If so, how did you feel? If not, how do you think you would feel?

3 Why do you think some people choose to put themselves in dangerous situations?

B SKIM **Read *Into the abyss*. What different emotions does the writer go through on their journey? Were any the same as your answers to Exercise A?**

C READ FOR DETAIL **Read *Into the abyss again*. Six sentences have been removed from the story. Choose from the sentences (a–g) the one which fits each gap. There is one extra sentence which you do not need to use.**

a It was his lack of words that finally allowed me to shake off the morning's nerves.

b It was myself who I was really trying to convince.

c It was that murky half-light, before the night gives in to the dawn, which I now watched.

d It is hard to describe moments like these.

e It is in situations like this that it occurs to me how often I put my life in the hands of complete strangers.

f It was reaching the summit that was my ultimate goal.

g It was just as Batsal disappeared over a rise that I lost my footing.

D INFER MEANING **Work in pairs. Decide which of the words in bold from the story match the meanings (1–5).**

1 ________________ (n) fear of something bad that might happen or that is going to happen

2 ________________ (n) a feeling of sadness and of being without hope

3 ________________ (n) a feeling of extreme excitement and happiness

4 ________________ (adj) relaxed and pleasant because shared with friends or friendly people

5 ________________ (adj) very serious, and not smiling or friendly

E SPEAK **Work in groups. Think of a time when you felt one of the emotions from Exercise D. Tell your group about your experience. Mention the following points.**

- when you felt this way
- the reason(s) for feeling the emotion

GRAMMAR

it clefting

A Find a sentence in Reading Exercise C that means the same as the one below. What is different about the version in the article? What is the focus in each sentence? Use the information in the box to help you.

I was really trying to convince myself.

> ***it* clefting**
>
> We can use *it* clefting to focus attention on part of a sentence (e.g. the subject, an object, a time clause, a *because*-clause, *to* + infinitive, etc).
>
> *My ultimate goal was reaching the summit.* → *It was reaching the summit that was my ultimate goal.*

B Rewrite the remaining sentences in Reading Exercise C so they don't use *it* clefting.

a ________________

b *I was really trying to convince myself.*

c ________________

d ________________

e ________________

f *My ultimate goal was reaching the summit.*

g ________________

C Go to the Grammar Hub on page VIII.

D SPEAK **Work in pairs and complete the sentences so they are true for you.**

1 It was because I wanted to … that I …

2 It's not … that's important …

3 It wasn't until …

SPEAKING

DISCUSS **Work in pairs. Can you think of a time when you felt a mix of emotions? Use the questions to help you.**

1 What was the situation?

2 How did you feel?

3 What happened?

INTO THE ABYSS

1 ___ I had arrived early at the café and now sat waiting at a formica table, tentatively sipping the strongest coffee I had ever tasted. The bitterness was cloying, my hands shaking, but a 6 am start meant that rocket fuel was what I needed. The front door burst open, my coffee spilling across the table. The light struggling through the smeared glass door was blocked out by the silhouette of a man. He paused there in the doorway for a second. Though I couldn't see his face, I knew he was watching me.

He crossed the café in two strides. A weathered face forced itself into a half smile. 'Carla?' 'Yes. Batsal?'. A curt nod and then, 'If we are going, we go now, before the weather turns.'

I shouldered my pack and we set off down the pot-holed street beneath the shuttered-up houses and the tangle of electricity cables dangling menacingly low above us. 'Where is everyone?' He gestured a few metres ahead where a teenage boy was struggling to kick-start a motorbike, way past its prime, into life. The boy, who was almost certainly Batsal's son, glanced at me shyly and stepped aside as his father took hold of the bike. With a swift movement the engine roared. Batsal jerked his head at the seat behind him.

We were off. Hurtling down the road and then out towards the distant mountains. 2 ___ I've been conned, ripped off and outright robbed during my travels even by friendly-faced guides. Batsal was different though … I found his **dour** demeanour weirdly reassuring. 3 ___

Perhaps I was feeling too calm as we set off on foot up a narrow trail. My mind didn't dwell on the terrifying exposure of the route or the crevasses that seemed to plunge down into the depths of the earth. Instead I let my gaze calmly return to the untouched snow of the peaks which glistened in the low sun. We climbed in **companionable** silence for an hour or so. Up and over some boulders the size of cars.

4 ___ A small lapse in concentration. I found myself on my back skidding towards the edge. The boulder felt smooth. I watched in panic as my hands and feet flailed, trying to get purchase on something, anything. My legs were disappearing into the abyss. I thought of my family. Then time slowed, my focus narrowed and I gripped the rock. As I held on I found myself in a place I'd never been, somewhere between **dread** and calm.

A searing pain jolted through me as I was yanked by my arm. I twisted my neck to see Batsal retreating up the boulder, dragging me behind him like a rag doll. He pulled me to my feet. The question in his eyes. 'I can carry on,' I replied. 5 ___ And my shoulder throbbed in protest.

We scrambled upwards for five more hours over loose shale. The air was thinning out – every breath was laboured. But something of that strange calmness remained. When we reached a ledge, we stopped. I looked again over at the peaks that seemed no closer than they had at sunrise. 'OK, but let me see it properly before we turn back.' With one last effort I pulled myself up onto the ridge above the ledge and looked out over the perfect vista. 6 ___ The sheer **exhilaration** but also **melancholy** of a journey's end. After ten minutes, we began our descent. My heart thumping.

Glossary

gesture (v) a movement that communicates a feeling or instruction

skid (v) to slide across the ground in an uncontrolled way

weathered (adj) appearance changed because of the effects of wind, rain, etc

VOCABULARY

Feelings

A **Match the quotes (1–10) with the adjectives in the box. How do the people feel?**

courageous	devastated	disgusted	frustrated	grumpy
humbled	hysterical	indifferent	resilient	superior

1 'I feel bad because there's nothing I can do about my situation.' __________
2 'I was overwhelmed by our local community's kindness and generosity.' __________
3 'I lost control of my emotions and started shaking and crying.' __________
4 'I feel terrible because I've lost all hope.' __________
5 'When I'm in a bad mood, I'm not very nice to other people.' __________
6 'You can do what you like. I really don't mind.' __________
7 'When other people do stupid things, it makes me feel better about myself!' __________
8 'I know it's dangerous, but I won't let my fear stop me.' __________
9 'When things go wrong, I just have to pick myself up and carry on.' __________
10 'I'm so angry! It makes me feel sick.' __________

B Go to the Vocabulary Hub on page XVII.

C SPEAK **Work in pairs. Think of examples of situations where people feel the ten emotions in Exercise A. Share your ideas with the class.**

LISTENING

A SPEAK **Work in pairs and discuss the questions.**

1 What morning TV programmes are there in your country?
2 What type of news stories are discussed on them?

7.1 **B** LISTEN FOR SPECIFIC INFORMATION **Listen to part of a TV programme, *the Breakfast Show*. Decide if the statements are true (T), false (F) or not given (NG).**

1 Arjun didn't see the accident happening. ___
2 The other driver helped Arjun to move the car. ___
3 The car that Arjun lifted weighed over 1500 kg. ___
4 Professor Ivănescu thinks Arjun has extremely unusual powers. ___
5 Tony (the presenter) doesn't think he'd ever be able to lift the car. ___
6 Arjun used hysterical strength. ___
7 Whenever our muscles hurt, it means we're damaging them. ___
8 The cyclist suffered permanent injuries. ___

7.1 **C** LISTEN FOR CAUSATION **Listen again. Which pairs of events are examples of correlation (a)? Which are examples of causation (b)? Use the information in the box to help you.**

Identifying causation

It's important to distinguish between ***correlation*** (= two or more things happen at about the same time) and ***causation*** (= one thing causes another thing to happen).
Common ways of signalling causation include:

- linking expressions (e.g. *as a result of, due to, thanks to, that's why*).
- conditionals (e.g. *If X hadn't happened, Y might not have happened*).
- past perfect in time clauses (e.g. *After I'd done X, Y happened*) rather than past simple (e.g. *After I did X, Y happened*).

1 Arjun wasn't paying attention to the other vehicles. The car ran over a bicycle. *a / b*
2 The driver freed the cyclist. Arjun put the car down. *a / b*
3 They used a mobile phone. A spark caused the car to explode. *a / b*
4 Arjun was brave. The cyclist wasn't seriously injured. *a / b*
5 Arjun's back hurts now. He lifted the car. *a / b*
6 Tony was unable to lift the car. His muscles hurt. *a / b*
7 The adrenaline wore off. Arjun felt extreme pain. *a / b*
8 Athletes feel stressed. They can break world records. *a / b*
9 The cyclist survived. She spent a few weeks in hospital. *a / b*

D SPEAK **Work in groups. Discuss the questions.**

1 How do you think you would react in an extreme situation like the one Arjun described?
2 Have you heard of any examples of people doing amazing things in extreme situations? What happened?

PRONUNCIATION

Intonation in question tags

7.2 **A** Complete the extracts from *The Breakfast Show* with the correct question tag. Then listen to check.

1 So the car could have exploded at any second, ________________?
2 I mean, you're a big guy, ________________?
3 It's weird, ________________?
4 I mean, a car weighs, what, a tonne and a half, ________________?
5 So that's what helped Arjun, then, ________________?
6 We can't harness this strength in everyday life, ________________?
7 I'm just a normal guy, ________________?
8 Anyway, let's have a break now, ________________?

7.2 **B** Listen again. Try to copy the intonation.

C SPEAK Work in small groups and discuss the extreme human abilities shown in pictures 1–5. Use question tags to ask questions, make suggestions, check assumptions and invite agreement.

Let's start with this one, shall we? It's bungee jumping, is it?

SPEAKING HUB

A PLAN You are going to conduct a daytime TV interview about examples of extreme achievements. Work in groups of three. Use pictures 1–5 to help you.

Student A: You are the **interviewee**. You can talk about a real experience from your life, or you can invent the details.

Student B: You are an **expert** (e.g. a university professor). You have been invited to explain Student A's abilities/achievements. You can use your real knowledge or invent details.

Student C: You are the **interviewer**. It's your job to make the interviewee and the expert feel comfortable, and to make the TV show entertaining for the audience at home.

B PRACTISE Practise your interview. Try to use the vocabulary, grammar and pronunciation from this lesson in your interviews.

C PRESENT Act out your interview for the class.

D REFLECT Which of the interviews was the most believable? Which was the most entertaining?

3

4

5

- Describe reactions to extreme experiences
- Describe extreme situations and achievements

7.2 Extreme jobs

- Discuss extreme jobs
- Deal with difficult interview questions

G – ***what* clefting and *all* clefting**
P – ***any* and *quite***
V – **polysemy; intensifiers**
S – **understanding reference within texts**

READING

A SPEAK Work in pairs. Look at the pictures. Why do people choose to work in such extreme places?

B READ FOR MAIN IDEA Read *Risky business*. Match the statements (1–6) with the workplaces (a–c).

1 It's dangerous if you go up too fast. ____
2 The weather may prevent you from working. ____
3 You'll need to work at least half a year. ____
4 You'll earn a lot of money. ____
5 It's hard to get a job there. ____
6 It takes over a week to get home. ____

a The Antarctic
b At extreme heights
c Under the ocean

C READ FOR REFERENCES What do the reference devices (1–10) in the article refer to? Use the information in the box to help you.

1 ____________ 6 ____________
2 ____________ 7 ____________
3 ____________ 8 ____________
4 ____________ 9 ____________
5 ____________ 10 ____________

Understanding reference within texts

Reference devices (e.g. pronouns, articles, contrast linkers, comparatives) link different parts of a text.

Anaphoric reference: refers back to something mentioned earlier in the text.

Cataphoric reference: refers forward to something mentioned later in the text.

Exophoric reference: refers to things outside the text, e.g. *you* (the reader), *they* (people in general).

D SPEAK Work in pairs and discuss the questions. Do any of the jobs in the article appeal to you? Which would you hate?

RISKY BUSINESS

[1]They say over half of us are doing jobs that we don't care about, and a further 16% actively hate our jobs. If you're **sick** of the nine-to-five, here are some of the more extreme places where you can actually make a living.

ANTARCTICA

Unfortunately, it's not exactly easy – or cheap – to visit Antarctica as a tourist. So if you really want to go, what you should do is get a long-term job, not a holiday job: no employer is going to pay your airfare if you're planning to stay for less than six months.

There are scientific jobs for biologists, glaciologists, geologists, meteorologists, oceanologists, and so on. Trouble is, there's plenty of **competition** for them, with hundreds of applicants for each vacancy. Your best chance of **landing** [2]one is to be a well-qualified specialist already, ideally with a doctorate or two.

There are also a few support jobs for engineers, technicians, divers, radio operators, etc. Just be warned: you'll spend most of your time on the base, where you'll quickly get bored with the same faces every day. Due to the extreme weather, it's usually too dangerous (or too expensive) to venture out into the wilderness for some sightseeing.

AT EXTREME HEIGHTS

For [3]those of us who get dizzy at the thought of standing on a chair, the prospect of climbing up a radio mast, wind turbine or skyscraper is the stuff of our worst nightmares. But for [4]the lucky few who have no fear of heights, there are plenty of career opportunities.

[5]It's not especially glamorous, but the easiest way to make a career at heights is as a window cleaner. You can literally start at the bottom – all you'll need is a ladder and a bucket – and gradually work your way up to office blocks and skyscrapers.

A rather [6]more lucrative career for real-life 'high-climbers' is as a tower climber. These brave people spend their time 100 to 150 metres above the ground, inspecting cellular phone towers for damage, changing light bulbs, replacing cables, etc. One of the biggest challenges is that they need to work in all **conditions**, including the cold, the wind and the rain, all of which add to the level of danger. The [7]one exception is thunderstorms, which tower climbers steer well clear of.

ON THE OCEAN FLOOR

[8]It's one of the most bizarre careers imaginable. [9]These people do construction, maintenance and demolition work 300 metres or more beneath the ocean's surface. To survive the extreme **pressure** at such depths, they spend weeks or months at a time living in tiny pressurised containers, either deep underwater or inside pressure tanks on board ships. Welcome to the world of the saturation diver.

Breathing pressurised air causes inert gases to dissolve in your blood and body tissues. If you were to release the pressure suddenly, by coming to the surface, the bubbles formed would quickly kill you. To avoid this, saturation divers spend several hours building up to the necessary pressure, saturating their bodies with inert gases. At the end of their work, they spend as much as eleven days de-pressurising, before finally returning to normal life.

Saturation divers carry out essential work for some of the world's richest businesses, so [10]it's no surprise to find that they're extremely well-paid. However, before sending off your **application**, you need to consider how you'd feel about spending months in a tiny metal container with your co-workers, constantly aware that the failure of a single pressure valve would mean certain death.

Glossary

lucrative (adj) bringing a lot of money
venture (v) to go somewhere unpleasant, dangerous or exciting

VOCABULARY
Polysemy

A Choose the correct definition of the words in bold from *Risky business*. Use the context in the article and the information in the box to help you.

Polysemy

Polysemy is where a word has two or more related meanings. Sometimes different meanings have different grammatical properties (e.g. countable/uncountable).

1 sick
- **a** feel unwell
- **b** bored or tired of something

2 competition
- **a** rivalry
- **b** a contest

3 to land
- **a** bring a plane down
- **b** get something you want

4 condition(s)
- **a** weather
- **b** an important part of a contract

5 pressure
- **a** a feeling of too much work
- **b** a 'pushing' force

6 application
- **a** a way of using something
- **b** a document stating why you want a job

B In which pair of meanings from Exercise A is one meaning countable and the other uncountable? In which pair is one meaning always plural?

C Go to the Vocabulary Hub on page XVII.

GRAMMAR
what clefting and *all* clefting

A Complete the rules with examples from the article.

***what* clefting and *all* clefting**

Form: *what/all* + FIRST FOCUS + *is/was* + SECOND FOCUS

Example: *What you need to succeed is mental strength.*

We can use *what* clefting to focus attention on two different parts of a sentence by keeping them separate.

1 You should get a long-term job. → ________________

All clefting has the extra meaning of *only*.

2 You'll only need a ladder and bucket. → ________________

B Go to the Grammar Hub on page VIII.

SPEAKING

DISCUSS Work in pairs. Think about the advantages and disadvantages of the jobs in the article. Your partner is planning to apply for one of the jobs. Give your partner advice using *what* clefting and *all* clefting.

LISTENING

A SPEAK Work in pairs. Have you ever had a stressful job interview? What happened?

B Read *Extreme job interviews*. Rank the questions in order from hardest to easiest (1–7).

7.3 **C** LISTEN FOR DETAIL Listen to a recruitment specialist giving advice about the questions below. For each question, make notes on the dos and don'ts for job interviewees.

7.4 **D** LISTEN FOR GIST Now listen to some extracts from an interview for a job as a marketing designer. Does Oscar (the interviewee) follow the recruitment specialist's advice for each question?

EXTREME job interviews

These days, recruiters are going to extremes to sort the best from the rest. The following questions, all taken from real job interviews, have no correct answer. But they are designed to show how you cope with stress and how creative you are. They might also reveal the real 'you' behind the business suit and the polished CV.

- *What would you take with you to a desert island and why?*
- *If you could be any dinosaur, which dinosaur would you be?*
- *What's your biggest weakness?*
- *Name four uses for a stapler, without the staples.*
- *How many square metres of pizza are eaten in the US each year?*
- *What's the most interesting thing about you that we wouldn't learn from your CV?*
- *How would your worst enemy describe you?*

7.4 **E** LISTEN FOR DETAIL Listen again. Choose the correct options (a, b or c) to answer the questions.

1 How would Oscar feel on a desert island?
   a lonely   b inspired   c upset
2 What would be Oscar's priority as a dinosaur?
   a pleasure   b beauty   c safety
3 How does Oscar feel at the end of each day?
   a relieved   b disappointed   c exhausted
4 Which one of the following is NOT mentioned as a use for a stapler?
   a tissue-holder   b child's toy   c doorstop
5 How many pizzas does Oscar think a typical American eats each year?
   a 12   b 144   c 300
6 How does Oscar feel about looking after his brothers and sisters?
   a grateful   b frustrated   c proud
7 How does Oscar feel about people who don't like him?
   a grumpy   b indifferent   c superior

F SPEAK Work in pairs. Ask and answer the questions from *Extreme job interviews*.

VOCABULARY
Intensifiers

A **Complete the sentences from the interview with intensifiers in the box. Sometimes more than one answer is possible.**

altogether immensely noticeably outright practically radically relatively remarkably somewhat utterly

1 I find writing poetry ________ calming.
2 I'd be ________ devastated if I couldn't record my ideas on paper.
3 Compared to the ground, the sky would be a ________ good place.
4 I tend to be ________ disorganised.
5 I learnt some ________ simple techniques, and I've improved ________ since then.
6 I'm not ________ sure how typical I am.
7 I'm not ________ different from the average American …
8 It was often ________ impossible to study.
9 I'm not the sort of person who has ________ enemies.

B **Work in pairs. Complete the sentences with an intensifier from Exercise A.**

1 ________ means 'to a huge extent'.
2 ________ is mainly used before negative adjectives and adverbs.
3 ________ means 'compared to other things'.
4 ________ means 'a little'.
5 ________ means 'so much that it's obvious or easy to see'.
6 ________ is often used in negative sentences, especially with 'sure'.
7 ________ is often used before nouns with a negative meaning.
8 ________ means 'not quite 100%, but as good as 100%'.
9 ________ is often used before 'different'.

C **Go to the Vocabulary Hub on page XVII.**

D **SPEAK Work in small groups. Offer advice for preparing for and coping with extreme job interviews. Use intensifiers in your advice.**

PRONUNCIATION
any and *quite*

7.5 **A** **Listen to the extracts from the recruitment specialist's advice. Underline *any* and *quite* when they are stressed.**

1 Almost any other answer is much better …
2 So don't just say any old number that pops into your head.
3 … on a desert island, without any other people …
4 … the sense of freedom would be quite exhilarating.
5 It takes quite a lot of self-discipline …
6 It's been quite challenging …

7.6 **B** **Listen and underline the sentence (a or b) in which *quite* or *any* is stressed.**

1 a The interview was quite difficult.
b The interview was quite impossible.
2 a Don't say anything!
b Don't say anything!
3 a Her house was quite dirty.
b Her house was quite dirty.
4 a Any questions can be answered.
b Any questions can be answered.

SPEAKING HUB

A **PLAN** **Work in groups of three. You are going to interview several candidates for a job. First, decide what the job is, what exactly it involves and what sort of candidate you are looking for. Then plan four or five extreme questions for your interview. Use the ideas below or your own ideas.**

- If you could be any …, what would you be?
- Name four uses for a …
- How many … could you fit inside this room?
- How would … describe you?

B **PREPARE** **Discuss what would be a 'good' or 'bad' answer for each of your questions, bearing in mind the type of candidate you are looking for.**

C **INTERVIEW** **Interview two candidates from other groups. At the end of each interview, provide feedback on what the candidate did well/badly and give advice on how to improve.**

D **DISCUSS** **Work in your original groups to choose the best candidate for your job. Make sure you justify your choice. Share your decision and reasoning with the class.**

Discuss extreme jobs
Deal with difficult interview questions

7.3 Push your limits

A fronting   S changing and recycling topics

Driving on the edge

A Work in pairs. Look at the picture and discuss the questions.

1 Where do you think this is?
2 What do you think it would be like to be a bus driver in these mountains?

B Watch the video. Check your answers to Exercise A.

Glossary

abrasive (adj) having a rough surface
canyon (n) a long deep valley with steep sides made of rock
maze (n) a set of small streets, roads, paths, etc that it is easy to get lost in
slope (n) a surface or piece of land that has one end higher than the other end

C Watch the video again. Complete the sentences with between one and three words.

1 The mountains of Northern Peru consist of a network of ______________, basic roads and deep canyons.
2 Glorioso is considered a ______________ amongst some of the villagers in Huancabamba.
3 The truck tyres need to be changed after ten weeks as the roads here are so ______________.
4 Annually, over a ______________ people die on the mountain roads of Peru.
5 The passengers on the bus are not ______________.
6 The secret to a long ______________ as a Peruvian bus driver is to take your time.

AUTHENTIC ENGLISH

A Work in pairs. Read the information in the box. Complete the sentence from the video.

And that's ______________ to a long career as a Peruvian bus driver – taking the mountains at their own pace.

Fronting

Fronting involves moving information to the front of a sentence, often to give it emphasis. It is often used in informal spoken English, for example, *Really good it was – best film I've seen for ages.*

Whole clauses can be fronted, for example, *Why they decided to buy that house, I couldn't tell you.*

B Work in pairs. Rewrite the sentences to create emphasis. Begin each sentence with the underlined word.

1 I'll never know <u>why</u> Maria married Tony.
____
2 He didn't know <u>whether</u> he'd got the job or not.
____
3 I'll be there <u>in</u> about twenty minutes.
____
4 It cost me <u>three</u> hundred pounds.
____
5 I just don't know <u>how</u> you put up with your boss.
____
6 It started to snow <u>all</u> of a sudden.
____
7 It must have cost <u>an</u> absolute fortune.
____
8 An old woman sat quietly <u>in</u> the corner.
____

C Compare your sentences in Exercise B with another pair.

Hello from the Andes

SAM MALCOLM AMANDA HARRY EMILY

A Work in pairs. Discuss the questions.

1 Do you prefer travelling with other people or on your own? Why?

2 Do you know anybody that has visited many countries? What motivates them to travel?

B ▶ Watch the video. Who calls Sam and where are they?

C ▶ Watch the video again. Answer the questions.

1 Who did Fred meet by chance?

______

2 What does Fred's meeting make Sam think of?

______

3 What does Fred say about the condition of the bus?

______

4 What could Fred see when he looked out of the window?

______

5 What did Fred find comforting?

______

6 What does Sam suggest doing when Fred returns?

______

SPEAKING SKILL

A What is the purpose of the phrases in bold in each of the examples from the video?

1 Sorry, not very good signal out here. **So where was I?** Oh yes …

2 **I tell you what** when you're back from the Andes, let's go for dinner.

B Work in pairs. Underline the words and phrases which are used to change or recycle topics in the extracts below.

1 I had just arrived in Lima and guess who I ran into?

2 Well, funny you should ask. I had a bit of an adventure getting to my adventure.

3 That reminds me of the time when I was in Spain and bumped into my next door neighbour.

4 Well, yeah … made worse by the fact it was quite an old bus.

5 For sure … which brings me back to what I was saying … Daniel suggested I come with him on a trek.

Changing and recycling topics

We use many different set phrases to try to steer conversations towards the topics we wish to talk about.

We can use them to recycle a topic we were speaking about, for example, *as I was saying*. We can also use them to change topic, for example, *that's like the time when*.

SPEAKING HUB

A PREPARE Student A: you are going to describe your exciting journey to your partner. However, your partner is going to try to distract you and talk about himself/herself.

Student B: you are going to listen to your partner describing a journey. However, you are not very interested in what your partner has to say and you want to talk about yourself and your experiences.

B PRESENT Perform your conversation. Change roles.

A: Why I'd decided to drive through the wilderness alone, I couldn't tell you.

B: Speaking of which, I'm going camping in the wilderness next month.

C REFLECT Work in small groups. Perform and listen to each other's conversations again. Give feedback using the points below.

- use of language
- pronunciation
- fluency
- interaction

— Tell a story about an exciting journey

➤ Turn to page XXV to learn how to write a cover letter for a dream job.

Unit 7 Review

VOCABULARY

A **Match numbers (1–10) to letters (a–j) to form full sentences.**

1 I'm frustrated because I
2 I thought she was so courageous
3 I became hysterical
4 I always get grumpy
5 I'm quite resilient
6 They were disgusted by
7 As a child, I was indifferent
8 I try to be humble
9 I felt devastated about
10 He acted superior

a when I'm tired.
b to my classmates' bad behaviour.
c about my success when I meet strangers.
d when she chased away the burglars.
e can't do anything to help.
f losing all that work.
g around the others, as if he were the best player.
h and couldn't calm down for ages.
i the condition he left the flat in.
j so I'm sure I'll get over this setback.

B **Complete the sentences with the correct form of the words in the box. Use each word twice.**

sick competition condition application

1 Unfortunately your ____________ for the job hasn't been successful.
2 We can't go out in these ____________! We'll get wet!
3 I'm ____________ of his excuses. He's just lazy!
4 The product can be used in a number of ways – it has many ____________.
5 I enter a lot of ____________ but I never win.
6 There's a lot of ____________ for each place on the course.
7 I find an early night helps if you are feeling ____________.
8 You can go out on ____________ that you're home by 10 pm.

C **Put the lines (a–h) in order so that they form a paragraph.**

__ a long periods – the world-record free-diver, Herbert Nitsch, can go an utterly
__ b dangerous changes of pressure. Nitsch's record of 253 metres was spoiled
__ c different to normal deep-sea diving, because the divers have practically
__ d easy compared to the challenge of coping with immensely
__ e somewhat by the medical problems he suffered as a result.
__ f Free diving is radically
__ g incredible nine minutes without breathing. But holding your breath is relatively
__ h no equipment. It involves holding your breath for remarkably

GRAMMAR

A **Complete the sentences with words from the box. Each word can be used more than once.**

is was until that not because who it

1 It was ____________ I was scared ____________ I decided not to climb the cliff.
2 It's ____________ adrenaline that I'm looking for; it ____________ a sense of flow.
3 It wasn't ____________ I reached the top ____________ I realised how high the cliff was.
4 When I said 'Stop being stupid', it was ____________ you I was talking to; ____________ was James I was talking to.
5 It ____________ at that moment ____________ I realised I was no longer afraid.
6 It ____________ to impress my friends ____________ I tried to lift the car.
7 It's you ____________ is causing most of the delays, ____________ us!

B **Find and correct the mistakes in five of the sentences.**

1 All what I'm trying to say is you should be careful.

____

2 What you should avoid to do is to pretend you don't have any weaknesses.

____

3 What I did was stretched my arms to calm my nerves.

____

4 All I remember is staring out into the abyss and feeling sick.

____

5 What happened next was that some people call an ambulance.

____

6 All they did was watch TV.

____

8 WELL-BEING

Sunset swimming washes away the day's cares.

OBJECTIVES

- discuss wellness treatments
- talk about health and technology
- talk about sports psychology
- discuss nutrition and fitness
- explain and give instructions about a process
- write a summary

Work with a partner. Discuss the questions.

1 Look at the picture. Do you often swim in lakes, rivers or the sea? How is it different from swimming in a pool?

2 Read the quote. What does Plato mean? Do you agree?

3 Do you think it's easy for people to stay healthy these days? Why/Why not?

8.1 Health and wellness

- Discuss wellness treatments
- Talk about health and technology

G relative clauses with complex relative pronouns
P building suspense
V health problems
S identifying writers' opinions

VOCABULARY
Health problems

A Work in pairs. Discuss the questions. Try to write down five words for each question.

1. Name five parts of the body connected to the five senses.
2. Name five joints.
3. Name five parts of the body that people have more than two of.
4. Name five parts of the body that can be used as verbs.

B Work in pairs. Match the words in bold in 1–9 with the definitions (a–i).

1. **fracture** a rib/your leg
2. **dislocate** your shoulder/thumb
3. a **sore** throat/back
4. **pull** a muscle
5. **sprain** your ankle/your wrist
6. **inflamed** joint/skin
7. skin **rash**
8. fast/slow **heart rate**
9. high/low **blood pressure**

a. the force at which the blood flows through the body
b. twist (a joint)
c. the speed that your heart beats
d. break or crack (a bone)
e. painful
f. force a joint out of its socket
g. red and swollen
h. red spots on the skin
i. overstretch or tear

C Go to the Vocabulary Hub on page XVIII.

D SPEAK Work in pairs. What can people do to avoid having the health problems in Exercise B? What can people do if they have these problems?

READING

A SPEAK Work in pairs. Have you ever tried any wellness treatments (e.g. a massage, a sauna, a spa)? Did you enjoy them? Did they have any lasting benefits?

B READ FOR MAIN IDEA Read *From forest bathing to halotherapy*.

Which treatments are good for …

1. your lungs?
2. your heart?
3. reducing stress?
4. your skin?
5. insomnia?

C READ TO IDENTIFY OPINIONS Work in pairs. Read the article again and discuss the questions. Use the information in the box to help you.

1. What is the writer's attitude to the things she is writing about? Find examples of three types of language which show her attitude.
2. What is the purpose of this article? Is it mainly written to inform, entertain or persuade?

Identifying writers' opinions

Writers can choose particular words and phrases to show their opinion of a topic.

- Adverbs can show a positive attitude (*interestingly, surprisingly, intriguingly*), a negative attitude (*disappointingly, infuriatingly, predictably*) or a sceptical or cautious attitude (*supposedly, allegedly, presumably*).
- Different structures can be used to show writers believe something is true (*it is good for the heart*), they have a neutral stance about reported information (*it is said/thought to be good for the heart*) or they are uncertain or even sceptical (*it is supposed/meant/claimed to be good for the heart*).
- Writers can also use colloquial asides, including tag questions and rhetorical questions (*sounds fascinating, doesn't it?*) to comment on information. They can use humour, sarcasm and irony to show a sceptical attitude.

D SPEAK Work in pairs. Do you agree with the writer's attitude to the treatments? Why/Why not?

SPEAKING

DISCUSS Work in groups. Discuss the questions.

1. Why do some people prefer alternative treatments to conventional medicine?
2. Should doctors be allowed to recommend wellness treatments and alternative medicine?
3. Should companies be allowed to offer scientifically unproven wellness treatments?

FROM FOREST BATHING TO HALOTHERAPY: THE FIVE LATEST WELLNESS TRENDS

Know your 'sound lounger' from your carbon dioxide bath with our guide to the latest and not-so-greatest spa innovations.

'Wellness' is all the rage these days, but we've noticed that some therapies doing the rounds at hotel spas right now sound suspiciously basic. Surely oxygen therapy is just breathing, right? Decide for yourself, as we explore a few of the more interesting treatments we've spotted on spa menus around the world.

Forest bathing or 'going for a walk'

Forest bathing is based on the Japanese practice of *Shinrin-yoku*. That may sound like some sort of elaborately mystical ritual, but in fact involves simply 'being in the forest'. You might call it walking, or even sitting, in, you know, a forest. The practice is supposed to exercise the mind as well as reduce stress by bringing you back to nature. Perhaps eager to jazz up the concept, The Mayflower Grace Hotel in Connecticut has put together a forest-bathing package that involves 90 minutes of skin-cleansing treatments, using plant-derived lactic acid and exfoliators made with peat enzymes and berries. Finally, a 'plant hydrosol ionising mist' supposedly boosts your lymphatic system with a 'stimulating breeze'.

Carbon dioxide dry bath or 'sitting in a bag'

Does lying fully clothed on a bed while wrapped in a bag of carbon dioxide sound fun? Didn't think so, but in the Czech Republic it's all the rage. In the west of the country – an area known for its natural gas – you can have a large bag wrapped around you all the way from your toes to under your arms and watch it slowly inflate with CO_2. The treatment is meant to slow your heart rate, reduce your blood pressure and improve circulation, but this happens by the gas seeping into your clothes and skin – that thought would put most people's blood pressure up, not down.

So Sound lounger or 'napping and listening to music'

Yes, Tibetan singing bowl therapy has been around for centuries, but it's now been upgraded for the digital age. The So Sound lounger is meant to help you relax by, well, sitting in a lounger and listening to music. Revolutionary stuff. You're supposed to be able to take a 'therapeutic nap' while the lounger sends musical vibrations through your body … A bit like an airport massage chair, perhaps?

Halotherapy or 'a salty room'

Halotherapy is actually a fancy name for salt therapy. In a natural setting, this treatment would mean sitting in a salt cave and breathing in the dry, salty air, which is supposed to be good for respiratory and skin conditions. Now hotels are replicating salt caves; the Windsor Arms Hotel in Toronto has created a room filled with salt and negative ions that has darkened ambient lighting to replicate natural salt caves found in Europe. Supposedly this also helps strengthen the immune system, among other health benefits.

Oxygen therapy or 'breathing'

Oxygen therapy is supposed to help with headaches, depression and sleep deprivation by – that's right – breathing oxygen. It involves being hooked up to a machine, sticking some tubes up your nose and, well, breathing.

Glossary

circulation (n) the continuous movement of blood around your body
lymphatic (adj) relating to the body's liquid lymph, or involved in moving lymph around your body
mystical (adj) relating to or involving mysterious religious or spiritual powers
nap (v) to sleep for a short period of time, usually during the day
ritual (n) a formal ceremony

LISTENING

A SPEAK Work in pairs. Discuss the questions.

1 Do you own any gadgets that monitor your health? If so, how often do you use them?

2 What are some of the benefits and drawbacks of these devices?

8.1 **B LISTEN FOR GIST Listen to a conversation between friends discussing technology to help you stay healthy and answer the questions.**

1 What kinds of health data can be provided by the devices they talk about?

2 What four devices do they talk about?

8.1 **C LISTEN FOR DETAIL Listen again and answer the questions.**

1 Why are they talking about wellness technology?

2 Why do Cheryl and Luke think that wellness technology is a good idea?

3 Why is Jake uncertain?

D DISCUSS Work in pairs. Discuss the questions.

1 Would you use any of the devices the speakers discussed? Why/Why not?

2 Do you think it's useful for people to collect data about their health?

GRAMMAR

Relative clauses with complex relative pronouns

A Read the extracts from the conversation. Underline the relative clauses and circle the relative pronouns.

1 Wellness technology is technology with which we can improve our health and well-being.

2 I've just read several news stories about people whose lives may have been saved because their smart watch alerted them to a problem.

3 I'm meeting the person [who is] writing the article with me for lunch today.

4 It's basically a thermometer which a smartphone can be attached to.

5 This device has an automated diagnosis feature whereby it checks the symptoms of the person to whom it's attached against a database.

B Complete the rules (1–6) with the words in the box and the example sentences from Exercise A. You may use the words in the box more than once.

informal formal whereby whom whose

Relative clauses with complex relative pronouns

Advanced relative pronouns

1 Use ______________ to add information about someone's possessions.

2 Use ______________ to add information about a method (mainly used in formal English).

3 Use ______________ to add information about a person where they are the object of the clause (mainly used in formal English).

Prepositions and relative pronouns

4 In ______________ English, prepositions usually come at the end of the relative clause.

Example: ______________

5 In ______________ English, prepositions come before the relative pronoun.

Examples: ______________
and ______________

Reduced relative clauses

6 In ______________ English, we can often omit *who*, *that* or *which* in relative clauses – and in relative clauses that use *be*, we can leave out the pronoun + the part of *be*.

Example: ______________

C Complete the sentences with the correct relative pronoun. Add a preposition if needed.

1 The device ______________ I'm most interested is something that helps me eat healthily.

2 Wellness devices are the technology ______________ people will be able to extend their lives.

3 Companies need to develop security systems ______________ it's impossible for hackers to gain access to users' private health data.

4 I don't understand people ______________ first thought when they are sick is to look up their symptoms online rather than go to the doctor.

5 The people ______________ wellness technology will make the biggest difference are older people.

D SPEAK Work in pairs. Do you agree with the sentences in Exercise C?

E Go to the Grammar Hub on page X.

PRONUNCIATION

Building suspense

8.2

A Listen to the example sentences from the conversation. Underline the word where the speaker changes pitch.

1 So check out my brand new smart watch!

2 You'll never guess what … I've just been commissioned to write an article about wellness technology.

3 For example, on this smart watch take this handy heart rate tracker.

4 And if you forget, it starts flashing red.

B Complete the sentences so they are true for you.

1 The app I use most on my phone is …

2 The person I send most messages to is …

3 In one of the messages I received recently, someone said …

C Work in pairs. Present the information in Exercise B to your partner. Use pitch and pauses to build suspense.

SPEAKING HUB

A PLAN Work in groups. Imagine that you work for a technology start up. Your group needs to think of a health and wellness product idea and pitch it to potential investors. Discuss your ideas and think about the following questions.

- Will your idea help prevent health problems, encourage healthy behaviour or help people who are already sick?
- What problem do people have that your idea could help to solve?
- Is your idea for a device, an app or a service?
- Who is the target market for your idea?
- How will you make it easy for users to use your product or service?
- What are the benefits for users of your product or service?

B PREPARE Prepare a presentation about your idea. Think of ways to sell the idea to your classmates.

C PRESENT Present your idea to the class. Then as a class, vote on the best idea.

Discuss wellness treatments
Talk about health and technology

8.2 Sport and wellness

- Talk about sports psychology
- Discuss nutrition and fitness

G – pronouns and determiners
P – pronunciation of idioms
V – idioms; describing taste
S – understanding speech with background noise

LISTENING

A SPEAK Work in pairs. Discuss the questions.

1 Do you know any players or teams that use a sports psychologist?
2 How do sports psychologists help athletes?

8.3 **B LISTEN FOR GIST Listen to the first part of a podcast about sports psychology. What are the two training techniques the sports psychologist mentions?**

8.3 **C LISTEN FOR DETAIL Listen again and answer the questions.**

1 What example situation does Professor Kumar give for using therapy?
2 How do Professor Kumar's positive thinking techniques help athletes?

8.4 **D LISTEN WITH NOISE Listen to the second part of the podcast. Some parts are quite hard to hear because of background noise. Which two main sports psychology techniques does the interviewee use in her training sessions? Use the strategies in the box to help you.**

1 ____________________
2 ____________________

Understanding speech with background noise

If there's a lot of background noise and you can't ask the speaker to repeat what they said:

- use the context of the situation to help you. Remember that you don't need to understand every word that is spoken to get the gist of what somebody is saying. Use your knowledge of the topic to help fill in the gaps.
- remember that speakers stress the most important words, so these words should be easier to hear. Use this information plus the context to help make intelligent guesses about what the people are saying.

8.4 **E LISTEN FOR DETAIL Listen to the second part of the podcast again and answer the questions.**

1 What problem had the football team been facing?
____
2 What kind of coaching style does she say many players won't accept?
____
3 What kind of coaching style does Bill prefer?
____

F SPEAK Work in pairs and discuss the questions.

1 Do you think sports psychologists are important?
2 Which techniques do you think would be most helpful for you when playing sport?
3 How difficult did you find it to understand what the speaker was saying when there was background noise?

VOCABULARY
Idioms

A Look at the three groups of idioms (1–12). Complete the headings for each group with the words in the box.

body sport food

____________ idioms

1 My gut feeling is we'll lose the match.
2 Their striker was head and shoulders above the rest of us.
3 Keep an eye out for John – we're supposed to meet him at the stadium.
4 ____________________

____________ idioms

5 It wasn't a big problem, but he was really making a meal of it.
6 He says he knows Ronaldo, but you have to take what he says with a pinch of salt.
7 What she said about coaching gave me food for thought.
8 ____________________

____________ idioms

9 The other athletes are really good. I think she's out of her depth.
10 I can't win, so I think it's time to throw in the towel.
11 I thought I'd finished my part of the work, but then they suddenly moved the goal posts.
12 ____________________

B Put the underlined idioms below into the correct group in Exercise A.

- They have times when they doubt their abilities or get cold feet because they're anxious about competing.
- It's all about staying calm and focused, so they can give it their best shot.
- I need someone to nag me and tell me to up my game, but I know that's not everyone's cup of tea.

C Match the underlined idioms (1–12) in Exercise A with the meanings (a–l).

a something to think about carefully ___
b change the rules or aims ___
c watch for ___
d feel nervous ___
e make something seem more important or serious than it really is ___
f be the most likely to win something ___
g lack the required ability or knowledge ___
h much better than ___
i be sceptical about something as it may not be accurate or true ___
j to have an instinctive feeling about ___
k try your hardest ___
l not something that everyone likes ___

D SPEAK Work in pairs and discuss the questions.

1. Do you usually have a gut feeling about who will win a sports game?
2. Have you ever felt out of your depth playing a game or sport?
3. Do you keep an eye out for new trends in fitness and nutrition?
4. What kinds of sport are not your cup of tea?
5. Do you know anyone who is head and shoulders above the rest at a sport?

PRONUNCIATION

Pronunciation of idioms

8.5 **A** Listen to the sentences. Circle the prominent words in the underlined idioms.

1. I had a gut feeling.
2. It's time to throw in the towel.
3. He was really making a meal of it.
4. Keep an eye out for the others.
5. You have to take what she says with a pinch of salt.

B Complete the advice for sports players with your own ideas.

1. If you feel out of your depth, …
2. If you have cold feet, …
3. You should always keep an eye out for …
4. If you want to give something your best shot, …
5. If your opponent is making a meal of something, …
6. Take it with a pinch of salt if …

C Work in pairs. Read the sentences you wrote in Exercise B to your partner. Do you agree with your partner's advice?

SPEAKING

A Work in groups. Rank the following in order of how important they are for success in sports.

- coaching
- diet and nutrition
- insights from technology
- natural ability
- physical fitness
- sports psychology
- training facilities

B DISCUSS Work in groups and discuss the questions.

1. Could students benefit from using sports psychology techniques? How?
2. Could people at work benefit from using sports psychology techniques? How?

C Share your ideas with another group.

READING

A SPEAK Work in pairs. What kind of diet should an athlete have?

B SKIM Read *Should athletes go gluten-free?* about someone trying out a diet. Which foods did the writer eat? Which did the writer have to avoid?

C READ FOR DETAIL Read the article again and answer the questions.

1 Why did he decide to try this diet?
2 What problems did he experience?
3 What was his conclusion about the effectiveness of the diet?

D Work in pairs and discuss the questions.

1 Have you tried a gluten-free diet?
2 Would you like to try a gluten-free diet? Why/Why not?
3 Would might be the advantages and disadvantages?

Should athletes go *gluten-free*?

For those who are gluten intolerant, a diet that is gluten-free is a necessity rather than a choice. But there are some who may be motivated to try this diet for other reasons. When tennis player Novak Djokovic became world number one, he credited going gluten-free as the reason for his success. Some athletes have followed suit and switched to a gluten-free diet and some are already swearing by its effects. So, I'm going gluten-free for two weeks to see if it makes me a better football player.

DAY 1 Going gluten-free means no bread and no cereal, so I had nice **tangy** grapefruit for breakfast. Then for lunch, I had a big salad full of nice **crisp** lettuce and **crunchy** carrots. I was briefly impressed by how healthy I was being. But then I worked out in the afternoon, and was suddenly ravenous.

DAY 2 I was overjoyed when I saw the gluten-free section of my local supermarket stuffed full of packets of bread, pasta, cakes, and biscuits – all long lost friends! [1]I put several in my basket. Then I added some more packets just in case. At home, I made myself my first sandwich for two days. Disappointingly, the bread was incredibly dry and incredibly **bland**.

DAY 3 [2]I'd been planning to have grapefruit some days and melon some days, but I was so hungry today that I had both. However, the grapefruit tasted **sour**, so I decided to try one of my gluten-free cupcakes instead. It didn't look that **appetising** but it was actually pretty good – **moist**, unlike the bread, and with very sweet, **sticky** icing. Relieved that I had found some comfort food, I had two more before lunch.

DAY 4 A revelation! Perhaps the gluten-free bread would be passable as toast? I spread a generous amount of honey on top. Maybe too much as it was a bit **soggy** – but it actually tasted OK. A relief, because I didn't fancy grapefruit or melon for breakfast again.

DAY 5 For variety, I decided to try some probiotic food – food rich in healthy bacteria that are said to be good for gut health. I'd been told kefir, a fermented milk drink, is a good way to kick things off. It looked like milk, but it smelled interesting – slightly **cheesy** but also vinegary. Tentatively, I poured some into a glass. It had a **creamy** texture, but it was also a little **gritty**. And it tasted like a slightly **acidic**, **fizzy** glass of milk. I'd found something else I could have for breakfast!

DAY 6 A Japanese friend had warned me that natto – another probiotic food made from fermented soya beans – is a bit of an acquired taste. I could see what she meant right away. It looked **slimy** and had a very **pungent** aroma – almost like burnt tyres. I think the beans actually had a pretty **mild** taste, but the smell was so strong that it was hard to tell. [3]I couldn't eat much, so I reached for some gluten-free cakes instead, which I ate with some kombucha, a sweetened tea that looked a little **murky**. Despite the **cloudy** appearance it was nice, although it didn't exactly taste like tea.

DAY 7 I met some friends for a game of football. The jury was still out as to whether the diet had had any effect. Unfortunately, there wasn't much to see. I hadn't morphed into an overnight football sensation. So, is going gluten-free better for sports performance? It seems highly unlikely. And if you do need to go gluten-free, you should work with a sports nutritionist to create a diet to suit your training needs.

Glossary

appetising (adj) appetising food smells or looks very good
morph (v) to change from one thing into another by small and interconnected steps
overjoyed (adj) extremely pleased
the jury is still out (phr) used for saying that people have not yet decided what they think about someone or something

GRAMMAR
Pronouns and determiners

A Look at the sentence from the article *Should athletes go gluten-free?* Which of the underlined words in the sentence is followed by a noun? What does the word not followed by a noun refer to?

Some athletes have followed suit and switched to a gluten-free diet and some are already swearing by its effects.

B Choose the best words to complete the rules.

Pronouns and determiners

Words such as *this*, *these*, *many*, *several* and *some* can be used as both pronouns and determiners. To understand whether the word is being used as a pronoun or determiner, we need to look at the context.

1. Pronouns ***are / are not*** followed by a noun. They are used in place of a noun. We need to use the context to understand what the pronoun refers to.
2. Determiners ***are / are not*** followed by a noun. They are used to say which thing or how many things are being talked about.

C Look at the underlined sentences (1–3) in the article in *Should athletes go gluten-free?* For each sentence, decide which words are pronouns and which are determiners. Then decide which nouns the pronouns refer to.

D Go to the Grammar Hub on page X.

VOCABULARY
Describing taste

A Complete the table with the words in bold from *Should athletes go gluten-free?* Some words can go into more than one category.

Look	Smell	Taste	Texture

B Go to the Vocabulary Hub on page XVIII.

C SPEAK Work in pairs. Discuss the questions.

1. Describe a food you have eaten because you wanted to be healthy. Did it have any effect?
2. Describe a food you have eaten from another country. Did you like it?
3. Describe the most unusual thing you have ever eaten. Would you recommend it to other people?

SPEAKING HUB

A PREPARE Work in small groups. Imagine you are a fitness instructor or personal trainer. You are pitching your services to a famous athlete. To win the pitch, you need to create the best plan to help him or her prepare for an important competition. First decide what kind of athlete you are pitching to.

B PLAN Create a plan to help the athlete. Use the questions to help you.

- What are the best mental techniques to help him or her prepare for the competition?
- What should he or she do to prepare physically?
- What is the best diet for him or her to follow?

C PRESENT Present your plan to the class.

D DISCUSS Discuss the plans with the class. Which plan was the best?

Talk about sports psychology
Discuss nutrition and fitness

Café Hub

8.3 Health hacks

A – reformulating S – repairing misunderstandings

Is it good for you?

A Work in pairs. Look at the picture and discuss the questions.

1 Are these foods healthy? Why?
2 Would you eat the food shown in the picture? Why/Why not?

B Read the terms below. Now watch a video about food packaging. Tick (✓) the terms you see or hear.

☐ source of fibre	☐ high in iron
☐ high in vitamins	☐ low in salt
☐ high in vitamin D	☐ source of calcium
☐ gluten free	☐ good
☐ low in calories	☐ 100% natural
☐ OK for veggies	☐ high fibre
☐ nature is power	☐ high in Omega 3
☐ organic	☐ no refined sugars
☐ no added nonsense	☐ veggie-friendly
☐ low sugar	☐ no added salt

Glossary

back up (phrasal verb) to show that an explanation or belief is probably true
bend the rules (phrase) to allow something that is not normally allowed
dupe (v) to trick someone into believing something that is not true or something that is stupid or illegal
manipulate (v) to influence someone or to control something in a clever or dishonest way
tricks of the trade (phrase) quick and effective methods used by experienced people in a particular profession

C Watch the video again. Complete the summary.

A normal supermarket has thousands of products with [1] __________ information. Food producers cannot make health [2] __________ about products unless they can support them with [3] __________.
However, they often manipulate the [4] __________ to make their foods appear healthier. People generally only notice certain [5] __________ when food shopping.
Some terms such as 'good' and 'natural' are [6] __________ and can be used without any evidence of health [7] __________.

AUTHENTIC ENGLISH

A Work in pairs. Read the sentences from the video and the information in the box. Which of Babita's words has Richard reformulated?

Babita: *So, we're being duped, we're being fooled, are we?*
Richard: *Well, we're being manipulated.*

Reformulating

We reformulate when we want to express that we don't necessarily agree with what another person has said or with their point of view. We often reformulate by using *well* and then the same structure the other person has used.

B Match the sentences (1–6) with the replies (a–f).

1 New York's the greatest city in the world.
2 They're definitely lying to us, aren't they?
3 What they're doing is illegal.
4 All health claims on food have to be backed up with scientific evidence.
5 You hated the film then?
6 So, Maria doesn't want to come to the party then?

a Well, they're not being completely honest.
b Well, they're definitely bending the rules.
c Well, some have to be backed up with evidence.
d Well, it's certainly the most exciting.
e Well, she wants to come but she's working really late.
f Well, I didn't like it very much.

C Work in pairs. Write responses to the sentences.

1 I bet the film was amazing, wasn't it?
2 What they're doing is immoral.
3 The apartment's filthy.

D Work in pairs. Practise the exchanges you wrote in Exercise C.

Healthy display

SAM MALCOLM AMANDA HARRY EMILY

A Work in pairs. Discuss the questions.

1 Where do you get recipes from?

2 Are you good at following recipes or do you prefer to improvise?

B ▶ Watch the video. Complete the recipe.

Amanda's HEALTHY BROWNIE RECIPE

INGREDIENTS

One [1] ________________ of coconut oil
Two egg whites
[2] ________________ yoghurt
small amount of sugar
[3] ________________ cocoa powder
[4] ________________ flour
[5] ________________ of dark chocolate

METHOD

Step one: [6] ________________ the oven.
Step two: [7] ________________ egg whites from yolks.
Step three: [8] ________________ egg whites, coconut oil, yoghurt and sugar.
Step four: Add cocoa powder and wholemeal flour to wet [9] ________________.
Step five: [10] ________________ mixture until incorporated.
Step six: Add chips of chocolate.
Step seven: Spread the [11] ________________ in a pan.
Step eight: Put the pan in the oven for [12] ________________ minutes at 260 degrees Fahrenheit.

C Where does Harry think he went wrong with the recipe?

SPEAKING SKILL

A Work in pairs. Complete the example in the video. Why does Sam use a question tag here?

Sam: Now you did separate the egg whites from the yolks, ________________?

B Read the information in the box. Which strategy (a–c) has been used in the sentences from the video (1–4)?

Repairing misunderstandings

When we don't understand another person or another person doesn't understand us there are a number of things we can do to repair the misunderstanding.

a Tag questions to check that we have understood correctly or that the other person has understood correctly.

b Clarifying instructions to signal that we are going to go over instructions again.

c Restating to clarify what we mean. We can also say what we don't mean.

1 OK … maybe let's go over them again. ___
2 Not whisk … mix. ___
3 Remember to add chips … not chunks … chips of dark chocolate. ___
4 Hold on, Fahrenheit? You mean Celsius, don't you? ___
5 OK, let's go through it one more time. ___

C Work in pairs. Take it in turns to read aloud the sentences (1–5) in Exercise B. Try to copy the intonation of Sam and Harry in the video.

SPEAKING HUB

A PLAN You are going to give instructions on a process you know well. Choose one of the ideas below or use your own idea.

- recipe
- how to repair something
- sport or exercise tips
- professional or academic process

B PREPARE Make notes on how you are going to explain the process to your partner.

C PRESENT Work in pairs. Explain your process to your partner. Ask your partner to retell you the process. Clarify any misunderstandings. Change roles.

Well, no … that's not quite right. You should make sure you stretch first.

Explain and give instructions about a process

➤ Turn to page XXVI to learn how to write a summary of a text about stress.

Unit 8 Review

VOCABULARY

A Choose the correct word to complete the sentences.

1. I went to see the doctor when I had a ***rash*** / ***sprain*** on my chest.
2. I'm really stressed at the moment, so my blood ***pressure*** / ***rate*** is a little high.
3. I'm on crutches because I've ***fractured*** / ***pulled*** a bone in my foot.
4. Do you have any eye drops? I've been looking at a screen all day and my eyes are really ***inflamed*** / ***sore***.
5. I ***pulled*** / ***sprained*** my wrist when the ball hit my hand.
6. I think I ***fractured*** / ***pulled*** a muscle at the gym, so I'd better put some ice on it.
7. Do you ever track your heart ***rate*** / ***pressure*** while you're exercising?

B Match the questions (1–12) with the answers (a–l).

1. Do you ever get cold feet before speaking in public?
2. Do you always give it your best shot when you play sports?
3. Do you always keep an eye out for good places to eat?
4. Which sports are not your cup of tea?
5. Have you heard something that you've had to take with a pinch of salt?
6. Did you feel like throwing in the towel when it got tough?
7. When was the last time you felt out of your depth?
8. Who is a sports player who is head and shoulders above his peers?
9. Do you offer to help out when you see someone making a meal of something?
10. What was the last thing you read that gave you food for thought?
11. Are your gut feelings usually right?
12. Has anyone ever moved the goal posts while you were working on something?

a Yes, because I'm incredibly competitive.
b Messi is clearly one the best players in history.
c At times in the race I wanted to give up, but you have to keep going.
d No, I don't usually get nervous.
e A teacher once changed the title of an essay.
f I'm not a big fan of rugby or cricket.
g There was a great article in the paper about innovation the other day.
h Yes, a friend told me a story. But he always exaggerates.
i Not usually, I find it a bit embarrassing.
j Not really. I search for things online.
k I once took an exam that was much too difficult for me.
l Rarely. I'm not good at predicting things.

C Choose the correct word to complete the sentences.

1. I don't like soft biscuits. They need to be ***crunchy*** / ***sharp*** / ***soggy***.
2. I don't often eat seaweed. It's a bit too ***crisp*** / ***murky*** / ***slimy*** for me.
3. Pasta can often be too ***bland*** / ***pungent*** / ***sour***, so I always add lots of parmesan cheese.
4. I tend to order a ***mild*** / ***gritty*** / ***sticky*** curry when I have Indian food.
5. I like lemon dressing on my salad to give it a ***creamy*** / ***soggy*** / ***tangy*** flavour.
6. I never buy ***mild*** / ***pungent*** / ***fizzy*** drinks in case they've been shaken up.
7. I love eating ***cheesy*** / ***gritty*** / ***sticky*** things like toffee apples and candy floss.

GRAMMAR

A Correct the mistakes in the sentences.

1. My smartwatch has a feature that you can share your exercise data with friends.
2. There's an app which in you can record your fitness data.
3. This is the device that being used to monitor people's blood sugar levels.
4. The inventor is someone which people like to read about.
5. I don't know who's smartwatch this is.
6. This is the diet tracking service which I subscribe.

B Complete the text with the words or phrases in the box.

a large number of	both	either
most people	one	others	some people

The raw food diet

These days, there are [1] ____________ diets that claim to be the best way to stay healthy. [2] ____________ is the raw food diet. According to this diet, [3] ____________ cooked and processed foods are unhealthy, so people should not eat [4] ____________. [5] ____________ follow a raw vegan diet, whereas [6] ____________ eat animal products, too. The diet includes fruits, vegetables, nuts, seeds and, for the non-vegans, meat. [7] ____________ who follow the diet, whether vegan or not, also eat fermented foods, such as sauerkraut and kimchi.

9 BEHAVIOUR

Behaviour is the mirror in which everyone shows their image.

Johann Wolfgang von Goethe

Caught red … and blue … and green handed.

OBJECTIVES

- talk about group behaviour
- discuss factors that affect behaviour
- discuss animal behaviour
- talk about behavioural experiments
- give and justify your opinion on social engagement
- write a conclusion to an academic report

Work with a partner. Discuss the questions.

1 Look at the picture. How do children learn to behave? What influences our behaviour as we grow?

2 Read the quote. What aspects of our image/character might we deliberately try to show through our behaviour? What might we reveal accidentally?

3 What would a stranger guess about your character from your behaviour? What might they assume incorrectly?

9.1 Language and behaviour

- Talk about group behaviour
- Discuss factors that affect behaviour

G noun phrases V slang P pronouncing vague expressions S understanding rapid colloquial speech

VOCABULARY
Slang

A SPEAK Read the dictionary definition. Work in groups and discuss the questions.

1 Can you think of any examples of slang (in English or your language)?
2 What problems can slang cause for language learners?

> **slang** – definition and synonyms
> NOUN Pronunciation /slæŋ/
> Words or expressions that are very informal and are not considered suitable for more formal situations. Some slang is used only by a particular group of people.

9.1 **B** Read and listen to some examples of informal English. In pairs, try to work out the meaning of the underlined slang expressions.

1 I could do with some new wheels but they'd set me back at least ten grand … and I'm completely skint.
2 Hey, can you lend me ten bucks? Ah, sweet. That's awesome, dude.
3 I don't mean to whinge, but the office do last night was a total shambles. I was so gutted!
4 This bloke offered me a brand new telly for fifty quid, so I'm like 'Sounds dodgy to me – it's probably nicked or something.'
5 I wanted to hang out with my buddies tonight but I'm totally beat, so I guess I'll just chill out and crash instead.
6 I'm well chuffed cos I got myself a new flat. So I'm sorted now.

9.2 **C** Now listen to a more neutral version of the same sentences to check your ideas.

D DISCUSS Work in small groups. Discuss the questions. Use words in Exercise B.

1 When was the last time you whinged about something?
3 What events have you been to that were a complete shambles? What happened?
4 When was the last time you felt well chuffed or gutted? Why?

LISTENING

A SPEAK **Work in pairs. Do you speak or behave differently depending on who you are with?**

9.3 **B** LISTEN FOR GIST **Listen to a group of people taking part in a psychology experiment. Then answer the questions.**

1 How many participants are in the group?

____

2 Where are the experimenters?

____

3 What's the purpose of the experiment?

____

4 What five tasks does the experiment include?

____

9.3 **C** LISTEN FOR DETAIL **Listen again. Are the statements true (T) or false (F)? Correct the false sentences.**

1 Lisa volunteered to take part for free. *T / F*
2 Lisa's group was due to start at 11:30. *T / F*
3 All four members of the group agree to eat the doughnuts. *T / F*
4 Lisa knew for certain that her answer about the lines was wrong. *T / F*
5 Sometimes PTU affects everyone in a group. *T / F*
6 The participants think 'yummy' is a cool word. *T / F*
7 Groupthink is mainly associated with teenagers. *T / F*
8 The experimenters were surprised by Lisa's behaviour. *T / F*

9.4 **D** LISTEN TO RAPID SPEECH **Listen to some extracts from the conversation. Cross out the words and sounds that the speakers leave out. Put brackets [ ] round the phrases they link together. The first two have been done for you. Use the information in the box to help you.**

Understanding rapid colloquial speech

Rapid colloquial English is especially difficult to understand because:

- speakers use a lot of slang and idioms.
- sounds, syllables or even whole words are often left out.
- common phrases like *what do you* and *going to* are linked together.

1 Go~~od~~ morning. How ~~are~~ [you doing?]
2 [Don~~'t~~ know] what they're testing.
3 Are we supposed to wait?
4 We've got to go and teach.
5 Shall we get cracking?
6 It's obvious.
7 Do you think they're for us?
8 What about you, Jake?
9 Shall we have some more?
10 What are you on about?

E SPEAK **Work in groups and discuss the questions.**

1 Do you think you would respond to the tasks in the same way as Lisa?
2 Have you ever experienced PTU? Think about your experiences as a language learner.
3 Have you ever encountered groupthink or something similar? What happened?

PRONUNCIATION

Pronouncing vague expressions

A **Underline the vague expressions in the extracts from the conversation. Use the information in the box to help you.**

Pronouncing vague expressions

Vague expressions are a way of showing that we're not being too precise. They are especially common in informal English.

Vague expressions are usually pronounced very quickly, with no stressed syllables. The word *of* is often reduced to *a* (e.g. *kinda*, *sorta*). The word *and* becomes *n*.

1 Something about perception skills and stuff like that.
2 There were two blokes here earlier, psychology professors or whatever.
3 How groups influence our behaviour, and so on.
4 I thought my eyes were playing tricks on me in some way!
5 Sometimes it's easier to follow the crowd, in a sense, than to trust your own eyes!
6 Everyone else is nodding their heads, or something like that.
7 I felt kind of stupid.
8 You must think I'm some sort of sheep!

9.5 **B** **Listen to check your answers. Then practise saying the sentences.**

SPEAKING

DISCUSS **Work in small groups and discuss the question. Use the vague expressions in the list and slang from this lesson in your discussions.**

How can we avoid the problems of group behaviour? Think of at least five practical steps.

- and so on
- and stuff like that
- in a/some sense/way
- kind/sort of (+ adjective/verb)
- more or less
- or something (like that)
- or whatever
- some kind/sort of (+ noun)

READING

A SPEAK Work in pairs. Do you think the language you speak could affect any of the areas below? Why/Why not?

- how rich you are
- how you play
- your health

B SKIM Read *Does your language affect your behaviour?* Were any of your ideas from Exercise A mentioned?

C READ FOR MAIN IDEA Read the article again. Answer the questions.

1. How did Chen try to show that language (not other factors) affects our behaviour?
2. Why does our language affect our behaviour, according to Chen?
3. How could Chen's ideas make the world a better place?
4. What other behaviours are connected with our language, according to Chen?
5. What other factor (apart from grammatical structures) might affect how speakers of certain languages behave?
6. What claim is the main focus of the article?
7. What's the problem with the classification of English?
8. Which language feature did Chen use to categorise languages?

D SPEAK Work in groups and discuss the questions.

1. Do you agree with Chen's claims?
2. How else could we explain his correlations?
3. Do you often make long-term plans for the future (e.g. saving for retirement)?
4. Do you consider yourself an impulsive person or someone who likes to plan?

DOES YOUR LANGUAGE AFFECT YOUR BEHAVIOUR?

In 2013, Keith Chen, a behavioural economist at Yale University, made headlines around the world with the extraordinary claim that the language we speak can have a significant impact on [1]our propensity to save, plan and prepare for the future.

Chen divided the languages of the world into two categories: strong FTR (future tense reference) languages, which need markers like 'will' to signal the future, and weak FTR languages, which don't. In English (a strong FTR language), you can't say 'it snows tomorrow'; you usually have to add 'will' or 'going to'. In weak FTR languages like Mandarin, it's normal to say, 'it snows now' and 'it snows tomorrow', using the same verb form in [2]both these cases.

Chen's remarkable finding was that speakers of weak FTR languages save 25% more money for the future than speakers of strong FTR languages. Chen's interpretation of this correlation is that for speakers of weak FTR languages, the future feels like part of the present, while speakers of strong FTR languages save much less because the future feels more remote to them.

Remarkably, Chen's correlations held not only for savings rates, but also for overeating, smoking, drinking, debt and lack of physical exercise. In each case, speakers of weak FTR languages were significantly healthier and took fewer risks, presumably because they felt [3]a strong connection with their future selves.

While Chen's study provoked considerable interest and enthusiasm from the general public, the backlash from linguists and other academics has been just as striking. One criticism involves the possible confusion of correlation with causation. The link between languages and behaviour may in fact be due to other factors, such as age, education or income levels. Chen took great care to control for all these factors, by comparing families where the only difference was [4]the language spoken at home. However, many academics still feel deeply uncomfortable with the idea of a causal relationship behind the apparent correlation.

One alternative possibility is that it's the connotations of a language that affect our behaviour, rather than any grammatical properties of the language itself. For example, languages such as English might encourage a live-for-today attitude as a result of people's associations of that attitude with English-speaking countries.

In a 2010 study, Dirk Akkermans and colleagues set out to find out more by asking bilingual speakers of English and Dutch to play a game. [5]Those who had lived in English-speaking countries were found to be considerably more competitive when playing in English rather than Dutch. However, those who had experienced only limited exposure to the culture of English-speaking countries were found to be no more competitive when playing in English or Dutch, strongly suggesting that it's the culture of English-speaking countries, not the language itself, that is making the difference.

A second major concern with Chen's study is that his division of the world's languages into two categories, strong and weak FTR, seems overly simplistic. For example, while English does require a future tense marker in predictions like 'it'll rain tomorrow', future markers are optional in other future constructions (e.g. 'I'm leaving tomorrow') and virtually outlawed in conditional clauses (e.g. 'If it rains …'). The future in English is complex, as [6]pretty much every learner can attest, so its classification as strong FTR feels debatable at best. Similar objections could be raised for many other languages.

Overall, despite [7]the many legitimate concerns, Chen's analysis of the correlation can't be dismissed out of hand. Further research is needed, ideally with a more sophisticated classification of languages. However, if [8]Chen's conclusions that grammar influences behaviour prove correct, the implications will be profound. Wouldn't it be great if we could solve [9]all our financial and health problems simply by outlawing words like 'will'!

"Chen, M Keith. 2013. "*The Effect of Language on Economic Behavior: Evidence from Savings Rates, Health Behaviors, and Retirement Assets.*" American Economic Review, 103 (2): 690-731."

Glossary

backlash (n) a strong, negative and often angry reaction to something that has happened, especially a political or social change
legitimate (adj) fair and reasonable
outlaw (v) to make something illegal
propensity (n) a natural tendency to behave in a particular way
provoke (v) to cause a reaction, especially an angry one
simplistic (adj) treating something in a way that makes it seem much simpler than it really is

GRAMMAR
Noun phrases

A Complete the rules with the examples (1–9) from the text.

Noun phrases

Long noun phrases (NPs) are especially useful in formal and academic writing because they can contain as much information as a full sentence.

Most NPs start with a number, a quantifier (e.g. *some*, *all*) and/or another determiner (e.g. *the*, *my*, *these*).

a *all* and *both* can be used before a determiner without *of*: ___ / ___
b *many*, *few*, *little* and numbers can be used after a determiner ___
c Some quantifiers can be modified with phrases like *almost* or *not quite*: ___

Common structures at the end of an NP include:

d relative clauses: ___
e reduced relative clauses: ___
f preposition phrases: ___
g *that*-clauses ___
h *to* + infinitive ___

B Go to the Grammar Hub on page XII.

C SPEAK Work in small groups. Build 'monster noun phrases' around the nouns in the box, as in the example.

behaviour experiments language

A: My friends' behaviour is strange.
B: A lot of my best friends' behaviour is strange.
C: Quite a lot of my best friends' behaviour when they're tired is strange.

SPEAKING HUB

A DISCUSS Work in small groups. Go to the Communication Hub on page XXII.

B PLAN Choose one of the ideas in Exercise A. Create a list of at least five pieces of evidence to support or challenge the idea.

C PREPARE Work in pairs. Explain your pieces of evidence to your partner. Listen to your partner's evidence. Give feedback and ask questions.

D PRACTISE Practise presenting your evidence. Use your partner's feedback to improve your presentation.

E PRESENT Report your evidence to the class. Be prepared to answer questions.

F REFLECT Decide which evidence you found most convincing and why.

– Talk about group behaviour
– Discuss factors that affect behaviour

9.2 Animal behaviour

- Discuss animal behaviour
- Talk about behavioural experiments

G – participle clauses and verbless clauses
P – intrusive stops
V – verb + object + infinitive; gestures and body language
S – identifying outcomes of scientific research

READING

A SPEAK Work in pairs and discuss the questions.

chimpanzees dolphins crows and jays dogs

1 Which of the animals listed in the box are intelligent?
2 How do we know?
3 How could we find out?

B SKIM Read *Understanding animal behaviour* quickly. What does the writer say about the questions in Exercise A?

Understanding animal behaviour

By Peter Aldhous

We gaze into the eyes of a chimp and see a reflection of ourselves. We glance at a crow and see an alien being. Such biases skew our understanding of what non-human intelligence looks like.

The best known experiment designed to probe animal minds is the 'mirror test'. Having been given time to interact with a mirror, chimps are marked with a dye and anaesthetised. After coming round, they look into the mirror while touching the marked area. From this behaviour, researchers have concluded that the chimps know they are looking at themselves – one of the hallmarks of an advanced mind. Other animals that have passed the test include manta rays and dolphins.

My issue with the mirror test isn't the meaning of success, but rather how to interpret failure. Do most animals fail because they lack a concept of self, or is the test irrelevant to species that don't use vision for social communication? How would you design a similar test using smells for a dog or ultrasound for a dolphin? When a dolphin **hears its own echoes coming** back in altered form, it might well be thinking: 'Yes, that's me' – but how would we know?

In New Caledonian forests, Gavin Hunt of Massey University **watched crows fashion** twigs into hooks to capture insects from holes. Seeming to understand cause and effect, crows are capable of astounding feats of meta-tool use: using one tool to manipulate another in order to achieve an ultimate goal.

In fact, they seem better than chimps at translating their skill in solving one problem to another conceptually similar one. In the trap-tube test, an animal must use a stick to obtain food from a tube. Pushing it in one direction **helps them get** the reward; pushing it in the other **makes the food fall** into a trap. Crows that have already solved this problem can apply their skills when presented with the trap-table test, which looks different but has the same rule: Don't **let the food drop** down the hole. For chimps, prior experience with the trap tube gives no advantage on the trap table.

Understanding the wider scope of corvid cognition meant entering the birds' world to devise experiments to probe their mental processes. Nicky Clayton did this while at the University of California in the late 1990s. After being told confidently by a psychologist colleague that animals lack 'episodic' memory – an ability to remember the 'what, where and when' of past events – Clayton decided to check for herself. While studying western scrub jays, she realised that the birds' habit of burying food provided a prime opportunity to test their memories.

Clayton first **had the jays bury** insect larvae and peanuts in sand-filled trays. Having learnt that the larvae tasted bad after a few days, if just four hours had elapsed, the jays sought out the places where they had hidden them. But if several days had passed, they went for the hidden peanuts. This was an impressive demonstration of 'episodic-like' memory. Clayton has also found that jays will selectively bury certain types of food when aware that it is likely to be scarce in future. So now we apparently have jays planning ahead, in addition to acting on specific memories of the past.

When I visited Clayton and her scrub jays, it was a while before I **saw one of the birds** bury an item of food – apparently my presence had interrupted them. 'They're checking you out,' Clayton told me. I stared back, struck by the gulf between us. Despite having read the scientific papers and knowing how cognitively sophisticated scrub jays are, I experienced no emotional connection.

Glossary

elapse (v) if time elapses, it passes
feat (n) something impressive and often dangerous that someone does
gulf (n) a large and important difference between people or groups
hallmark (n) typical feature

C READ FOR OUTCOMES Complete the notes about the research. Use the information in the box to help you.

Identifying outcomes of scientific research

When you read about scientific research, it's important to distinguish between:

- results (what happened?)
- conclusions (what did we learn?).

You can then decide if you agree with the conclusions.

Mirror test

1 Results: Chimps look in mirror and ________________.

2 Conclusions: Chimps know ________________.

Trap-tube/-table test

3 Results: Crows ________________ from one test to another; for chimps ________________.

4 Conclusions: ________________ at translating skills to conceptually similar problems

Insect larvae vs peanuts

5 Results: Jays went to larvae locations after ________________, but to peanut locations after ________________.

6 Conclusions: Jays possess ________________.

D SPEAK Work in pairs and discuss the question. How might research like this change the way we treat animals?

VOCABULARY

Verb + object + infinitive

A Look again at the examples in bold in *Understanding animal behaviour*. Then complete the rules with verbs from the text.

Verb + object + infinitive

A very small number of verbs are followed by an object and an infinitive without *to*.

1 Sense verbs: ________, ________, ________ and *feel* are followed by an infinitive to describe a complete event, or an *-ing* form to describe a process or series of events.

2 Causative verbs: ________, ________ and ________. After *help*, both an infinitive and *to* + infinitive are possible.

B Go to the Vocabulary Hub on page XVIII.

GRAMMAR

Participle clauses and verbless clauses

A Complete the sentences from the article with one word.

1 ________ been given time to interact with a mirror, chimps are marked with a dye.

2 After coming round, they look into the mirror while ________ the marked area.

3 Nicky Clayton did this ________ at the University of California in the late 1990s.

4 After ________ told confidently by a psychologist colleague that animals lack 'episodic' memory … Clayton decided to check for herself.

5 Having ________ that the larvae tasted bad after a few days … the jays sought out the places where they had hidden them.

6 Clayton has also found that jays will selectively bury certain types of food when ________ that it is likely to be scarce in future.

7 I stared back, ________ by the gulf between us.

B Match the sentences (1–7) in Exercise A with the rules (a–c).

Participle clauses and verbless clauses

Participle clauses use participles (e.g. *doing, done, being done, having done, having been done*) instead of a subject + verb.

a When a clause starts with a participle, the meaning is often *when/after* ___, ___ or *because* ___.

b Many participle clauses start with prepositions (e.g. *before, after, despite*) ___.

c After some conjunctions (*if, when, while, although*), we can leave out the subject and *be*. Usually this leaves a participle ___.

When *be* was the only verb, we are left with a 'verbless clause' ___, ___.

C Go to the Grammar Hub on page XII.

SPEAKING

SPEAK Work in groups. Discuss your experiences and opinions of animal intelligence. Then use participle clauses to report back to the class.

LISTENING

A SPEAK Work in groups. Discuss the questions.

1 Do you have any lucky charms that you use before exams or other stressful situations? Do you know anybody who uses these lucky charms?

2 Do you have any lucky rituals or routines that you follow, e.g. before watching your favourite sports team? Do you know anybody who follows these lucky rituals?

9.6 **B LISTEN FOR MAIN IDEA Listen to a radio show about behavioural psychology and answer the questions.**

1 How did the pigeons get food?

____

2 What's the connection between the experiment with pigeons and the one with people?

____

3 How do the three people at the end try to influence events?

____

9.6 **C LISTEN FOR DETAIL Listen again. Choose the correct endings.**

1 In the famous pigeon experiment, the mechanism always delivered food …
  a after the same amount of time had passed.
  b at random times.
  c when the pigeons performed a particular action.

2 As the food continued to be delivered, the pigeons …
  a changed their actions.
  b became more sure they could affect the delivery.
  c became more desperate.

3 The experiment with people …
  a showed humans weren't so easily convinced.
  b showed very similar results.
  c used food as well to trick the participants.

4 The person who seems most convinced of their power to control events is …
  a the football fan.
  b the exam-taker.
  c the lottery player.

D SPEAK Work in groups and discuss the questions.

1 Do the behaviours and rituals described in the radio show prove that pigeons and people are stupid/irrational? Or is there a benefit in believing we can influence things beyond our control?

2 What other examples can you think of, where people (or animals) try to control things that are beyond their control?

3 What are some dangers of this type of behaviour?

PRONUNCIATION

Intrusive stops

9.7 **A Listen carefully to some extracts from the radio show. Which sound (/p/, /t/ or /k/) can you hear in each of the underlined words?**

1 A kind of bizarre pigeon dance. /p/ /t/ /k/

2 Such actions can influence something beyond our control. /p/ /t/ /k/

3 After completely random lengths of time. /p/ /t/ /k/

4 I was a youngster, and my aunt gave me a lucky hamster mascot. /p/ /t/ /k/

B Work in pairs. Practise saying the sentences in Exercise A.

9.8 **C Which six words in the box can have intrusive stops? Listen to check. What's different about the other three words?**

becomes influence intense once prince strength things warmth wins

D Work in pairs. Write a sentence using at least three of the words in Exercise C. Then give it to another pair for them to attempt to say correctly.

The more influence the prince has, the more intense he becomes.

VOCABULARY
Gestures and body language

A **Match the gestures (1–7) with the body parts (a–g). Choose each body part once. When would you use each gesture?**

1	blink / wink	**a**	your finger(s)
2	shrug	**b**	your eyebrows
3	point / bend / wiggle	**c**	your head
4	nod / shake	**d**	your legs
5	fold / cross	**e**	your eyes
6	cross / bend	**f**	your shoulders
7	raise	**g**	your arm(s)

B **Complete the sentences with the correct form of a verb in the box. Which body part does each verb involve?**

beckon fidget gaze glare grin lean smirk stare

1. Stop ________ at those people's clothes! It's really rude! They're looking back now!
2. You look so happy in that photo! You're ________ from ear to ear!
3. I love ________ out to sea and dreaming of what's on the other side.
4. Stop ________ with your keys and pay attention!
5. During the test, the teacher ________ for me to come to the front of the class.
6. Don't ________ against that cupboard! It's not very stable.
7. When he beat me at tennis, Harry just ________ and said, 'I guess I'm better than you.'
8. I could tell you were angry by the way you ________ at me.

C **Go to the Vocabulary Hub on page XVIII.**

D SPEAK **Work in groups and discuss the questions.**

1. Which gestures can you use to show that you're happy/interested/bored?
2. How might you show that you don't like someone?
3. How could you communicate with a stranger who doesn't speak your language?

E **Work in groups to play a game. One of you is the facilitator; the others are players. Facilitator – go to the Communication Hub on page XXI. Players – go to the Communication Hub on page XX.**

SPEAKING HUB

A PREPARE **Work in groups. You are going to design and conduct a behavioural experiment to test an assumption. You can use one of the ideas below or your own ideas.**

Assumption 1: Our body language communicates more information than the words we use.

Assumption 2: We can't help nodding or shaking our heads when we say *yes* or *no*, or shrugging our shoulders when we say *I don't know*, even if the movements are extremely tiny.

Assumption 3: We can't help mirroring other people's gestures and body language. We copy them subconsciously.

B PLAN **Work out how you could test the assumption on other members of the class.**

- How will you set up the experiment?
- What will you tell the participant(s)?
- What will you be looking out for?
- How might your observations confirm or undermine the initial assumption?

C CONDUCT **Take turns to conduct your experiments with other members of the class.**

If you're participating in another group's experiment, try to act naturally. Don't try to guess what the experimenters are testing – and don't try to influence their results.

If you're an observer, watch both the experimenters and the participants carefully. Try to work out what the experiment is testing.

D DISCUSS **Report back to the class on what you learnt from your experiment. Ask other observers for their conclusions. How could you refine your experiment to learn more?**

– Discuss animal behaviour
– Talk about behavioural experiments

Café Hub

9.3 Model behaviour

A– *end up* S– backtracking and reformulating

All together now

A Work in pairs. Look at the picture and discuss the questions.

1. What is happening in the picture?
2. Which other animals behave in this way? Why?

B ▶ 00.00–01.51 Work in pairs. Watch the first part of a video. Check your answers to Exercise A.

Glossary

evacuation (n) the process of removing people from a building or an area that is not safe
scenario (n) a situation that could possibly happen
simulate (v) to produce the features of something in a way that seems real but is not
swarm (v) to go somewhere as part of a large crowd

C ▶ 00.00–01.51 Watch the first part of the video again. Complete the sentences with the best option (a, b or c).

1 Doctor Ed Codling is a …
 a mathematician.
 b biologist.
 c mathematical biologist.

2 The experiment replicates how people on their own react in …
 a a fire.
 b an earthquake.
 c a plane accident.

3 Doctor Codling wants to observe participants that …
 a look confident and assume they can find the exit.
 b remain calm and find the exit.
 c panic and follow another person.

4 When Doctor Codling blows his whistle he wants them to leave out of …
 a the north exit.
 b the south exit.
 c either the north or south exit.

D Work in pairs. Discuss the questions.

1. What do you think the result of the experiment will be?
2. How many people do you think will go the right or the wrong way?
3. Why did people behave in the way they did?

E ▶ 01.51–02.35 Watch the second part of the video. Check your answers to Exercise D.

AUTHENTIC ENGLISH

A Work in pairs. Read the sentence from the video. Choose the correct options in the box.

*I mean, I've done it before, you just **end up** following someone who looks the most confident in the room.*

end up

We use *end up* to describe being in a particular place or state after doing something or because of doing it. It is used when the subject ***did / didn't*** intend or expect this.

B Work in pairs. Respond to the sentences using *ended up*.

1 You missed your plane.
I ended up sleeping at the airport.

2 The film you wanted to see was sold out.
____

3 After travelling around the world for years, Marta unexpectedly settled down in Ireland.
____

4 I thought I'd passed the exam but I failed.
____

5 Alan kept on arriving late for work.
____

6 We had booked a holiday but had to cancel it because my boyfriend was ill.
____

C Compare your answers with another pair.

Follow the herd

SAM MALCOLM AMANDA HARRY EMILY

A Work in pairs. What do you think the phrase *follow the herd* means?

B ▶ Watch the video. Answer the following questions.

1. What is Amanda writing an article about?
2. What motivated people to use the Social Stairs?
3. What doesn't Harry understand?
4. Why does Sam want Amanda to tell him what she finds out?

SPEAKING SKILL

A Work in pairs. Complete the examples from the video.

1. Oh, ______________________ like that piano staircase in Stockholm?
2. ______________________, the piano staircase had an escalator next to it.
3. You ______________________ about that other example – the Social Stairs or something like that?
4. Oh, yeah. The Social Stairs. ______________________.
5. Or ______________________, they liked hanging out together.

B ▶ Watch the video again to check your answers to Exercise A.

C Choose the correct options to complete the information.

Backtracking and reformulating

When we correct something that has been previously said we [1]*backtrack / reformulate*. When we say something previously said in a different way we [2]*backtrack / reformulate*.

D Work in pairs. Decide which of the examples in Exercise A are backtracking (b) and which are reformulating (r).

1 ___ 2 ___ 3 ___ 4 ___ 5 ___

SPEAKING HUB

A PREPARE You are going to discuss the following question.

Do you think a sense of community is declining in modern society. Why/Why not?

Make notes on what you are going to say and how to justify your opinion. Be prepared to reformulate your arguments.

B DISCUSS Work in small groups. Present your opinion to the rest of the group. Respond to what the other members in your group say.

We've ended up being very isolated … or to put it another way … lonely.

C REFLECT Give feedback to the other members of your group. Consider the following points.

- reformulation
- fluency
- pronunciation
- interaction

Give and justify your opinion on social engagement

➤ Turn to page XXVII to learn how to write a conclusion to an academic report.

Unit 9 Review

VOCABULARY

A Complete the conversation with the words in the box.

awesome bloke chill out chuffed dodgy dude gutted quid shambles was like

A: Hey, [1] ________________. You look happy. What's up?

B: I'm well [2] ________________! I just got ten [3] ________________ for taking part in an experiment.

A: [4] ________________! What did you do?

B: I had to use sticks to push food out of a tube, but it kept dropping into a hole. Total [5] ________________! I was well [6] ________________, but the [7] ________________ who was in charge [8] ________________, [9] '________________, man! Don't worry!'

A: Sounds a bit [10] ________________ to me. What were they testing?

B: Whether people are smarter than crows! Crazy, huh!

B Find and correct the mistake in three of the sentences.

1 The researchers watched one chimp hide the food.

____

2 We weren't let to watch the experiment.

____

3 I'll have my assistant to contact you next week.

____

4 I felt a mosquito bite me last night.

____

5 I can't help you to pass the exam, but I can help you avoid mistakes.

____

6 A crow was seen use one tool to make another.

____

C Choose the correct words to complete the blog post.

How to listen – and show you care

- [1]*Lean / Glare / Raise* towards the other person slightly.
- Don't [2]*fold / gaze / wink* your arms or [3]*fidget / shake / wiggle* with pens, keys, etc.
- Keep neutral facial expressions – a smile might look like a [4]*gaze / raise / smirk*.
- Don't speak. Instead, [5]*bend / nod / wink* your head slowly to show understanding, [6]*cross / point / raise* your eyebrows to show interest, or [7]*bend / shrug / wiggle* your shoulders to show you don't know.
- Keep eye contact but don't [8]*cross / grin / stare*. You're allowed to [9]*beckon / blink / glare*!

GRAMMAR

A Reorder the sentences to make noun phrases.

1 You usually have to use / forms / available / future / the / two / that / of / one / are /

____.

2 The research focused on / for / are making / the / that / worrying / of / preparation / the future / lack / extremely / most people /

____.

3 all / behaviour / Practically / into / research / my / animal / shows they're smarter than we think

____.

4 The accident occurred because of / the event / for / failure by / such / the organisers / almost / to plan / the / large crowds / complete / to attend /

____.

5 problem / the / ways / these / approaching / Both / of / are flawed

____.

6 We are aware of / that / be expressed / the / only / animal intelligence / of / many / a / can / few / ways /

____.

B Complete the sentences with participle clauses. Use the verbs in brackets.

1 ________________________ a big breakfast earlier, I skipped lunch. (*eat*)

2 The octopus uses a coconut shell as a shelter if ________________________. (*attack*)

3 ________________________ to understand the rules, the pigeon solved the puzzle quickly. (*seem*)

4 ________________________ to be at the airport at 4 am, we weren't happy about the 10-hour delay. (*tell*)

5 When ________________________ your bags, remember to leave space for souvenirs. (*pack*)

6 Despite not ________________________ at university, she has produced some excellent research. (*study*)

10 SOCIETY

Society exists only as a mental concept; in the real world there are only individuals.
Oscar Wilde

A castle village in Burj Al Babas, Bolu, Turkey

OBJECTIVES

- discuss issues related to tourism
- present solutions to urban problems
- talk about political activism
- discuss how to make a difference
- debate for and against a motion
- write a persuasive essay

Work with a partner. Discuss the questions.

1 Look at the picture. What type of person might live in a place like this?

2 Read the quote. What do you think Wilde means? Do you agree?

3 What would be the advantages and disadvantages of living in an unusual place like the one in the picture?

10.1 Urban problems

- Discuss issues related to tourism
- Present solutions to urban problems

G – discourse markers
P – introducing new information
V – culture and heritage; nouns with *to*
S – integrating information from different texts

READING

A SPEAK Work in pairs. What are some advantages and disadvantages of increased tourism for a city?

B SCAN Read the three newspaper articles. What problem of tourism are they discussing?

Has tourism reached its limit?

Being **designated** as a UNESCO World **Heritage** site helps **preserve** a site and **refurbish** its facilities – as well as boosting tourism. Yet, it can end up **endangering** the site. A famous example is Machu Picchu, the **ruins** of an Inca **settlement** in Peru, which is being destabilised owing to tourists littering, climbing on the ruins or even taking pieces of it home.

In response to similar problems, Venice has capped the number of tourists allowed to enter its most famous areas. Niagara Falls requires visitors to buy tickets which say when they can enter the site, whereas the Taj Mahal has increased entrance fees for tourists to actually try to put people off visiting.

Glossary

booming (adj) if an activity is booming, it is becoming very popular
destabilise (v) to cause problems for a country, government, or person in authority so that they become less effective
elitist (adj) supporting or based on a system in which a small group of people have a lot of advantages and keep the most power and influence

C SYNTHESISE INFORMATION Imagine that you are writing an essay about tackling the problem you identified in Exercise B. Complete the notes using information from all three articles. Use the information in the box to help you.

Integrating information from different texts

Sometimes you need to get information from multiple sources to understand a topic.

- Be clear about your purpose for reading. What questions are you trying to answer?
- Underline the main ideas in the texts and look for arguments connected to your topic.
- Use headings to organise the information you are looking for. Make notes under these headings as you read more texts.

Notes

Issues caused by the problem

Ideas for dealing with the problem

Criticism of these ideas

D DISCUSS Work in pairs. Look at your notes in Exercise C and discuss the best methods for solving the problem.

Is tourism tax fair?

The New Zealand government recently announced that it will start charging tourists a tax of approximately NZ$35 (£18). The government claims this **fund** will be spent on infrastructure and the natural **habitat** of New Zealand's wildlife.

Is this reasonable? Tourists already contribute to the economy by paying for hotels, food and souvenirs. It's not as elitist as charging higher entrance fees to attractions, but it is still enough to put some tourists off.

Some might question if the fee is masking a failure to manage tourism properly. Should governments be responsible for not only attracting tourists, but better ensuring they are able to handle the influx of visitors?

VOCABULARY
Culture and heritage

A **Match the words in bold in the articles with the meanings (1–10).**

1 ________ = the type of place where an animal lives or a plant grows
2 ________ = the parts of a building that remain after it has been damaged
3 ________ = a large amount of money
4 ________ = to take care of something and prevent it being damaged
5 ________ = a place where people live
6 ________ = relating to the style or design of a building
7 ________ = to formally choose someone or something for a role or special status
8 ________ = objects, traditions and beliefs important to a society's history or culture
9 ________ = to put something at risk of being destroyed or becoming extinct
10 ________ = to repair or improve a building

B **Go to the Vocabulary Hub on page XIX.**

C **SPEAK Work in pairs and discuss the questions.**

1 Are there any habitats where endangered species live in your country?
2 Should your country's government provide a larger fund to preserve cultural sites?
3 How important is architectural style to your country's heritage?

Tackling tourism with tech

Tourism in Amsterdam is booming, with over 14 million visitors a year to enjoy the canals and the mix of **architectural** styles. The Amsterdam tourism board felt limiting tourist numbers was too extreme, so they turned to technology to deal with potential overcrowding.

Many tourists visit the Van Gogh Museum in the morning and take a cruise on the canal in the afternoon. So the tourism board has launched an app providing information on how busy the attractions are and suggesting alternative destinations.

GRAMMAR
Discourse markers

A **Choose the correct discourse markers to complete the sentences.**

1 A top tourist attraction is the Grand Bazaar in Istanbul ***owing to / despite*** its spectacular architecture and wide range of shops.
2 The Zócalo in Mexico, another very popular attraction, hosts a large number of events throughout the year. ***Yet / Moreover***, it is home to the Metropolitan Cathedral and the National Palace.
3 Some of the most popular tourist attractions are in the US – ***as a matter of fact / namely*** Times Square, Central Park and Union Station.
4 Theme parks are also among the most popular tourist destinations. Disneyland in Florida, ***in any case / for instance***, is a very popular destination.
5 ***Conversely / Whereas*** several of the world's most popular tourist attractions are in the US, one of the most popular destinations in Europe is Paris.

B **Complete the rules with words and phrases in Exercise A.**

Discourse markers

1 Use *despite*, ________ and ________ to join two clauses. They can come at the beginning of the sentence (followed by a comma) or in between the two clauses.
2 Use *as a matter of fact*, *conversely*, *in any case*, ________ and ________ to connect ideas in two sentences.

C **Go to the Grammar Hub on page XIV.**

D **Work in pairs. Make sentences using the prompts below plus a discourse marker.**

1 there are some great tourist sites in my city
2 people who live near tourist sites often get angry with tourists
3 tourists have a reputation for bad behaviour
4 many cities around the world are keen to attract tourists

SPEAKING

A **SPEAK Work in pairs and discuss the questions.**

1 How important is tourism to your country?
2 Do you believe tourism is mainly good or bad for a city? Why?

B **DISCUSS Work in groups. Try to gain a consensus on question 2 in Exercise A. Use the steps below to help you.**

- Get everyone's view.
- Allow speakers time to justify their views.
- Establish agreement: think about ways of doing this fairly.

C **PRESENT Present and justify your position to the class.**

LISTENING

A SPEAK Work in pairs and discuss the questions.

1 What kind of place do you like to work or study in? Why do you like this place?

2 What are your favourite buildings in your city? Why do you like them?

10.1 **B LISTEN FOR GIST Listen to the first part of a radio report about building design. Generally speaking, how can the design of a building affect people?**

10.2 **C LISTEN FOR DETAIL Listen to the next part of the radio report and note down how these specific features can affect people.**

1 Light: __________

2 Shapes and lines: __________

3 Colours: __________

4 Shop facades: __________

5 Spaces between buildings: __________

D SPEAK Work in pairs and discuss the questions.

1 What do you think of the different ideas? Do you think they make a difference?

2 Why do you think many buildings don't follow the recommendations discussed in the programme?

VOCABULARY

Nouns with *to*

A Circle the nouns followed by *to* in the extracts from the radio programme. Use the information in the box to help you.

> **Nouns with *to***
>
> Several nouns are often followed by *to* + the infinitive. You can remember which ones they are by thinking about the adjective or verb forms of these words – because they are also normally followed by *to* + infinitive, e.g. *Architects normally start with the wish to design innovative buildings.*

1 And if people feel better about their environment, they have a higher inclination to interact positively with the people around them.

2 People have a tendency to be less productive if their desk is more than 7.5 metres away from a window.

3 … whereas plain, monotonous facades make people anxious and give them the urge to hurry past.

4 The project's failings were a reminder for architects to think not just about the look of buildings, but also about how people would interact within the spaces they create.

B Match the underlined nouns (1–10) with their meanings (a–j).

1 Most architects have a desire to create beautiful rather than functional buildings. ___

2 Most people in big cities show a reluctance to talk to strangers. ___

3 Governments have an obligation to limit the population of their cities. ___

4 Cities need to be doing a lot more in readiness to deal with swelling populations. ___

5 The refusal of many cities to provide seating in public places is a mistake. ___

6 A failure to learn from environmental psychology will lead to higher crime rates. ___

7 People need frequent reminders to behave considerately in cities. ___

8 Companies have a responsibility to make sure building design has a positive effect on their staff. ___

9 People in cities have a tendency to feel isolated because they are too busy to socialise. ___

10 There should be a greater urge to limit noise and sound pollution in cities. ___

a something that helps you remember something
b an unwillingness
c preparation
d not doing something that you were expected to do
e a wish
f saying that you will not do something
g a strong feeling of wanting or needing to do something
h responsibility
i a habit of behaving in a particular way
j a duty

C Work in pairs. Do you agree with the sentences in Exercise B?

D Work in pairs. Complete the sentences with your own ideas.

1 Architects have a tendency to …
2 In my city, most people show a reluctance to …
3 Most people have no desire to …
4 Local planners have a responsibility to …

Google Global HQ

PRONUNCIATION
Introducing new information

10.3 **A Listen to the extracts from the radio programme. Does the pitch of the speaker's voice go up or down on the underlined words?**

1. As the city evolves, its population has swelled to over 21 million, making Beijing one of the most populated cities in the world. And the more people there are, the more challenging it becomes to provide comfortable environments for people to live and work in.
2. They found that people strongly preferred daylight to electric light – and, as a matter of fact, other research has shown that people have a tendency to be less productive if their desk is more than 7.5 metres away from a window.
3. Apparently, people feel more comfortable in places with round shapes and curved lines. On the other hand, straight lines and sharp edges have been shown to create feelings of fear.
4. One interesting study showed that people are more relaxed when they see lively and interesting shop facades, whereas plain, monotonous facades make people anxious and give them the urge to hurry past.

B Work in pairs. Practise saying the sentences. Listen carefully. Did your partner use a higher pitch on the correct word?

1. Although most people think that living in a city is exciting, it's actually quite boring for many people.
2. Rather than developing urban areas, we should be developing rural areas.
3. Companies are now embracing ideas from environmental psychology rather than ignoring them.
4. The offices of large companies are being designed to encourage positive feelings in staff. People's homes, however, are much less likely to receive the same attention.

SPEAKING HUB

A PLAN Work in small groups. Imagine that your city is holding an election for a new mayor. Make a list of some of the biggest problems about living in your city and brainstorm some solutions to these problems.

B PREPARE You support a candidate in the election. Prepare a short speech to try to persuade people to vote for your candidate. You should:

- decide which three problems your candidate will solve
- be ready to explain the problems
- be ready to explain how your candidate will fix them
- make sure that each member of your group has something to say.

C PRESENT Give your speeches and listen to the other groups' speeches.

D DISCUSS As a class, decide which candidate you want to be mayor.

For me, the best speaker by far was ...
While I liked all the candidates, the one that really stood out was ...

Discuss issues related to tourism
Present solutions to urban problems

10.2 How to change the world

- Talk about political activism
- Discuss how to make a difference

G ellipsis and substitution **V** word building **P** managing conversations **S** recognising shifts in register

READING

A SPEAK Work in pairs and discuss the questions.

1. If you were concerned about a local issue, would you contact your local politician about it?
2. Do you think that political activism (e.g. demonstrations or petitions) can make a difference?

B READ FOR MAIN IDEA Read the article *Political activism* and choose the best summary.

1. The younger generation are becoming very active in politics and many are choosing to become politicians so they can make the world a better place.
2. The younger generation are more interested in campaigning for specific causes than getting behind a particular political party.
3. The younger generation are completely uninterested in politics and prefer to focus on their friendships, hobbies and interests.

C READ FOR DETAIL Read the article again and answer the questions.

1. Is the writer part of the younger or older generation?
2. Why is the younger generation disillusioned with the political system?
3. What three issues has the Harry Potter Alliance taken an interest in?
4. What does the writer mean when he says that 'we're moving from a vision of civics that is party-based and partisan to one that's personal and pointillist'?

D SPEAK Work in pairs. Discuss the question. Some people label the kind of political activism described in the article as 'slacktivism'. Do you think this is a fair criticism?

Political activism is as strong as ever, but now it's digital – and passionate

The new generation of digital natives are not apathetic about politics, but they see online campaigns as more effective than lobbying a politician or joining a party.

Like most Americans of my generation – born in 1973 – I learnt about civics from television. On Saturday mornings, our childhood diet of cartoons was regularly interrupted for *Schoolhouse Rock*, three-minute animated musical lessons on science, grammar and the workings of government. Today it's hard to teach civics in three-minute snippets because the way we participate in civic life is changing shape – and changing very quickly. The vision of participatory citizenship that I grew up with – read a newspaper, vote in elections and if you're really incensed, write to your congressional representative – is utterly unpersuasive and unappealing to the students I teach. Digital natives, born and raised in an atmosphere of interactivity, are acutely aware of how insensitive most governments are to participation and how little meaningful interaction they can expect from their elected representatives and other government officials.

This distaste for participation in dysfunctional political systems is easily misread as apathy, leading legislators and educators to declare 'a crisis in civics' as young people participate in elections at a much lower rate than their parents. But that misses a key shift: digital natives are participating in civic life in ways where they feel they can have an impact and these points of impact are often outside government.

Take the Harry Potter Alliance, a group of teen and twenty-something fans of JK Rowling's books and movies, who are organising online and searching for ways to live out the values of Harry Potter and Dumbledore's Army here in the Muggle world. Their past campaigns have purchased thousands of books for underfunded public libraries and sent planeloads of health supplies for Haitian crisis response. Now they're working to persuade Warner Bros to buy Fairtrade chocolate for the sweets sold as tie-ins to the movies, bombarding the company with 'howlers', open, digital letters that demand it consider the ethical concerns of Harry Potter's fans.

VOCABULARY

Word building

A Complete the Example column with words from the article. Use the information in the box to help you.

Word building

We use suffixes to change the form of words. For example, we can add *-ness* to the end of an adjective to turn it into a noun (*ready* becomes *readiness*). Being aware of different suffixes can help you to understand what kind of word is being used.

Suffix	Add to …	to make…	Example
-al	a noun	an adjective	ethical
-ate	a noun	an adjective	
-ic	a noun	an adjective	
-ical	a noun	an adjective	
-ive	a verb	an adjective	
-hood	a noun	a noun	
-ity	an adjective	a noun	
-ship	a noun	a noun	

B Go to the Vocabulary Hub on page XIX.

SPEAKING

DISCUSS Work in small groups. Discuss the questions.

1 What do you think are some of the biggest problems in the world today? Make a list and rank the problems.

2 What could people do to raise awareness of the top three issues on your list? How could people try to get companies, individuals or governments to change their behaviour?

3 If a friend of yours wanted to become involved in political activism, would you encourage him or her or dissuade him or her from doing so? Why?

Not every digital native is an engaged, active citizen (and not every young person is a digital native) and not every online campaign has an impact. But it's too easy to dismiss digitally-rooted activism as naive 'slacktivism'. Online activism is having an impact, but it often focuses in areas outside formal political participation. Civic participation of the young uses a broad suite of tools to affect a wide range of targets.

Coders write open-source security software in the hope of frustrating NSA surveillance, while community organisers fund neighbourhood gardens through Kickstarter. This emergent civics targets governments, corporations, communities and the media. It harnesses social media, crowdfunding, social entrepreneurship and open-source software as well as law and politics, to bring about change.

No wonder it's hard to get our heads around it. We're moving from a vision of civics that's party-based and partisan to one that's personal and pointillist. Parties offer a way to have an opinion (often an ill-informed one) on every issue, while participatory civics centres on issues that people are passionate about. While my generation tends to see the world in terms of issues important to Republicans or Democrats, my students often see the world in terms of the issues their friends care about, a political identity built on the passions of people important to them. This isn't civics in crisis – it's civics in flux, civics that's changing with the people who practise it.

Glossary

dysfunctional (adj) not working normally
howler (n) a silly and embarrassing mistake
incensed (adj) extremely angry
lobby (v) try to influence politicians or people in authority on a particular subject
snippet (n) a small piece of something, especially information or news

LISTENING

A SPEAK Work in pairs. Discuss the questions.

1 What job did you want to do when you were younger?

2 Do you still want to do that job? Why/Why not?

10.4 **B LISTEN FOR MAIN IDEA** Listen to a conversation about finding a job after university. Answer the questions below.

1 What kind of job was Robin interested in before?

______

2 What kinds of jobs is Robin thinking about doing now?

______

10.4 **C LISTEN FOR DETAIL** Listen again and answer the questions.

1 What made Robin think about pursuing a different career?

______

2 What does Joanna think about the jobs Robin is thinking of doing?

______

3 What advice does Mr Evans give Robin about finding the job he wants to do?

______

4 How did the philosophy graduate decide to help people?

______

5 Does Joanna agree with Mr Evans' advice?

______

10.5 **D LISTEN TO REGISTER** Listen to extracts from the conversation. For each, decide if Robin is using formal or informal register. Use the information in the box to help you.

Recognising shifts in register

People speak differently in formal and informal/casual situations.

In formal situations, speakers:

- use longer, more complete sentences
- use careful pronunciation
- are less direct
- use formal words and phrases.

In informal/casual situations, speakers use:

- short sentences, contracted forms and often omit words
- less careful pronunciation
- more informal words and phrases (phrasal verbs, vague language and slang).

1 *informal / formal*

2 *informal / formal*

3 *informal / formal*

4 *informal / formal*

5 *informal / formal*

6 *informal / formal*

E SPEAK Work in pairs and discuss the questions.

1 What kind of job do you think Robin should do? Why?

2 What do you think about the idea of working in finance to help charities?

3 If you want to donate to charity, what's the best way to choose the charity?

GRAMMAR
Ellipsis and substitution

A **Look at the extracts from the conversation. The speakers omitted some words. Complete the sentences with the omitted words.**

1 I've just been trying to sort out my CV and ______________ looking for some interesting stuff to apply to.

2 ______________ any idea what you're going to do?

3 You could train to be a teacher or ______________ just volunteer in your spare time.

B **Look at the underlined words in the sentences. What words do they replace?**

1 **A:** So … you going to work at your dad's company then?
B: Hmm … hope <u>not</u>.

2 If you haven't read it, you should <u>do</u>.

3 **A:** I was thinking about some kind of voluntary work.
B: You should definitely <u>do it</u>.

C **Complete the rules using examples in Exercises A and B.**

Ellipsis and substitution

Ellipsis means omitting unnecessary words. We can omit:

1 the subject + modal: ______________

2 the subject + auxiliary verb: ______________

3 a verb phrase

4 an adjective: ______________.

In spoken English, it's also common to leave out words if our meaning is obvious from the context. We can omit:

5 the subject

6 the subject + auxiliary verb.

Substitution means avoiding repeating something by using words like:

7 *do*: ______________

8 *not*: ______________

9 *do so / do it / do that*: ______________.

D **Go to the Grammar Hub on page XIV.**

E **SPEAK** **Work in pairs. Cross out the words that can be omitted in these sentences. Then discuss whether you agree or disagree with them.**

1 Charity workers should not receive high salaries and they should not get bonuses.

2 Some charity workers are very persistent and I wish they weren't so persistent.

3 Animal charities often receive the most money, but they shouldn't receive the most money.

F **Work in pairs. Replace parts of the questions with *do so*, *not* or *so*. Then ask your partner the questions.**

1 Would you ever go overseas to do voluntary work? If you went overseas to do voluntary work, where would you go?

2 Do you think having voluntary work on your CV makes a big difference to recruiters or does it not make a big difference to recruiters?

3 If your company or university allowed you to take a week off to do voluntary work, would you take a week off to do voluntary work?

PRONUNCIATION
Managing conversations

10.6 **A** **Listen to extracts from the conversation. For each extract, decide if the intonation on the second speaker's words rises (↗) falls (↘) or rises then falls (↗↘).**

1 ___ 2 ___ 3 ___ 4 ___ 5 ___

B **SPEAK** **Work in pairs. Think of an anecdote for one of these topics. Listen to your partner and use appropriate reactions to keep the conversation going.**

- some good advice a teacher gave me
- a time I made a difference

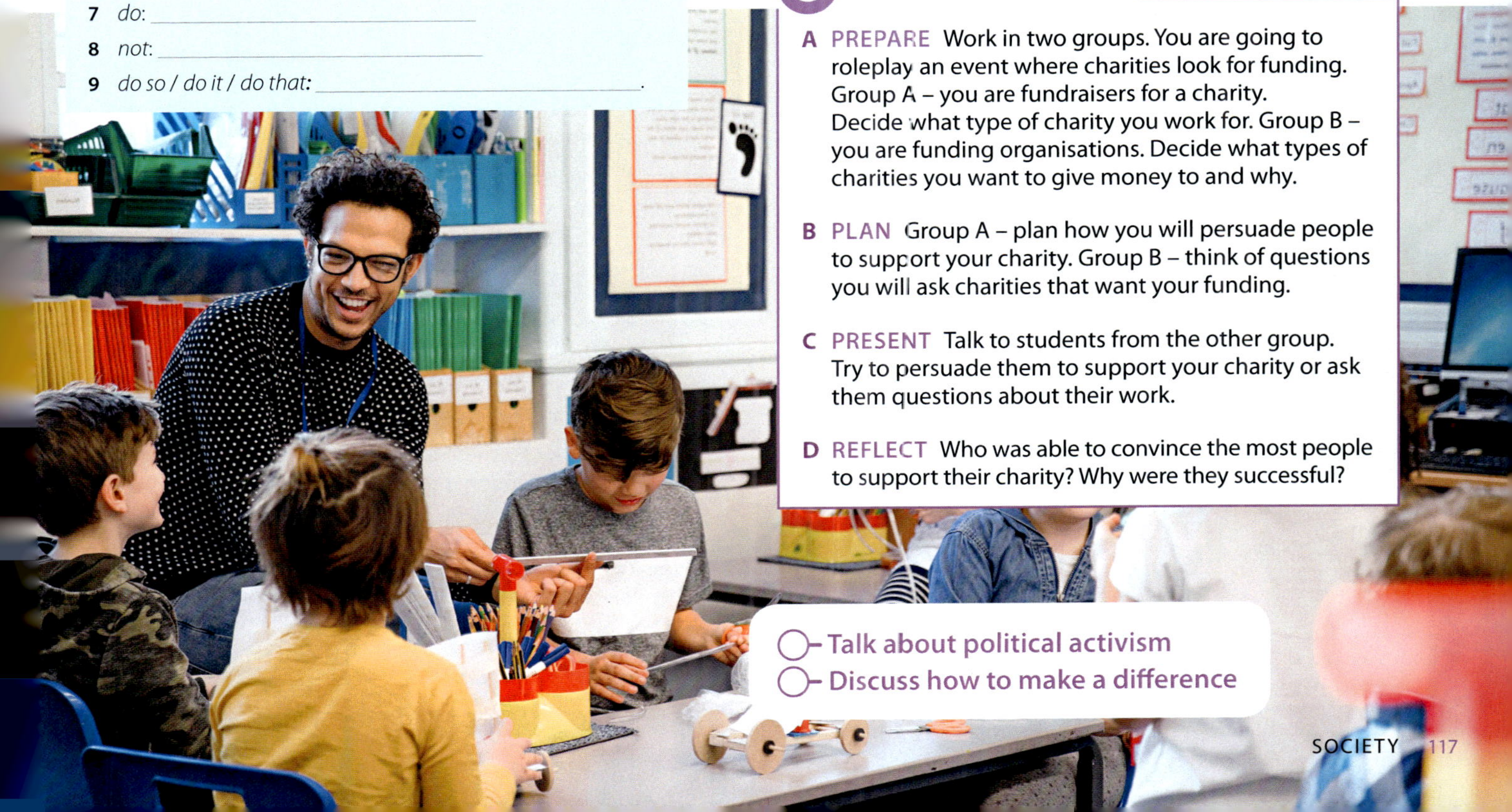

SPEAKING HUB

A **PREPARE** Work in two groups. You are going to roleplay an event where charities look for funding. Group A – you are fundraisers for a charity. Decide what type of charity you work for. Group B – you are funding organisations. Decide what types of charities you want to give money to and why.

B **PLAN** Group A – plan how you will persuade people to support your charity. Group B – think of questions you will ask charities that want your funding.

C **PRESENT** Talk to students from the other group. Try to persuade them to support your charity or ask them questions about their work.

D **REFLECT** Who was able to convince the most people to support their charity? Why were they successful?

- Talk about political activism
- Discuss how to make a difference

Café Hub

10.3 Changing cities

A – describing a scene in real-time S – using vague language

Mexicable

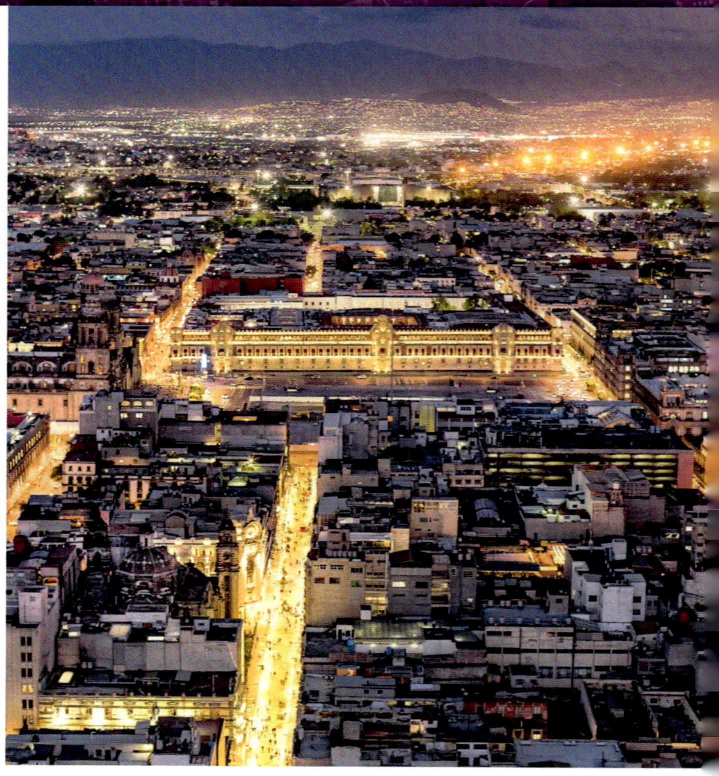

A **Work in pairs. Look at the pictures and discuss the questions.**

1 What are some of the different uses of cable cars?

2 Are there cable cars in your city or country? How are they used?

B **Watch the video. Tick (✓) which of the following you see.**

1 A man admiring spectacular views from a cable car. ☐

2 A man in a wheelchair going up a ramp. ☐

3 A man in a wheelchair entering a cable car. ☐

4 Tourists taking photos from a cable car. ☐

5 Mechanics repairing an engine. ☐

6 A man wheeling himself along a pavement. ☐

C **Watch the video again. Complete the sentences with between one and three words.**

1 Ade likes the cable car station because there's a wheelchair entrance and ______.

2 From the cable car, Ade points out a mural of ______.

3 The cable cars from Stations 1 to 4 are moved by ______.

4 *Mexicable* connects some of the poorest and ______ areas of the city.

Glossary

feat (n) something difficult needing a lot of skill, strength, bravery, etc to achieve it

haphazard (adj) done in a way that does not seem to be carefully planned or organised

loop (n) a round shape or curve made by a line curling back towards itself

mural (n) a large painting on the wall of a room or building

D **Work in pairs. Try to remember what you heard. What do these numbers and dates refer to? One number isn't mentioned.**

1	22 million ______	5	30,000 ______
2	2016 ______	6	4 ______
3	6 ______	7	7 ______
4	26 ______	8	3 ______

AUTHENTIC ENGLISH

A **Work in pairs. Read the sentence from the video and the information in the box. Underline the descriptive words. What do they mean?**

The views from the Mexicable – you've got this sprawling city and these murals and the amazing colours on the houses, it's just breathtaking!

Describing a scene in real-time

When we describe a scene in real-time we often use visually descriptive language to bring the scene to life and paint a mental picture in the listener's mind.

B **Read the sentences. What is being described in each sentence?**

1 There's this sea of golden shifting sand, spectacular dunes and a fierce, burning sun.

2 Just look at the gorgeous lush green meadows and peaceful grazing sheep.

3 I've never seen such deep valleys and magnificent snow-capped peaks.

4 Everywhere you look there are towering skyscrapers, bustling streets and stunning street art.

5 You've got these picturesque narrow streets, an enchanting medieval square and beautiful, cosy cottages.

C **Work in pairs. Describe a scene to each other using descriptive language. Student A – go to the Communication Hub on page XXIII. Student B – go to the Communication Hub on page XX.**

Everything's changing

SAM MALCOLM AMANDA HARRY EMILY

A Work in pairs. Discuss the questions.

1 What developments are happening where you live?
2 Are the developments positive or negative? Why?

B Watch the video. Does everybody have a similar opinion about the new cable car?

C Watch the video again. Answer the following questions.

1 Why is parking and traffic worse according to Emily?
2 What is being built over the river?
3 What does Malcolm say will happen to the area soon?
4 How much would it cost Emily to rent a bigger business space?
5 Why is Harry looking forward to the cable car?
6 What improvements have there been to the area according to Amanda?
7 How was Sam able to set up his café according to Harry?

SPEAKING SKILL

A Work in pairs. Look at the extracts from the video. Why have the speakers used the underlined phrases?

Amanda: Also, the area was quite run down with high unemployment and <u>all the rest of it</u>.

Malcolm: I had to park all the way over on <u>whatsitsname</u> and walk here.

B Read the information in the box. Underline the vague language in the sentences from the video.

Using vague language

We often use vague words when we can't find the exact expression we need.

a List completers – when someone is unable to complete everything on a list.
b Placeholders – a speaker cannot remember something.
c Evasion – not wanting to say something exactly.
d Quantities – when we're not sure of the exact figure.

1 It doesn't help either that they're building that thingy over the river.
2 I hardly recognise the neighbourhood any more with all the new shops, the road system and stuff like that.
3 It was two thousand odd pounds for the month.
4 Well, yeah, sort of … it is convenient … but if I can't afford to stay in the area they won't be much good to me.
5 It will also encourage tourism and who knows what else.
6 Crime in the area is down about 20% in the past four years.

C Work in pairs. Match the examples (1–6) from the video with the functions (a–d) in the box.

SPEAKING HUB

A PREPARE You are going to debate the following motion. Decide who in the class will be *for* and *against* the motion.

All vehicles should be banned from city centres.

B PLAN In your groups, make notes for your side of the argument. Think about:

- environment
- public transport
- convenience
- cost

C PRESENT Join together with the other group and hold a debate.

Without cars you could have more public spaces, street cafés and all the rest of it.

D REFLECT Hold a vote on whether you agree or disagree with the motion.

Debate for and against a motion

➤ Turn to page XXVIII to learn how to write a persuasive essay about living in the city or countryside.

Unit 10 Review

VOCABULARY

A Complete the article with the words in the box.

architectural designated endangered fund habitat heritage preserve refurbish ruins settlement

UNESCO
World Heritage Sites

The aim of the World [1] ________ list is to help countries [2] ________ sites of 'outstanding universal value'. To be [3] ________ as a World Heritage site, a place must meet one of ten criteria, such as being an [4] ________ masterpiece, a human [5] ________ or the [6] ________ of one representative of a particular culture, a place of exceptional natural beauty, or a place that is the natural [7] ________ of an [8] ________ species.

Once a site is selected for the list, the World Heritage [9] ________ can provide money to protect or [10] ________ the site – and being on the list usually provides a significant boost to the number of tourists visiting the site.

B Choose the correct words to complete the sentences.

1 Architects have ***an urge*** / ***a responsibility*** to provide people with enough daylight.
2 People have a ***reluctance*** / ***tendency*** to be less productive if there is background noise.
3 The government needs frequent ***desires*** / ***reminders*** to tackle the problem of air pollution.
4 The government's ***readiness*** / ***refusal*** to invest in rural areas has led to overcrowding in cities.
5 Architects have ***a failure*** / ***an obligation*** to talk to the people who will use a building before they design it.

C Choose the correct words to complete the sentences.

1 Young people don't like politics because it is too ***formal*** / ***formality***.
2 People often vote for the person with the strongest ***personal*** / ***personality*** rather than the best plans.
3 The ***public*** / ***publicity*** should have a vote on major political decisions.
4 Social media enables much easier ***interactive*** / ***interactivity*** with politicians.
5 Politicians' ***personal*** / ***personality*** lives should remain private.
6 People who don't vote have let down their ***communal*** / ***community***.

GRAMMAR

A Complete the article with the words or phrases in the box. There are five you do not need to use.

as a matter of fact conversely despite for instance in any case moreover namely owing to whereas yet

Tourism
Cycle Model

Tourist sites go through similar stages as they grow. First of all, adventurous tourists start coming to a place. [1] ________ this interest, local people set up businesses to cater for tourists. They open hotels and restaurants, [2] ________. After that, larger companies start to invest in the area – [3] ________, by building large hotels and catering to large groups. The tourism industry begins to dominate the area, while, [4] ________, other industries begin to shrink. As the number of visitors increases, the area becomes less attractive and visitors begin to go elsewhere. [5] ________, the facilities begin to become dated and damaged. If there is no further investment, the area will go into decline.

B Match numbers (1–6) to letters (a–f) to form full sentences.

1 It's better to give money to a charity than
2 You should donate clothes or
3 Some charities are really wasteful with their donations
4 If a friend asks you to donate to a charity,
5 Some people are really good at volunteer work,
6 It's a good idea to choose one or two charities to support

a volunteer your time rather than give money.
b and when you do, you can give bigger donations.
c you should do so.
d to an individual.
e and I wish they weren't.
f but I'm not.

Endmatter Contents

Grammar Hub

Vocabulary Hub

Communication Hub

Writing

Grammar Hub

6.1 Past modals of speculation and deduction

- We use *must* + *have* + past participle for things we believe logically happened.

  *It's a huge book, so it **must have taken** her a long time to research and write.*

- We use *could/might/may well* + *have* + past participle for things we believe likely happened.

  *They're still not sure what caused the fire but it **may well have been started** deliberately.*

- We use *could/might/may* + *have* + past participle for things we think possibly happened.

  *The plane **might have crashed** in the mountains but they never found the wreckage.*

- We use *can't/couldn't* + *have* + past participle to say something was not logically possible.

  *They **couldn't have built** this massive fort in just a week.*

Be careful!

- Although *could/might/may have* + past participle all mean the same thing, *might/may not have* expresses possibility, whereas *couldn't have* expresses certainty.

  It's possible that Aled didn't see the email. = Aled may/might not have seen the email. NOT ~~Aled couldn't have seen the email.~~

- We can use phrases that start with *There is* + *a/an/the* + adjective + noun + (*that*) to speculate, with adjectives such as *distinct*, *fair*, *high*, *remote*, *slim* and *slight*, and nouns such as *chance*, *likelihood* and *possibility*.

  ***There is a distinct possibility that** he picked up the illness while in the jungle.*

- We can also use phrases that start with *It is* + adverb + adjective + (*that*) to speculate, with adverbs such as *extremely*, *highly*, *reasonably*, *somewhat* and *quite*, and adjectives such as *likely* and *possible*.

  ***It's quite possible that** rival explorers sabotaged their plans.*

6.2 *-ing* and infinitive forms

- We use *-ing* after a preposition.

  *She praised the journalist **for exposing** the injustice.*
  *They're not interested **in finding** out the truth.*

- We also use *-ing* after expressions such as *It's no good…*, *It's not worth…*, *There's no point (in)…* and *…have a good time/difficulty/fun/problems…*.

  *It's **not worth publishing** the article if it will get you fired.*
  *There's **no point (in) helping** people who are ungrateful.*
  *You'll **have difficulty justifying** that answer.*

- We use *to* + infinitive after adjectives, nouns, quantifiers and the word *time*.

  *She's **eager to get** started on her work.*
  *They urged **people to take** shelter in the new facility.*
  *The report is lengthy, and there's **too much to read** in one night.*
  *Let's pick a good **time to review** the materials.*

Be careful!

- We use *to* + infinitive after the word *time*, but after the phrase *have a good/great time…*, we use *-ing*.

  It's time to make a decision. NOT ~~It's time making a decision.~~
  We had a great time painting the wall. NOT ~~We had a great time to paint the wall.~~

- Some verbs can be followed by *-ing* (e.g. *appreciate*, *suggest*) and some can be followed by *to* + infinitive (e.g. *attempt*, *manage*). Some can be followed by *either*, *usually* with a change of meaning (e.g. *remember*, *stop*, *try*).

  *Why don't you **try doing** some research online? (= experiment)*
  *I **tried to get** in touch with Jan but couldn't find her anywhere. (= attempt)*

- We can use *-ing* or infinitive without *to* after the object of sense verbs like hear, see, etc. The infinitive without *to* emphasises a complete action that is seen or heard, while the *-ing* emphasises an ongoing activity.

  *I **saw her drinking** the coffee. (= The action was in progress. I didn't see her finish the coffee.)*
  *I **saw her drink** the coffee. (= The action was completed. I saw her finish the coffee.)*

6.1 Past modals of speculation and deduction

A Find and correct mistakes in some of the sentences.

1. You may have been exhausted after such a long journey.
2. She must be lying. She might not have travelled all that distance in one day. It's impossible!
3. They could have taken a wrong turning, but it's hard to tell at this stage.
4. He must well have taken his bike with him as he loves cycling.
5. Janessa couldn't possibly have climbed Mt Kilimanjaro with a broken ankle.
6. She can't have been a globetrotter in her youth because she has souvenirs from all round the world.
7. Jonathan must not have got our message. I suppose we'll only find out when we hear from him.
8. They must have already left because their room is empty and their bags are gone.

B Choose the correct options to complete the sentences.

1. There is ***a distinct possibility / extremely possible*** that they checked in under a false name.
2. It is ***a slim chance / somewhat likely*** that the courier company had the wrong address.
3. There's ***highly possible / a remote chance*** that the Sphinx was carved more than 10,000 years ago.
4. There isn't ***the slightest possibility / highly unlikely*** that anyone survived that plane crash.
5. It's not ***a distinct likelihood / completely impossible*** that she made her way out of the cave alive.
6. There's ***somewhat possible / a reasonable chance*** that Geoff kept copies of all the correspondence.

C Complete the text with the words in the box.

couldn't it might must there well

Cabeza de Vaca may [1] ________ have been one of the luckiest and unluckiest explorers ever. Of the 600 men on his 1527 expedition to the Americas, he was one of only four to survive. While they probably imagined a difficult journey, they [2] ________ have known the misfortune that awaited them. They risked it because [3] ________ was a possibility of finding gold. Before they even set foot on land, 100 men deserted. They [4] ________ have been too exhausted to continue.

Shortly before reaching the coast, a hurricane killed 60 more. On land, the Apalachee people they encountered weren't very hospitable. [5] ________ is likely they sensed the explorers' ill intentions. The Spanish tried to escape, and they [6] ________ have been successful except for another hurricane! More men died, the natives in Texas enslaved them, and it was ten years before Cabeza de Vaca and his last three men were finally free.

➤ Go back to page 63.

6.2 *-ing* and infinitive forms

A Choose the correct options to complete the sentences.

1. It's no good ___ him for information. He doesn't give anything away.
   a to ask b asking
2. It's time ___ our invention to the test!
   a putting b to put
3. Despite putting his heart and soul into the project, he had a hard time ___ it.
   a to finish b finishing
4. Even though the city has got money, they have little ___ to those in need.
   a to give b giving
5. It's correct ___ that her life was a true rags-to-riches story.
   a saying b to say
6. I'm not very keen on ___ a meeting on a Saturday.
   a to arrange b arranging
7. The police didn't have enough evidence ___ the crime.
   a to solve b solving
8. Jason found it harder ___ with his colleagues after the disagreement.
   a to work b working

B Write the correct form of the verb in brackets.

1. Justin was disciplined for not ________ (*finish*) his assignment.
2. She brought food for the picnic, but there wasn't enough ________ (*go*) round.
3. It's not worth ________ (*do*) such hard work for so little money.
4. I'm sorry, but this is a bad time ________ (*discuss*) this topic.
5. Is she having difficulty ________ (*adjust*) to her new life?
6. They advised him on ________ (*invest*) in new business ventures.
7. There are many ideas here ________ (*help*) you get started on the project.
8. Your plan failed miserably. Have fun ________ (*explain*) that to the boss!
9. I saw them ________ (*steal*) the bike. I witnessed the whole thing from start to finish.

➤ Go back to page 67.

Grammar Hub

7.1 *it* clefting

- We can use the structure *It* + *is/was* + 'focus' + defining relative clause to focus on a particular piece of information in a sentence. This focus could be:

a person/people	It was **Tenzing Norgay and Edmund Hillary** who first reached the summit of Mount Everest.
a time	It was **1953** when Sir John Hunt successfully led the expedition to reach the summit of Mount Everest.
a place	It is **Mount Everest** which has always captured people's imaginations.
a thing or idea	It was **the challenge of the climb** which inspired generations of climbers.
a clause with *because*	It was **because he had almost reached the summit one year previously** that Tenzing Norgay was hired for the expedition.
a clause with *to* + infinitive	It was **to show his respect for the people of Nepal** that Sir Hunt asked Tenzing to make the final climb to the summit.
a clause with *until*	It wasn't **until years later that Tenzing revealed** which climber had first stepped onto the summit of Mount Everest.

Be careful!

- In sentences like this, we usually leave out the second defining relative clause to avoid repeating the same information.

  It wasn't John Hunt who first climbed Everest – it was Edmund Hillary.
  NOT ~~It wasn't John Hunt who first climbed Everest – it was Edmund Hillary who first climbed Everest.~~

7.2 *what* clefting and *all* clefting

- We can use a *what* clause + *be* + second clause in order to emphasise the information in the second clause.

  With this structure, the information in the *what* clause is usually known or understood whereas the information in the second clause is usually new and therefore the main focus of the sentence.

  What Prianka wants is to escape the rat race.
  What they needed, after their walk in the snow, was a hot bath.
  What he decided to do was to change careers.
- To emphasise a verb in the second clause, we can use the structure: *what* clause with *do* + *be* + second clause. We can use the infinitive with or without *to* after the verb *be*.

  What he does is (to) climb cellular phone towers.
- We can use *All* instead of *What* at the beginning of the first clause. This emphasises the idea of there being 'only one thing'.

  All you need to do in the interview is (to) act naturally. (= the only thing you need to do)
- It is also possible to use *Why*, *Where*, *How*, *When* to begin this kind of cleft sentence.

  Why he enjoys extreme sports is a mystery to me.

Be careful!

- The structure *what* clause + *be* + second clause is reversible.

  What he enjoys about his job is living in the wilderness. OR Living in the wilderness is what he enjoys about his job.
- The structure *what* clause with *do* + *be* + second clause is not reversible.

  What they did was move to the countryside. NOT ~~Move to the countryside was what they did.~~

7.1 *it* clefting

A Write one word in each gap to complete the responses.

1 Did you know that Jack was going to come with us?
No, it ________ a surprise that he decided to come.

2 What time did Antonio arrive home?
It was seven o'clock ________ I heard his key in the lock.

3 Was he worried about the cost of fixing his laptop?
No, it was losing all his work ________ he was more worried about.

4 You've met my sister, haven't you?
No, it was your brother ________ I met.

5 Did you recognise Stella straight away?
No, it wasn't ________ somebody introduced us that I realised it was her!

B Read the questions. Use *it* clefting and the information in brackets to complete the answers.

1 What first got you interested in rock climbing? (*my friend Seb*)
________________ first got me interested in the sport.

2 What do you think attracts people to Yosemite? (*the idea of being in the wilderness*)
I think ________________ attracts so many people to go there.

3 When did you set out to climb the Half Dome? (*early in the morning*)
________________ we set out.

4 When did you realise how high the Half Dome is? (*only when I reached the top*)
________________ I realised how high up it is!

C Complete the second sentence so that it has a similar meaning to the first sentence, using the word given. Write between two and five words.

1 Susan wasn't hysterical, Jane was.
WAS
It ________________ hysterical, not Susan.

2 Not until after we were rescued did I realise the danger we had been in.
UNTIL
It ________________ were rescued that I realised the danger we had been in.

3 We took part in the charity walk because we wanted to raise money.
IT
________________ money that we took part in the charity walk.

4 What caused her to fail the interview was her over-confidence.
WAS
It ________________ caused her to fail the interview.

5 I believe yoga will help you to relax.
THAT
It ________________ yoga will help you to relax.

6 Somebody else upset Mzia, not you.
YOU
It ________________ upset Mzia.

➤ Go back to page 74 .

7.2 *what* clefting and *all* clefting

A Reorder the words to make sentences.

1 about the winter / dislike / is / What / the long nights / I
________________.

2 I / want / a normal life / All / is
________________.

3 we're / a solution to our problems / to find / is / here / What
________________.

4 the last train / we missed / happened / that / What / was
________________.

5 I / to ask you / did / All / a simple question / was
________________.

6 I / remember / All / is / really difficult / the questions / were / that
________________.

B Rewrite these sentences using *what* clefting or *all* clefting.

1 I've found that working underwater isn't as bad as it sounds.
What ________________.

2 I'm only saying that you should think twice before moving to Antarctica.
All ________________.

3 I'm going to look for a job as a window cleaner.
What ________________.

4 I only asked for your opinion.
All ________________.

5 I bought a ladder and a bucket.
What ________________.

➤ Go back to page 79.

Grammar Hub

8.1 Relative clauses with complex relative pronouns

- We use *whose* to add information about someone's possessions.

  I was happy to meet Georgia, ***whose*** *sister had helped me find a place to stay.*
- We use *whereby* to add information about a method (formal).

  They introduced a new system in the company ***whereby*** *everybody has a full induction on their first day.*
- We use *whom* to add information about a person where they are the object of the clause (formal).

  The people ***whom*** *I asked were all in favour of the plan.*
- In very formal English, we place the preposition (generally only with *whom*, *whose* and *which*) before the relative pronoun.

  The Prime Minister, ***in whose*** *honour the event was being held, welcomed all the guests.*

  The person ***on whom*** *I depend the most …*

  The place ***to which*** *I often return …*
- In less formal English, we put the preposition at the end of the clause.

  Martin, ***whose house I was staying in****, was a very tidy person.*

  *The person (****who****) I depend* ***on*** *the most …*

  *The place (****which****) I often return* ***to*** *…*
- Formal constructions can use a variety of prepositions depending on meaning.

  The person ***in whom*** *I have the most confidence …*

  The person ***to whom*** *I sent the letter …*

  The person ***for whom*** *the money was being raised …*

Be careful!

- The relative pronoun *whom* is very formal. We don't usually use it with a preposition at the end of the clause.

  The person to whom you gave the money …

  NOT ~~The person whom you gave the money to …~~

8.2 Pronouns and determiners

- We use determiners before nouns to identify a number, an amount or a group.

  We have ***a few*** *tomatoes.*

  I had ***a couple of*** *cups of coffee while I was waiting.*

  You need to get ***some*** *fresh air.*
- Some common determiners include: *a/an, the, this/that/these/those, all, some (of), none, (a) little, (a) few (of), my/your/their/its*/etc, *any, much, more, both (of), enough, a lot of, other, each/every, one/two/three*/etc, *either (of)*.
- We can use some common determiners like *millions of, loads of, tons of* when we want to exaggerate a point, especially in informal English.

  I feel so guilty because I ate ***loads of*** *chocolate last night.*
- Pronouns can be the same words as determiners but they are not followed by a noun. They replace the noun, often to avoid repeating it.

  You look like you need water – I'll get you some.

  NOT ~~You look like you need water – I'll get you some water.~~
- Some common pronouns include: *I/he/they*/etc, *me/you/him/her*/etc, *this/that/these/those, there, some, mine/yours/his*/etc, *both, several, anyone/something*/etc, *others, none, either*.
- We can also use *one* or *one's* as pronouns to refer to people in general. These are especially used to make generalisations in formal English. *One's* indicates possession.

  Diets make ***one*** *realise how much food can impact* ***one's*** *life.*

Be careful!

- Some pronouns cannot be used as determiners.

  That glass is mine. NOT ~~That is mine glass.~~
- Some determiners cannot be used as pronouns.

  That is my glass. NOT ~~That glass is my.~~

8.1 Relative clauses with complex relative pronouns

A Choose the correct options to complete the sentences.

1 Do you know the name of the person to ***who*** / ***whom*** the letter must be addressed?
2 That's Melanie, ***whose*** / ***who*** mother is the manager of our company.
3 This is the mobile ***which*** / ***whereby*** I am most interested in.
4 His father, ***to whom*** / ***whom*** he would often go for financial help, had refused to give him more money.
5 We need to find a solution ***whereby*** / ***which*** everyone will be happy.
6 The new supermarket will benefit the villagers, ***among whom*** / ***for whom*** there are a number of families without cars.

B Complete each sentence with a word or phrase from the box.

for whom	into which	into whose	whereby	whose	with which

1 A pedometer is a mechanical or digital device ________ we count steps taken while walking.
2 The owner, ________ pocket the pedometer can be slipped, can then use it to calculate their distance travelled.
3 More recently, mobiles have started featuring fitness apps, ________ pedometers or 'step counters' have been incorporated.
4 Some experts claim that people ________ daily number of steps is lower than 10,000 should be concerned about their health and fitness.
5 Most fitness experts agree that any method ________ our steps can be counted is a useful one.
6 Pedometers make people ________ exercise is not a priority aware of their daily activity and motivate them to do more.

C Match the sentence beginnings (1–6) with the endings (a–f) to make sentences.

1 We reached an agreement ___
2 He was uncomfortable because it was a situation in ___
3 Paula is a person whose ___
4 This will be popular with the team, among ___
5 The explorer contracted an illness from ___
6 We still hadn't met Mr Dawson, in whose ___

a mood never changes.
b which he never recovered.
c house we were all staying.
d whereby everyone was satisfied.
e whom any extra support is appreciated.
f which he had never been before.

➤ Go back to page 88.

8.2 Pronouns and determiners

A Underline the determiners in each sentence. Some sentences have more than one determiner.

1 I could do with a little help starting this fitness programme.
2 The doctor said I should leave the car at home and do more walking.
3 Both of the sports centres in my area are too far to walk to.
4 There was little point in talking to him since he wouldn't listen.
5 One of the techniques is bound to suit you.
6 The canteen had two healthier options but I didn't fancy either of them.

B Change one determiner into a pronoun in each sentence by crossing out some words.

1 Some people have a gluten-free diet because they genuinely can't eat it without getting sick, but many people believe that avoiding gluten is just healthier.
2 I try to drink a couple of litres of water every day, but I'm pretty sure that I don't drink enough water.
3 A lot of people I know are cutting back on sugar and caffeine, but I don't want to cut back on either sugar or caffeine.
4 I've started following a vegan diet so I like to try vegan restaurants, but there are only a few vegan restaurants in my area.
5 I prefer fruit and vegetables that have been grown organically to those fruit and vegetables that haven't.
6 The government should make companies that produce food with a lot of sugar use less sugar to help people have better diets.

C Complete each sentence with the correct pronoun. More than one answer is sometimes possible.

1 Jack couldn't decide which of the two sandwiches to get so he just bought ________.
2 Some people enjoy running, while ________ find it really boring.
3 Now I can't tell which shoes are ________ – they look the same as yours.
4 'Which of the two matches do you want to watch on TV?' '________ – I really don't mind.'
5 I know we said we'd buy oranges but ________ don't look very nice.
6 We haven't got any football boots in stock but we'll be getting some new ________ in next week.

➤ Go back to page 93.

Grammar Hub

9.1 Noun phrases

- We can use possessive adjectives, quantifiers, numbers and modified quantifiers before nouns to make noun phrases.

Article/determiner	**Those** researchers are highly qualified.
Possessive adjective	**Their** study is well funded.
Quantifier	**Many** eager participants started immediately
Number	**Two of the five** speakers disagreed.
Modified quantifier	**Almost every single** student showed up early.

- We can use relative clauses, prepositional phrases, *that* clauses and *to* + infinitive after nouns to make noun phrases.

Relative clause	**The clinic where she works** just closed.
Reduced relative clause	**The woman sitting down** is my colleague.
Prepositional phrase	They shared **a wealth of knowledge**.
that clause	I question **the idea that humans are still evolving**.
to + infinitive	They looked for **a cheap place to eat and sleep**.

- We can use phrases such as *the fact that*, *the idea that* and *the belief that* to turn a sentence into a noun phrase.

A language dies every two weeks. That is regrettable. (= The fact that a language dies every two weeks is regrettable.)

People believe language strengthens social ties. This is supported by research. (= The belief that language strengthens social ties is supported by research.)

9.2 Participle clauses and verbless clauses

- We use present and past participles as well as combinations of both to form participle clauses.

Feeling unsure of the results, Mary tested the configuration once more.

Left to their own devices, children can solve complex problems.

Having just finished his research, Travis went for a walk to relax.

- We can use prepositions such as *before*, *after* and *despite* before participle clauses with present participles (but not past participles).

Before arriving at the office, Susan texted her boss.
NOT ~~Before arrived at the office, Susan texted her boss.~~

- We can use conjunctions such as *if*, *when* and *while* before participle clauses with both present and past participles.

While waiting for the bus, Paula had a marvellous idea.

When pressed to answer questions, Jonathan became very nervous.

Be careful!

- Participle clauses appear near the nouns they refer to. When that noun is missing, or the clause appears closer to another noun which it doesn't refer to, it becomes a 'dangling participle' and is grammatically incorrect.

While doing research, Frank noticed the room getting cold. NOT ~~While doing research, the room got cold.~~ (Incorrect: the room wasn't doing research)

- When the participle clause involves using the verb *be*, we can omit the verb altogether and the clause becomes 'verbless'.

Too impatient to wait, Paul barged in and demanded the results. (= Being too impatient to wait, …)

- We can start a clause with just a participle, with words such as *when*, *after* or *because* being implied.

Hearing the news, Alex leapt for joy! (= After hearing the news, Alex leapt for joy!)

9.1 Noun phrases

A Choose the option which is closest in meaning to the sentence.

1 Lisa questioned many of her professors, and only one gave a clear answer.
  a Many of the professors Lisa questioned only gave one clear answer.
  b Only one of the many professors Lisa questioned gave a clear answer.
2 I have two younger brothers, and they are language experts.
  a Both of my younger brothers are language experts.
  b Two of my younger brothers are language experts.
3 Very few of the participants enjoyed the study.
  a Almost all of the participants disliked the study.
  b Quite a few of the participants enjoyed the study.
4 Jake is standing at the workstation, and he's running reports.
  a The man standing at the workstation is running reports.
  b The man standing at the workstation and running reports is Jake.
5 They're looking for a safe location so they can try out their experiment.
  a They're searching for a safe location to try out their experiment.
  b They're looking to try out their experiment at a safe location.
6 Many people applied for the trial, but few were qualified to join.
  a Many of the few people applying for the trial were qualified to join.
  b Few of the many people applying for the trial were qualified to join.

B Rewrite these sentences using noun phrases. Use the words in bold to help you.

1 I speak **three** languages and **two** of **them** are Latin-based.
  ______ languages I speak are Latin-based.
2 I have **little** money, but I save **it all** … well, **almost**.
  I save ______ money I have.
3 I've read **very few** pieces of research, but this is **one of them**.
  This is ______ pieces of research I've read.
4 **The writer** draws **two** conclusions and they **both** seem dubious to me.
  ______ conclusions seem dubious to me.
5 **The researchers** interviewed **many** people. **Quite a few** had no savings at all.
  ______ interviewees had no savings at all.
6 They **can't conduct the experiment** in peace. That is annoying.
  ______ is annoying.
7 That **man** is in charge of the experiment. He's wearing a **white lab coat**.
  The ______ is in charge of the experiment.
8 Many linguists **believe language is alive**, and this is factored into their theories.
  ______ factored into linguists' theories.

➤ Go back to page 101.

9.2 Participle clauses and verbless clauses

A Choose the correct options to complete the sentences.

1 *Sensing* / *Sensed* danger, Henry shut down the machine immediately.
2 *Having already left* / *Leaving the building*, Danielle didn't feel like returning to get her phone.
3 Before *notifying* / *notified* her supervisor, Anna wanted to make sure the experiment was a success.
4 When *asking* / *asked* about the research, Kyle refused to reply.
5 *Too* / *Too being* cautious to take risks, Martin decided to stay on at his job.
6 Despite *handed* / *handing* in her notice, Sarah put in great effort during her last days at work.
7 *Having been told* / *Being told* to speed up the study, David cut corners to make his deadlines.
8 If *successful* / *being successful*, we can publish the results in a science journal.

B Rewrite these sentences using participle clauses or verbless clauses and the word in bold.

1 I understand animal behaviour better now that I've read the article. **having**
  ______.
2 The octopus hid in the coconut shell because it felt threatened. **feeling**
  ______.
3 These experiments can teach us a lot if you do them properly. **done**
  ______.
4 I guessed the answer because I didn't know. **knowing**
  ______.
5 The crow had never seen the tool before but used it perfectly. **despite**
  ______.
6 She wasn't fast enough to win the race, but she came in a close second. **too**
  ______.

➤ Go back to page 103.

Grammar Hub

10.1 Discourse markers

- We use discourse markers to connect ideas, or to give further information regarding our attitude to what we're saying or writing.
- We use some discourse markers to join two clauses within a sentence. They can be positioned either at the beginning of a sentence (followed by a comma) or in between the two clauses. They may be used to express cause and consequence, or to describe a contrast.

despite	**Despite** having a degree in Business Studies, Karla didn't get the job. Karla didn't get the job **despite** having a degree in Business Studies.
owing to	**Owing to** his lack of qualifications, Omar was unable to find a job in the field. Omar was unable to find a job in the field **owing to** his lack of qualifications.
whereas	**Whereas** Kim is determined to succeed, her sister lacks ambition. Her sister lacks ambition, **whereas** Kim is determined to succeed.

- We use some discourse markers to connect ideas in two separate sentences. These discourse markers can be positioned at the beginning of the second sentence, in which case they should be followed by a comma. Some can also be placed after the subject of the second sentence, and should in this case be followed by a comma, or at the end of the second sentence.

as a matter of fact	He's doing research into Arctic animals. **As a matter of fact**, he's leaving for Greenland next week. / He's leaving for Greenland next week, **as a matter of fact**.
conversely	The novel was a huge bestseller. **Conversely**, the film version was never as successful. / The film version, **conversely**, was never as successful.
for instance	Mediterranean resorts are making a comeback. **For instance**, Mykonos is now seen as a holiday hotspot for Europe's young celebrities. / Mykonos, **for instance**, is now seen as a holiday hotspot for Europe's young celebrities. / Mykonos is now seen as a holiday hotspot for Europe's young celebrities, **for instance**.
in any case	It seems that no crime had taken place. **In any case**, it wasn't a matter for the police. / It wasn't a matter for the police, **in any case**.
moreover	Tax income increased because of tourism. **Moreover**, it has created hundreds of new jobs. / It has, **moreover**, created hundreds of new jobs.

10.2 Ellipsis and substitution

- Ellipsis involves leaving out words and phrases to avoid repeating them.
- In written English, there are a number of grammatical items that are often left out.

repeated subject	**He**'s into politics and (**he**) is passionate about activism.
repeated subject + modal	**They should** organise a campaign and (**they should**) create some positive publicity.
repeated subject + auxiliary verb	**We're going to** start a petition and (**we're going to**) organise a protest meeting.
repeated verb phrase	'I thought you were **going on the march**.' 'Yes, I am (**going on the march**).'
repeated adjective	So many students are **apathetic**, but Kiera isn't (**apathetic**).

- In spoken English, we can also leave out some grammatical items for the sake of brevity, when it's clear who/what we're talking about.

subject: *Can't believe we managed to save the forest from developers! (= I can't believe …)*

auxiliary verb: *You planning to join the group? (= Are you planning …)*

auxiliary verb + subject + verb: *Any preference as to which route we take? (= Do you have any preference …)*

- We often substitute the following words and phrases to avoid repeating words.

do: *Are you going into town? Will you post my letter if you **do**?*
(to avoid repeating 'go into town')

not: *I may have to organise the campaign, but I hope **not**.*
(to avoid repeating 'that I don't have to organise the campaign')

do so: *Deactivate the burglar alarm. In order to **do so**, you'll need to key in this code number.*
(to avoid repeating 'deactivate the burglar alarm')

do it: *I often read English-language newspapers. I **do it** to improve my vocabulary.*
(to avoid repeating 'read English-language newspapers')

do that: *I specifically asked you not to read my emails. Why did you **do that**?*
(to avoid repeating 'read my emails')

10.1 Discourse markers

A **What is the function of the discourse markers in bold? Read the sentences and choose the correct options.**

1. Large hotel complexes consume huge amounts of water, **whereas** smaller family-run hotels tend to use less.
   - **a** contrasting two different ideas
   - **b** comparing two related ideas
2. Walking holidays, **for instance**, are an environmentally-friendly choice.
   - **a** suggesting a possibility
   - **b** giving an example
3. Huge building projects tend to attract investors. **Conversely**, small businesses sometimes struggle to raise money.
   - **a** repeating and reinforcing an idea
   - **b** contrasting two different ideas
4. The room wasn't at all expensive. **As a matter of fact**, it was one of the cheapest places we stayed.
   - **a** adding more information
   - **b** giving an example
5. Farmers are warning that crops may fail **owing to** the lack of rain.
   - **a** offering an explanation
   - **b** trying to persuade someone
6. **Despite** placing adverts on various websites, Aisha didn't manage to sell her products.
   - **a** describing a situation
   - **b** contrasting two different ideas

B **Choose the correct options to complete the sentences.**

1. We haven't visited all the monuments yet. ***Owing to / In any case***, Farid isn't that keen on sightseeing.
2. We managed to visit all the most important museums in the city ***whereas / despite*** our limited budget.
3. Because the cost of living in Venice is so high, many people are leaving. ***Moreover / For instance***, many inhabitants are worried about the danger of flooding.
4. Many of the streets in Venice are very narrow. The 'Calleta Varisco', ***conversely / for instance***, is just 53 centimetres wide!
5. ***Owing to / Despite*** rising water levels, Venice city authorities are building flood barriers to protect the city.
6. Riding on a gondola is a bucket list experience for many visiting Venice. Some say it is one of the most iconic tourist experiences, ***as a matter of fact / moreover***!

➤ Go back to page 111.

10.2 Ellipsis and substitution

A **Cross out the words that can be omitted in the conversation.**

Dom: Do you know who I saw the other day?
Ali: No, who did you see?
Dom: Klaus.
Ali: Do you mean your old roommate from college?
Dom: Yeah! I can't believe it – I saw him again after all these years.
Ali: What happened when you saw him?
Dom: He gave me his phone number and he gave me his email address.
Ali: Are you planning to meet up soon?
Dom: He's going to be visiting the area again next month, so he'll give me a ring when he does visit the area again.

B **Replace the phrases in bold with the words and phrases in the box.**

do | do it | do so | doing that | don't

1. 'Do you have time to help out at the animal shelter?'
   'No, I'm afraid **I don't have time to help out at the animal shelter.**'
2. 'I'd like to volunteer with you at the weekend.'
   'That's great. You'll have to fill out this form in order to **volunteer with us at the weekend**.'
3. 'I volunteer at an animal shelter every weekend.'
   'I really admire you for **volunteering at the animal shelter**.'
4. 'Are you enjoying your voluntary work?'
   'Yes. I didn't know how fulfilling it would be, but now I **know how fulfilling it is**.'
5. 'I've always wanted to volunteer at the cats' home.'
   'So why don't you **volunteer at the cats' home**?'

➤ Go back to page 117.

Vocabulary Hub

6.1 Journeys and adventures

A Complete the sentences with a word or phrase. Use the definitions in brackets to help you.

1 Can you think of a time that you went ______________________ (*away from frequently visited places*)?
2 How do/would you pass the time on a ______________________ (*long distance*) flight?
3 Do you prepare in advance before you ______________________ (*leave*) on a trip? What do you do?
4 Is there any ______________________ (*places not covered by maps*) left in the world? Where?
5 Imagine you had to camp in the ______________________ (*middle*) of a rainforest.
What ______________________ (*supplies of food, drink, equipment*) would you take with you?
6 Would you like a job that required you to be a ______________________ (*frequent traveller*)? Why/Why not?

B Work in pairs. Discuss the questions in Exercise A.

➤ Go back to page 63.

6.2 Binomial expressions

Work in pairs. Complete the sentences with a binomial expression from the box.

by and large	far and wide	heart and soul	life or death
safe and sound	side by side	slowly but surely	time after time

1 Marco Polo travelled ______________________ in Asia.
2 Brothers Louis and Auguste Lumière worked ______________________ to create film and cinema.
3 Edmund Hillary and Tenzing Norgay were the first to climb Mount Everest and return ______________________.
4 The American conservationist Dian Fossey won the trust of the gorillas ______________________.
5 The German physicist Albert Einstein is, ______________________, thought to be the smartest person that ever lived.
6 Passengers on the sinking *Titanic* faced a ______________________ situation.
7 ______________________, numerous climbers have tried to reach the summit of the mountain. But all have failed.
8 Van Gogh put his ______________________ into his art and inventions, working tirelessly on both.

➤ Go back to page 69.

7.1 Feelings

Choose the correct options to complete the text.

Home | Articles | About | Contact

The psychology of everyday life

Extreme and stressful situations can always be difficult to cope with. But it's actually how we deal with mundane, everyday tasks, that has the biggest impact on our well-being. Here are some tips on how to cope.

- Learn to control your emotions – be the calm and collected person rather than the [1]***hysterical** / **courageous** / **devastated*** one when the pressure is on.
- Try not to fire back emails when you're [2]***humble** / **grumpy** / **resilient*** – an angry message may make you feel better immediately. But, you'll be [3]***indifferent** / **disgusted** / **devastated*** when your boss fires you and you're suddenly jobless.
- If you just aren't getting anywhere with something and are [4]***frustrated** / **devastated** / **disgusted***, recognise that you may need a break or even to ask for help.
- Sometimes it's important to be [5]***courageous** / **humble** / **superior*** and take risks rather than play it safe. Bravery is something you can practise and get better at.
- Just because you are busy, don't be [6]***indifferent** / **hysterical** / **resilient*** to other people's problems – it's important to help out the people around you.
- No matter how well you think you're doing at the moment, try to stay [7]***humble** / **courageous** / **resilient*** about your achievements. Nothing annoys people more than a [8]***superior** / **disgusted** / **hysterical*** attitude.

➤ Go back to page 76.

7.2 Polysemy

Complete the sentences with the correct form of a word. You can use some words more than once.

1 It can be quite difficult to ________ a job with the right balance between intellectual challenge and not too much ________ to succeed.

2 One of the most important ________ of barometers (which measure atmospheric ________) is to calculate the height at which a plane is flying.

3 There's too much ________ between hundreds of people who have sent in their ________ for the job; there should be a ________ to find the successful candidate instead!

4 The pilot says he will ________ the plane shortly as ________ have improved.

➤ Go back to page 79.

7.2 Intensifiers

Choose the correct intensifiers to complete the advice about job interviews. What other intensifiers are used?

1 It's perfectly normal to exaggerate your achievements *remarkably* / *somewhat*, but you should never tell *noticeably* / *outright* lies.

2 If you're not *altogether* / *immensely* sure what the interviewer is asking, it's completely fine to ask for clarification.

3 *Practically* / *Radically* all interviews are highly stressful, but as long as you're extremely well-prepared, it should be *relatively* / *utterly* painless.

4 Remember that for the interviewers, it's *practically* / *exceptionally* boring to hear the same answers from every single interviewee. If you give *immensely* / *radically* different answers, you'll stand out from the crowd.

➤ Go back to page 81.

Vocabulary Hub

8.1 Health problems

Cross out one word in each sentence which does not make a collocation.

1 Tony fractured a(n) ***muscle / arm / bone*** when he went skiing last year.
2 Do you sell anything for a ***twisted / sore*** throat?
3 Some studies have claimed that ***low / slow*** blood pressure may be more common amongst athletes.
4 When I was running I may have ***pulled / dislocated / sprained*** a muscle.
5 After intense exercise your ***skin rash / blood pressure / heart rate*** is usually higher.
6 You can buy a number of products over the counter to help relieve skin ***fractures / inflammation / rashes***.

➤ Go back to page 86.

8.2 Describing taste

Complete the sentences with words from Exercise A. More than one answer is possible for some sentences.

1 I love ________________ drinks, but I'm trying to be healthy so I usually order sparkling water at restaurants.
2 I know I should eat more citrus fruits to get my daily dose of Vitamin C, but they are just too ________________ for me.
3 Presentation is so important for me – if food doesn't look ________________, I can't eat it.
4 I ate a delicious curry at the weekend, which wasn't too spicy at all – in fact, it was quite ________________.
5 My dad loves blue cheese, so I get some really ________________ aromas when I open the fridge sometimes.
6 I try to eat salad for lunch occasionally, but it doesn't taste of much. It's really ________________ unless I put some unhealthy dressing on the top.
7 I'm trying to eat healthy snacks, like carrot sticks – they're nice and ________________.

➤ Go back to page 93.

9.2 Verb + object + infinitive

Complete the sentences with the correct form of the verbs in brackets.

1 The scientists observed the dolphin ________________ itself in the mirror for hours. (admire)
2 Snakes' heat sensors help them ________________ prey ________________. (detect, approach)
3 Scientists must be seen ________________ procedures very carefully. (follow)
4 Oh! You're here! I didn't notice you ________________! (arrive)
5 I woke up because I could feel a spider ________________ on my arm. (crawl)
6 I was made ________________ for over an hour before they let me ________________ in. (wait, come)
7 The experimenters had the participants ________________ a form before they could start. (sign)

➤ Go back to page 103.

9.2 Gestures and body language

Complete the sentences with the correct form of the words in the box.

beckon	fidget	glare	grin	lean	wink	nod	gaze

1 Sally was ________________ across the bay, looking at nothing in particular, when the ship suddenly came into view.
2 Phillip just can't sit still in meetings – he's always ________________.
3 James ________________ at Emma, so she knew he was joking.
4 'Shhh … we have to be quiet … just ________________ if you agree with me.'
5 The bookshelf fell over when I ________________ against it.
6 Steven was so happy when he got the job that he couldn't stop ________________.
7 The teacher ________________ his student over to the board.
8 Elizabeth was so angry that she just ________________ at them without saying a word.

➤ Go back to page 105.

10.1 Culture and heritage

Complete the text with the words in the box.

architectural endangered funding habitat heritage preserve refurbishment settlement

HOMETOWN GLORY

My hometown has a very rich history – it is where a famous treaty was signed and is close to the site of an ancient [1] ____________. In fact some of ruins of the site are still standing today and are of special [2] ____________ interest as they show the precise engineering methods of the Romans.

For these reasons alone, the town is a very important part of my country's national [3] ____________. The nearby forests are the [4] ____________ of a lot of different wildlife, including some rare species which are unfortunately now [5] ____________. As such they have been designated as an area of outstanding natural beauty and are protected.

Unfortunately we don't receive a lot of [6] ____________ from the government to [7] ____________ areas of the old town. Some of the unlisted buildings are in real need of [8] ____________ – so please come and visit us. Tourism is a valuable source of income and helps us to keep our heritage and culture alive!

➤ Go back to page 111.

10.2 Word building

A Write the correct form of the word in brackets to complete the sentences.

1 A good politician is someone who grew up in the ____________ (commune) that they represent.
2 Most politicians are more interested in ____________ (person) success than helping the public.
3 Becoming ____________ (act) in politics is the best way to make a difference in the world.
4 I feel ____________ (passion) about politics and follow the news closely.
5 Most people's political beliefs are formed in ____________ (child) by listening to their parents.
6 Many people are ____________ (apathy) about politics, because they don't trust politicians.
7 The best politicians are those who had other careers before entering ____________ (politics) life.
8 Local politics is often more ____________ (effect) at improving people's lives than national politics.

B Work in pairs. Do you agree with the sentences in Exercise A? Why/Why not?

➤ Go back to page 115.

10.3 Student B

SPEAK Describe the following scene to your partner.

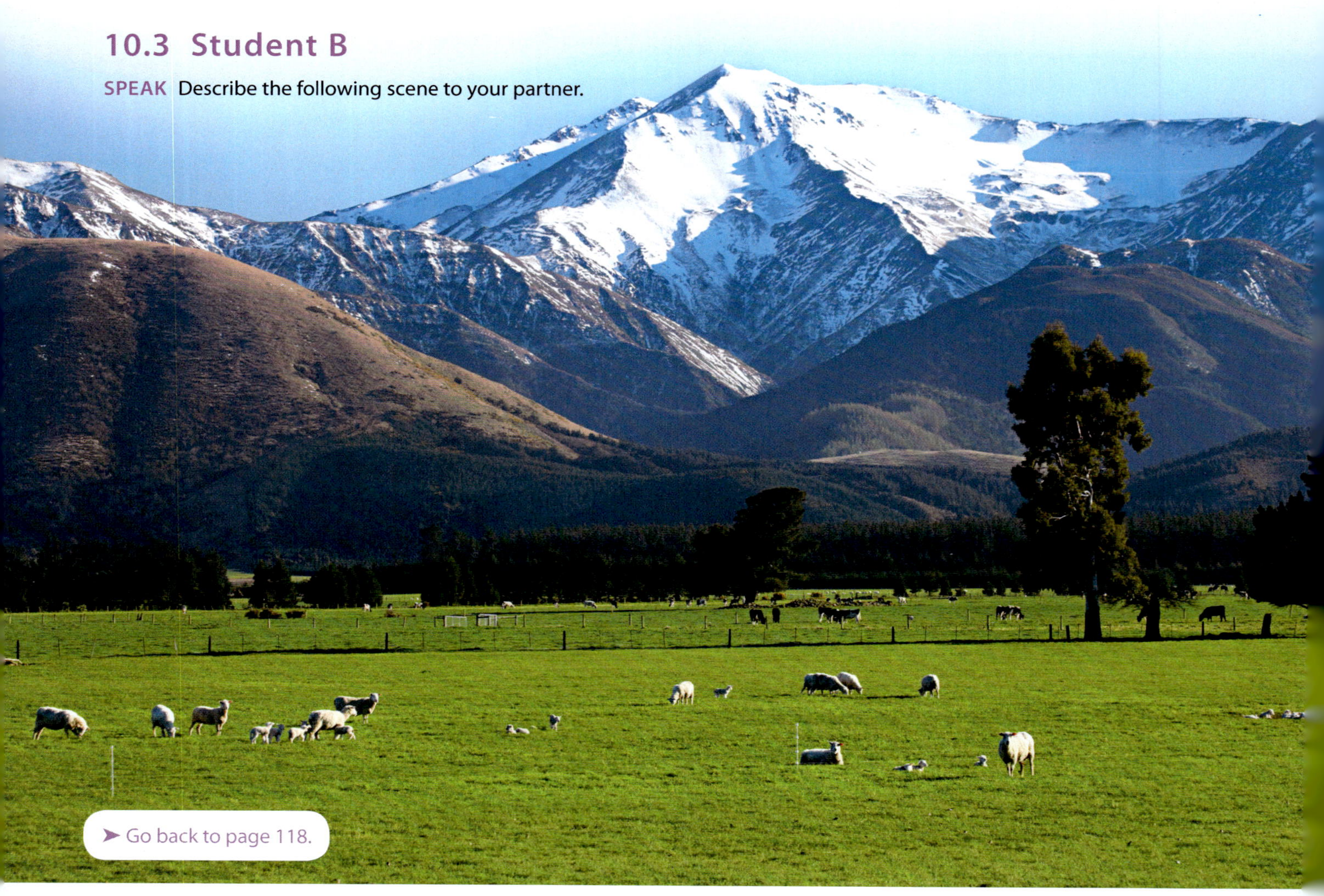

➤ Go back to page 118.

9.2 Players

You have three minutes to get ten points, but you have to work out the rules to the game by yourselves. For example, perhaps you get a point for nodding your head, for blinking your eyes or for saying a particular word (or perhaps all three at the same time). Work as a team to see if you can win ten points in three minutes. Good luck!

➤ Go back to page 105.

9.2 Facilitator

The 'game' is in fact an experiment to see if you can trick the players into behaving strangely. They think they have to 'win' points, but in fact they simply get a point at regular intervals. When the game starts, count to ten slowly and silently in your head, again and again, saying 'one point' aloud every time you reach ten. Don't let the players work out the real rules – but you can share the secret with them at the end!

➤ Go back to page 105.

6.1 Group A

Work in small groups. Read about an historical mystery. Speculate about what happened.

THE LOST COLONY OF ROANOKE

In 1585, an English settlement was established on a small island off the Eastern coast of the US. In the first year there, they began to run out of food, so the Mayor returned to England to get supplies – but it was three years before he could come back. He left behind his daughter, son-in-law and grandchild among the colonists.

When he returned, the colony and all 117 members of the colony were gone. The only thing left was a fence around the area and a newly built fort on the other side of the island. He never saw or heard from the colonists again.

The Mayor had told the settlers to carve a symbol into a tree if they had been forced to leave the area, but he only found the word CROATOAN. Croatoan was the name of a nearby island, inhabited by a tribe of indigenous people with the same name.

In recent years, some objects of European origin from that period were found at two different locations. Part of a sword was found on Croatoan Island and some pottery was found about 50 miles inland.

Despite modern efforts to solve the mystery, nothing of the actual colonists is known for sure. Several theories exist, but the quest to find out what happened continues.

➤ Go back to page 63.

Communication Hub

9.1 Students

In your groups, discuss the questions.

- Experiments have shown that speaking English encourages people to be more competitive, thanks to the connotations of English-speaking countries. What effect might your own language have on its speakers?
- Unlike English, many languages have formal and informal words for *you*, so you always have to think about your relationship with the other person before speaking to them. How might that affect your behaviour?
- The present perfect in English treats past events as part of the present. How might that affect English speakers' views of the past … and their behaviour?

➤ Go back to page 101.

6.3 Students

Underline examples of summarising, repetition and dynamic words in the transcript.

Hydrogen atoms, carbon atoms, oxygen and sulphur atoms – these basic building blocks react and combine to make everything.

A woodland is a complex place – there are oak trees and grass and mosses and ferns, and countless animals and plants all living together in a tangled ecosystem. But there's a simpler level of description – everything is made of atoms. So an oak tree is really just carbon, nitrogen, oxygen and hydrogen and a few other bits mixed together. So, when you look at it like that, it's really not that complicated at all.

The atoms that make up this woodland have been on an extraordinary journey to get here. Think of a carbon atom in this acorn. It was assembled in the heart of a star billions of years ago out of protons that were built just after the Big Bang. It got thrown out into the universe in a supernova explosion, collapsed as part of a dust cloud to form the sun and then the earth four and a half billion years ago.

It will have spent a lot of time in rocks. It was probably part of some of the first living things on Earth. It would have got breathed out as carbon dioxide by someone that walked through this wood 400 years ago. It will have got into some ancient oak tree through the action of photosynthesis constructed into this acorn and fallen down to the ground. And there it is. It's got a history that goes back billions of years. In fact, a history in terms of the building blocks of carbon, the protons that goes back right to the origin of the universe. And in billions of years time when the sun dies and the Earth is vaporised they'll be thrown back out into space and probably condensed into a new world billions of years in the future.

So life is just a temporary home for the immortal elements that build up the universe.

➤ Go back to page 70.

10.3 Student A

SPEAK Describe the following scene to your partner.

➤ Go back to page 118.

6.1 Group B

Work in small groups. Read about an historical mystery. Speculate about what happened.

THE NAZCA LINES

Approximately 2000 years ago, people living in southern Peru drew pictures of shapes and animals into the dry desert landscape by removing red rocks to reveal the white sand below.

Some of the pictures are as large as the Empire State Building, but when seen from above are very accurate. How did the people draw the pictures without being able to see them from above? And since the pictures are not visible from the ground, who was supposed to see them?

One scientist found that one of the lines pointed directly to the sun during the winter solstice.

Another scientist believes the drawings were used to mark the location of underground rivers and wells.

One image is of a spider, but this species of spider is not found in this area. It comes from the Amazon, over 900 miles away.

➤ Go back to page 63.

W– structuring an expository essay

A SPEAK Work in pairs. Read the essay prompt and brainstorm possible answers.

> What are the benefits of deep-sea exploration?

B Read the essay. What benefits does the writer mention? What evidence or examples does the writer give for each benefit?

The benefits of DEEP-SEA EXPLORATION

Did you know that humans have only explored 5% of the world's oceans? This means there is clearly a lot left to be discovered. There are benefits of deep-sea exploration, such as learning more about climate change, addressing the problems of food shortage, and finding cures for diseases.

First, deep-sea exploration is providing vital information about climate change. For example, researchers have been observing how rising temperatures affect the movements of sea creatures. In addition, some studies have found that the sea is able to absorb carbon from the atmosphere.

Second, exploration of the seas will help governments ensure there is enough food for everyone in the future. According to the UN Food and Agriculture Organisation, fish stocks are already getting low. However, improvements to fish farming methods will allow countries to support sustainable fishing.

Finally, exploring the seas is leading to advances in medicine to help fight disease. For example, medicines have already been discovered to help with chronic pain, asthma and even cancer. Many scientists believe we are much more likely to discover new medicines in the sea than on land.

In summary, there are many benefits to deep-sea exploration. It can help scientists to understand climate change better as they try to prevent it. It can also help people to ensure the ocean remains a valuable source of food. In addition, discovering new species of plant and animal could lead to the development of new medicines. People have already discovered a lot from just 5% of the ocean. Imagine what they could find in the other 95%.

C Read the essay again and answer the questions. Use the information in the box to help you.

Structuring an expository essay

The typical structure of an expository essay is:

- **Introduction:** Includes a 'hook' to get readers' attention, background information and the thesis statement, which states what the essay will describe or explain
- **Body paragraph one:** Describes or explains the first point
- **Body paragraph two:** Describes or explains the second point
- **Body paragraph three:** Describes or explains the third point
- **Conclusion:** Summarises the points that were made and leaves the reader with a 'final thought'.

1. Which sentence is the hook? How does the writer get the reader's attention?
2. Which sentence is the thesis statement? What do you notice about the order of the points in the thesis statement?
3. The first sentence of each paragraph is called a topic sentence. What information is included in this sentence?
4. What kind of information is included in each paragraph to support the idea introduced in the topic sentence?
5. The conclusion contains a summary of the points made in the essay. What do you notice about the order of the points in the summary?

WRITING

A PREPARE Work in groups. Read the essay prompt in Exercise A again. Come up with ideas and make a list of possible benefits.

B PLAN Choose the best ideas and organise them into paragraphs.

C WRITE Use your plan to write an expository essay. Write approximately 250 words.

D REVIEW Work in pairs. Edit your partner's essay. Check:

- spelling and punctuation
- use of language
- clarity of the structure

7 Writing — Write a cover letter

W – using power verbs

A Read the job advert.

Which skills and abilities:

1 will candidates need to prove from their qualifications and experience?

2 will candidates try to show from their life experience and character?

3 are useful but not essential?

Research Technician – Antarctica

The **International Antarctic Research Station (IARS)** is recruiting a research technician. The job involves setting up and maintaining equipment for scientific experiments, collecting data and providing support as part of the IARS team.

No research skills are required but experience of work in glaciology, geology, meteorology or oceanology would be valuable. The main requirements are technical skills (including electrical and mechanical engineering). You will need to cope with extreme conditions (including severe weather, dangerous environments and hazardous materials), work as a reliable member of an international team and follow instructions accurately and intelligently.

Applications to: Dr Adelia Ross, IARS

B Read the cover letter. Which skills and abilities from Exercise A does Francesca mention? What doesn't she mention?

Dear Dr Ross,

I am writing to apply for the position of Research Technician at the IARS.

You will see on my CV (attached) that I have six years' experience as a laboratory technician at an international energy company, where I investigated energy efficiency. During this time, I gained invaluable insights into real-life research, where quick thinking and creativity are just as valuable as patience and precision.

I have explored the Polar regions many times. Last summer, I successfully led an international expedition to a remote part of Greenland, where I demonstrated exceptional organisational skills, resilience in the face of extreme challenges and, above all, the ability to work in a team.

I look forward to the opportunity of an interview.

Best regards,

Francesca Matienzo

C Read the information about using power verbs to apply for a job. Add five power verbs from Francesca's letter to the list of examples.

Using power verbs

In CVs and cover letters, it's more powerful to use verbs to describe your achievements (*I managed the project*) rather than nouns (*I was the manager of …*) or adjectives (*I was responsible for …*).

Examples: *achieved, coordinated, designed, implemented, improved, negotiated, organised, persuaded, strengthened, updated,* ______, ______, ______, ______, ______

D Make these extracts more powerful.

1 I was involved in negotiations to buy raw materials.

2 My manager agreed to my idea to switch suppliers.

3 I was in charge of a team of six.

4 Our old records were out of date, so I fixed them.

5 I did general office tasks, like answering the phone and checking emails.

WRITING

A PREPARE You are going to apply for your dream job or one of the jobs below. First, list the skills, abilities, experience and qualifications required for the job.

- stunt performer
- safari or mountain guide
- zoo keeper
- astronaut

B PLAN Draft your cover letter, using Francesca's letter as a model.

C WRITE Make your letter more powerful by adding at least five power verbs.

D REVIEW Read some of your classmates' letters. Which letters would persuade you to invite the candidate for an interview? How could you improve the other letters?

paraphrasing

A SPEAK Work in pairs. How does stress affect the body?

B Read *The effects of stress on the body* and circle the specific health problems the article mentions.

The effects of stress on the body

Chronic stress can affect several different parts of the body, including the musculoskeletal system, the cardiovascular system and the gastrointestinal system.

Stress causes muscles to tense and when this happens for an extended period of time, it can cause tension and pain in the back, shoulders and head. For many people, this results in tension headaches and migraines.

It is well known that acute stress causes a temporary increase in heart rate and blood pressure. However, long-term stress means that heart rate and blood pressure remain high, potentially leading to inflammation of the arteries and an increased chance of hypertension, heart attack or stroke.

Stress can have a direct or indirect effect on the gastrointestinal system. Stress often causes people to eat more unhealthy food than they usually would. This can lead to heartburn and acid reflux, which can affect the throat. Stress can upset the stomach too, leading to digestive problems, nausea and even stomach ulcers.

In summary, long-term stress puts extra pressure on the body that can lead to health problems for various parts of the body, such as the muscles, the heart and stomach.

C Look at three draft summaries of the article. What are the problems with each of these summaries?

1 Long-term stress can lead to heart attacks and strokes because of the extra pressure it puts on the cardiovascular system. During periods of stress, our heart rate and blood pressure are raised. This is a natural response to stress, but it becomes harmful if it continues for an extended period of time.

2 It is important to use strategies to help you relax, so that stress does not lead to health problems with your muscles, heart and digestive system. For example, having an increased heart rate and increased blood pressure for an extended period of time can result in heart disease or stroke. Stress can also cause headaches, digestive problems and even panic attacks.

3 Chronic stress can affect different parts of the body, including the musculoskeletal system, the cardiovascular system and the gastrointestinal system. Stress causes muscles to tense, and people to eat more unhealthy food, which can upset the stomach.

D Read the information in the box about writing a summary. Then identify the main points in *The effects of stress on the body.*

Paraphrasing

It's important to focus on the main points of the source text, but not just to copy the text. You need to explain the information in your own words.

1 Identify the main points in the piece of text that you want to summarise. In an academic paper, look at the introduction, the topic sentences at the start of each paragraph and at the conclusion. In a newspaper article, look at the opening paragraph and the conclusion.

2 Note down any words you need to re-use from the text (i.e. proper nouns, technical words).

3 Explain the information in your own words. Use different structures and different words to make sure you aren't copying from the text. You can also put the information in a different order.

4 Check your summary. Make sure you have not copied parts of the original, introduced new information or changed the meaning.

WRITING

A WRITE Write a short summary of *The effects of stress on the body.* Do not write more than 60 words.

B REVIEW Exchange your summaries. Give your partner any suggestions for improvements.

C EDIT Use your partner's feedback to improve your summaries.

W– linking in academic writing

A SPEAK Work in pairs. Say the following sentences aloud five times. Do they make you feel happier/sadder? Why?

1 Two new blue shoes flew to the moon.
2 These green leaves seem free and easy.
3 Our alarm can't harm the calm farmer.

B Read the conclusion to an academic report. Does it agree with your responses to Exercise A?

CONCLUSION

1 Our research set out to test the facial feedback hypothesis that our facial expressions can affect our moods. Strack *et al* (1988) famously asked respondents to evaluate cartoons while holding a pen in their mouths. Some held it between their teeth, forcing them to smile; others held it between their lips, forcing a frown. The 'smilers' found the cartoons significantly funnier than the 'frowners'. Similarly, Zajonc *et al* (1989), demonstrated a causal relationship between vowel sounds and mood: the repetition of 'smile vowels' (/e/, /iː/) and the 'aha vowel' (/ɑː/) put the respondents in a significantly better mood than 'frown vowels' (e.g. /uː/). However, recent research by Wagenmakers *et al* (2016) has cast serious doubt on this hypothesis.

2 Our own research provides limited support for the hypothesis. We found that repeating sentences with 'smile vowels' did indeed provoke a mood improvement compared to 'frown' vowels. However, in neither case were the results conclusive: the majority of respondents reported no change in mood. The one exception was that the 'aha vowel' had a significant positive effect on almost every respondent's mood.

3 Our evidence suggests that facial expressions do indeed affect mood, but it is principally the open-mouthed 'aha smile' rather than the wide-mouthed grin that has the greatest impact. This may explain the failure of Wagenmakers *et al* to repeat the effects of the pen experiment: they were focusing on the wrong type of smile.

4 If refined and confirmed by further research, the facial feedback hypothesis could be used by psychotherapists and carers to improve patients' moods. Additionally, marketers may use vowel sounds in product names to influence customers' connotations. If products such as 'New You' are renamed as 'Calming Spa', it may well be because of the effect of vowel sounds on our mood.

C Match the topics (a–d) with the paragraphs (1–4).

a Analysis: What did you learn? ___
b Implications: What do your findings mean? ___
c Background: What question were you trying to answer? ___
d Key findings: What information did you collect? ___

D Answer the questions. Use the information in the box to help you.

Linking in academic writing

Use linking words (e.g. *however*) to show the relationships between ideas.

Use colons (:) to show that one idea 'explains' another.

Use semi-colons (;) to show that two related ideas are 'equal' in importance.

1 Find a semi-colon in paragraph 1. In what way are the two ideas equal?
2 Which two linking words in paragraph 1 link all the research together?
3 Find three colons in paragraphs 1–3. How does the second idea explain the first in each case?
4 What linking word in paragraphs 2 and 3 relates expectations to reality? What grammar structure is often used with this word?
5 How does the writer link the main ideas in paragraph 4?

WRITING

A PREPARE Choose one of your own ideas or a piece of academic research from this unit.

B PLAN Make notes about the points you will cover in your conclusion.

C WRITE Write a four-paragraph conclusion. Use linking words, colons and semi-colons in your writing.

D REVIEW Exchange your conclusion with a partner. Do you agree with their analysis? Comment on how they use linking words.

E EDIT Read your partner's comments. Rewrite any parts of your conclusion that you think could be improved.

W– using counter-arguments and rebuttals

A SPEAK Work in pairs. Look at the essay title and discuss the questions.

1 What is gentrification?
2 What do you think of gentrification? Is it a good or bad thing?

B Read the example essay and answer the questions.

1 What is the writer's opinion of gentrification?
2 What reasons does the writer give for her opinion?
3 What reason to support the opposite opinion on gentrification does the writer mention?

DOES GENTRIFICATION HAVE A POSITIVE OR NEGATIVE IMPACT ON CITIES?

In cities all over the world, 'gentrification' is changing entire neighbourhoods. Some people argue that this improves the areas by making them cleaner and safer. However, on the whole, gentrification actually has a negative impact. It prices people out of the areas where they have lived for years, destroys the unique character of neighbourhoods, and it only benefits the rich.

The most obvious negative impact of gentrification is that it forces long-term residents to move away from their homes. As an area becomes trendy, landlords are able to increase the rent and attract wealthier tenants to the area. Meanwhile, lower income families are forced to move away from their friends, schools and jobs to find cheaper places to live.

Gentrification also results in the area losing its individual character. People may have first been attracted to an area by its unique shops and restaurants. However, as this area becomes gentrified, these establishments are unlikely to be able to pay increased rent. Gradually, these shops and restaurants are replaced by high street chains so the area becomes just like many other neighbourhoods in the city.

Some people argue that gentrification has a positive impact because the area becomes cleaner and safer. While it is true that gentrification leads to less crime and better facilities, the local people who deserve to benefit from these changes are unable to stay in the area. Rather than improving the city for all, gentrification only benefits the wealthiest.

In conclusion, gentrification predominantly has a negative impact on cities. It forces long-term residents from their homes, results in areas losing their individual character, and only provides real benefits for those with the most money. The government needs to find a way to ensure that redevelopment of the city can have a positive effect for everyone.

C Find the phrases the writer used to introduce the counter argument and rebuttal in the example essay. Use the information in the box to help you.

Using counter-arguments and rebuttals

In order to strengthen your argument in a persuasive essay, you can anticipate the points that could be used to support the opposite side of the argument (the counter-arguments) and respond with your answer to those arguments (a rebuttal). The rebuttal must respond directly to the counter argument.

Introduce a counter argument with phrases like:

- *Opponents/Supporters of .... claim/argue/believe that ...*
- *Some studies have shown that ...*
- *There is an argument that ...*

Introduce a rebuttal with phrases like:

- *However, this is only partially true.*
- *Studies have shown this is not true.*
- *Nevertheless, ...*

WRITING

A PREPARE Work in pairs. Look at the essay prompt and brainstorm reasons to support each side.

Which is better: living in the city or living in the countryside?

Reasons why living in the city is better	Reasons why living in the countryside is better

B PLAN Decide on your best points from Exercise A and make a plan of your essay.

C WRITE Write a persuasive essay to answer the essay prompt. Use a counter-argument and rebuttal in the third body paragraph. Use the example essay to help you.

D REVIEW Exchange your essay with a partner. How could your partner's essay be improved? How effective are their counter-arguments and rebuttals?

E EDIT Read your partner's comments. Rewrite any parts of your essay you think can be improved.

6 DISCOVERIES

Lesson 6.1, Listening, Exercise B

6.1 **P = Presenter K = Kyle**

P: Today we're talking about unusual travel challenges. Forget remote beaches and idyllic islands or precarious mountain treks and volcano hiking. None of that is enough to impress anybody these days. If you really want to stand out from the crowd, you need a travel challenge. At least that's what travel journalist Kyle Chen, who's been following this trend closely, is here to tell us today. Welcome to the show, Kyle.

K: Thanks for having me, Jo.

P: So … first of all, what exactly is a travel challenge?

K: Well, basically, it's travelling with a goal or some sort of self-imposed restriction – or both in some cases.

P: OK. Can you give us some examples?

K: Sure. So you can limit yourself to a particular method of transport, you can visit locations with a theme, or you can choose a particular route.

P: Actually, that sounds kind of fun. But why do you think these kinds of challenges are so popular all of a sudden?

K: Different reasons I guess. Well, in general, I think people want to be different. Perhaps they want to have a goal to make their trip more interesting. And, I think for some of them, they want to share their adventure. Or maybe they're doing something for charity, or hoping to write a book.

P: So, can you tell us about some interesting challenges that people have done?

K: OK. Well, this was a pretty ambitious one. A guy called Adam Leyton challenged himself to visit as many countries as possible in 24 hours using public transport.

P: Woah! I'm guessing you can't visit that many countries in 24 hours, though?

K: Well, amazingly, he visited 12.

P: Twelve countries in a day!

K: Right. It wasn't an easy 24 hours by the sounds of it either. He came up against a few challenges. He had no time to sleep, on the whole, except for a couple of hours on a night train. But he had to wake up, and get off and on the train, to set foot in the Czech Republic. He had to jog to the border with Hungary and only had 22 minutes to get from there to the Austrian border.

P: That's sounds quite … intense. What gave him the idea to take on the challenge?

K: Supposedly, he wanted to break a record but he also wanted to raise £900 for charity.

P: Hmm … it does sounds like an incredible trip. But … the fact is, you need some spare time to plan a challenge like that. What are some other challenges you've come across?

K: Well, one of my favourite challenges is a guy called Dixe Wills. He decided he was going to visit places in Great Britain, except he was only going to visit places that started with the letter Z. And he was going to visit all of them.

P: How many places is that?

K: There are 41 apparently! He wrote a book about it called *The Z-to-Z of Great Britain*. It's a great book, actually. It's about all these obscure places you might never have heard of – small farms in the middle of nowhere, a rock on the Isles of Scilly.

P: Hmm. That sounds like an interesting read. What else have people done?

K: Well, another really quirky one is Daniel Tunnard, a British man who lives in Buenos Aires. He decided to ride all of the 140 bus lines in the city.

P: One hundred and forty bus lines? Why?

K: It's a travel challenge. It took him about six months. Remarkably, he was sometimes travelling for 14 hours at a time.

P: OK. That actually doesn't sound like much fun at all to me.

K: Hmm … me neither. But you have to admire his dedication. He set himself a goal and then he went through with it, taking three bus routes a day. He also blogged about his experiences – in English and Spanish – and he published a book about them. Actually that's a really fascinating read.

P: Good for him. So how do these people fund their trips, on the whole?

K: Well, I think most of the examples I gave were self-funded. Mind you, travelling on the buses was actually very cheap. I think it cost about £55 altogether.

P: Right, got you.

K: However, some people ask for donations through crowdfunding sites like GoFundMe.

P: Isn't that a bit … cheeky? Surely, you should pay for your own adventures.

K: I think it's OK. The idea is that if people enjoy reading your blog or looking at your photos, they can make a small donation. People don't have to give anything unless they want to.

P: And what would your advice be for someone thinking about trying a travel challenge?

K: OK, first it's super important to be realistic about what you can do. Think about your budget. Think about how much time you can spare. Think about what you would be comfortable doing. The most important thing is to enjoy yourself. You don't have to travel far to have an adventure.

Lesson 6.2, Listening, Exercise C

6.4 **P = Presenter**

P: Today, I'd like to talk about someone who I particularly admire. In my opinion, he's far and away one of America's greatest inventors. His innovations have fixed everyday problems but also probably saved thousands of lives. In addition, he was one of the first African-American inventors to gain public recognition for his work. His name was Garrett Morgan and he was a prolific inventor and entrepreneur who lived between 1877 and 1963. And while you may not all know his name, you're likely to have experienced his innovations.

One of Morgan's early successes was actually an accident. He was repairing a sewing machine in his shop when he noticed that some oil he was using had straightened the hairs on a cloth. Realising that he might be on to something, he decided to test the oils on something bigger. So he borrowed his neighbour's dog and used the oils to straighten its hair. It worked. So well, in fact, that his neighbour didn't recognise his own dog and tried to chase it away. Morgan bottled his new invention, labelled it 'G.A. Morgan's Hair Refiner' and he was soon selling it far and wide.

His second big success, a safety hood, turned him from an innovator into a hero. Morgan had noticed how smoke inhalation made the work of firefighters both difficult and dangerous. His solution was a hood worn over the head with two tubes that extended to the ground, where the air was breathable. He soon had an opportunity to test out his invention An explosion in a tunnel near his home trapped 32 workers underground with smoke, dust and poisonous gases. With emergency services unable to enter the tunnel, it was truly a life-or-death situation. Morgan and his brother Frank raced to the scene and went in side-by-side, each wearing one of Morgan's safety hoods. It was a tense moment, but they soon re-emerged safe and sound with survivors. Morgan's fame began to spread slowly but surely, with his device being used by fire and police departments across the country.

Another of Morgan's life-saving inventions was an improved version of the traffic light. By and large, in the early 1920s, American roads were dangerous places. They were filled with horses, carriages and wagons – and increasingly, the newly invented automobile. On top of this, there were only two traffic signals – stop or go. Time after time there were stories of injuries and fatalities in traffic accidents.

One day, Morgan and his family saw such an accident – a collision between a car and a horse-drawn carriage at a busy intersection. The driver of the car was knocked unconscious, a little girl was thrown from the carriage, and the horse had to be put down. Determined that accidents like that shouldn't happen, Morgan's innovation was to add a third light – a 'caution' light. This gave vehicles that had entered the intersection enough time to get out before the signal changed to 'go'. Morgan sold the patent to the General Electric Motor Company, which installed the new traffic lights in cities all over the country. As a result, roads became safer and many lives were saved.

So why is Morgan so widely admired? Not only did his inventions save the lives of millions, but he also put his heart and soul into the community, even running for the city council. So while his life was a classic rags-to-riches story, it was also the story of a man who took a leadership role and truly cared about others.

7 EXTREMES

Lesson 7.1, Listening, Exercise B
7.1 **A = Arjun C = Catina T = Tony**

T: Welcome back to *The Breakfast Show* with me, Tony Scott. Now I'd like you to meet a real-life superhero, Arjun Prasad. Good morning, Arjun. What's your story?

A: Good morning. Well, I was driving home from work about three months ago, not really paying attention to the other vehicles, when suddenly I heard a loud bang from the road behind me. I looked in my mirror and saw a car had run over a bicycle. The cyclist was still trapped under the car, which was leaking fuel onto the road.

T: Sounds terrifying! So the car could have exploded at any second, couldn't it?

A: Exactly. So I ran over and lifted up the car while the other driver pulled the cyclist free. As soon as she'd freed the cyclist, I put the car down again. Then together we carried the cyclist to safety and called an ambulance. And we were just in time – the car exploded a few seconds later. A spark must have caused the fuel to catch fire.

T: My goodness! Now, you said you lifted up the car. But that's incredible. I mean, you're a big guy, aren't you? But a car!

A: Yeah. It's weird, isn't it?

T: It certainly is. This seems like a good point to introduce my second guest, Catina Ivănescu, a professor of kinesiology. Catina, how is it possible for a person to lift a car? I mean, a car weighs, what, a tonne and a half, doesn't it?

C: Good morning. Yes, a typical family car weighs between 1500 and 2000 kilograms. The world record for weight-lifting is just over 500 kilograms.

T: Are you saying that Arjun lifted over three times the world record?

C: No, not at all. If he'd lifted the car above his head, that would have been a superhuman feat. But in fact Arjun just lifted part of the car a few centimetres off the ground. Three or even all four of the car's wheels were still on the ground, supporting most of the car's weight.

T: Right. So Arjun's achievement is nothing special, then?

C: Far from it! First of all, as Arjun said, it was an incredibly dangerous situation, with a high risk of explosion at any second. So Arjun's actions were unquestionably courageous. There's no doubt that the cyclist escaped serious injury thanks to Arjun's heroic actions. But in addition, it still takes exceptional strength to lift a car, even by a few centimetres.

T: OK. Let's conduct a little experiment now. We have here in the studio a car of the same model as the one you lifted, Arjun. Could you lift it for us now?

A: Er, not really. I've had a bad back for several months, and the doctor advised me against doing any more heavy lifting.

T: Oh. That's a shame!

C: Why don't you lift it, Tony?

T: Me? Er, OK. Wow! That's heavy! There's no way I could lift that!

C: Well, not here and now. But who knows? Maybe if you were in the situation Arjun found himself in, you might be able to. It's all about something called 'hysterical strength': the strength that you get in extreme situations.

T: So that's what helped Arjun, then, was it? Hysterical strength?

C: Exactly. Basically, we're all a lot stronger than we think we are. But when we push our muscles to the limit, it's really painful.

T: Yeah, I know. I was in too much pain to lift the car – it was agony!

C: But that pain is just our body's way of telling us to stop exerting ourselves before we break anything. We feel it when our muscles are operating at around 60% of their potential. But, you could, theoretically, push yourself a lot further without damaging your muscles.

T: OK. But surely it would hurt so much that you'd want to stop.

C: Exactly. But in a high-stress situation, your body is flooded with adrenaline, which blocks your body's pain sensors – but only temporarily. That's how Arjun was able to go way beyond 60% of his strength. He didn't notice the pain until the adrenaline had worn off.

A: Exactly. I literally didn't feel any pain at all until about an hour after the accident. And then every muscle in my body was in agony!

T: I'm sure. Er, I'm just wondering, Catina. We can't harness this strength in everyday life, can we?

C: Well, world-class athletes are able to harness it to some extent. During training, they can often push themselves up to 80% of their potential. But in high-stress situations, such as when they're chasing an Olympic medal, it's often possible to go much higher. That's why so many world records are broken at such events, rather than in regular training sessions. The adrenaline blocks the pain, allowing you to go way beyond your normal limit.

T: Aha. OK, one last question, Arjun. What happened to the cyclist?

A: She made a full recovery. When I met her last week, after a few weeks in hospital, she said if it hadn't been for my actions, she might not be alive today. But I don't feel like a hero – I'm just a normal guy, aren't I?

T: Well, I'm not so sure about that, Arjun! Anyway, let's have a break now, shall we? We'll be back very soon.

Lesson 7.2, Listening, Exercise C
7.3 **RS = Recruitment specialist**

RS: OK, so let's look at those questions now. Interviewers often use the 'desert island' question to determine what sort of person you are. A practical survivor type might take a knife or even a satellite phone. A more creative dreamer would take something original and fun. There's no correct answer – it depends what type of employee they're looking for. Just don't pretend to be something you're not. Focus instead on the image you want to convey about yourself.

Next, the 'dinosaur' question tests your ability to avoid obvious answers. Ninety per cent of people say T. Rex, the first dinosaur they think of. But unless the employer is looking to recruit cold-blooded predators, T. Rex would be pretty unsuitable as a potential employee. Almost any other answer is much better – as long as you justify it.

The 'weakness' question is an old classic. Whatever you do, don't claim to have no weaknesses, as you'll come across as arrogant and lacking in self-awareness. A good trick is always to describe a weakness that you've overcome.

With the 'stapler' question, the key is to think beyond the obvious applications, and to explore the properties of the object in question. I wouldn't recommend saying 'a paperweight' – it's what everyone always says.

OK, so the 'pizza' question tests your ability to make estimates and work out a plan. So don't just say any old number that pops into your head. You don't need to produce an accurate answer – which would be about 150 million in this case. But of course it's better if you're in the right ballpark, which in this case would be between around 75 and 300 million.

Next, the 'not on your CV' question is a great opportunity to remind the interviewers that you're a real person, not some invented character whose life revolves around landing this particular job. It's fine to get personal, but don't forget to bring your story back to how you're suitable for the job.

Finally, for the 'worst enemy' question, it's always worth mentioning that you don't have any enemies. But resist the temptation to leave it there; talk about perceived weaknesses that are actually strengths. Demonstrate your ability to see yourself through others' eyes – a crucial skill for any employee.

Lesson 7.2, Listening, Exercise D

7.4 **I1 = Interviewer 1 O = Oscar I2 = Interviewer 2**

I1: What would you take with you to a desert island and why?

O: Er, a notebook and a pen. I find writing poetry immensely calming, so an extended stay on a desert island, without any other people to distract me, would really get my creative juices flowing. I'd be utterly devastated if I couldn't record my ideas on paper.

I2: Thank you. If you could be any dinosaur, which dinosaur would you be?

O: Oh, a pterodactyl, a flying dinosaur, soaring high above the plains. The views would be spectacular, and the sense of freedom would be quite exhilarating. But much more importantly, compared to the ground, the sky would be a relatively good place for staying out of harm's way!

I1: Right. What's your biggest weakness?

O: Hmm, well I tend to be somewhat disorganised. When I was a student, I often missed deadlines. But then I learnt some remarkably simple techniques, and I've improved noticeably since then. For example, I make a to-do list every day, and I can't have any rewards until I've cleared my list. It takes quite a lot of self-discipline, but it's so satisfying to know that, at long last, there's nothing hanging over you.

I2: Thank you. Name four uses for a stapler, without the staples.

O: You could use it to pick up tissues without getting your hands dirty! You could also use it as a hammer for bashing things. I suppose you could also give it to a child as a toy – the child might have fun pressing it and listening to the noises. And I suppose you could also use it as a paperweight, to hold down papers when it's windy.

I1: Hmm. How many square metres of pizza are eaten in the US each year?

O: A standard pizza is, what, thirty centimetres across? So you could easily fit nine inside a square metre. In fact, if you cut them up, there'd be room for perhaps three more in the spaces, so, twelve. That's a year's supply for me. I'm not altogether sure how typical I am – I guess some people would eat that many in a single month! But if we assume I'm not radically different from the average American, then we're looking at around one square metre per person per year. The USA has around 300 million people, so that's my estimate: 300 million.

I1: Not bad. What's the most interesting thing about you that we wouldn't learn from your CV?

O: Well, I have six younger brothers and sisters, who are all quite adorable. I'm the oldest, so I've spent most of my life looking after them while my parents were working. It's been quite challenging, because I never had any time to myself and it was often practically impossible to study, but it's also incredibly rewarding when I see how far they've come.

I2: Great. How would your worst enemy describe you?

O: Hah! I'm not the sort of person who has outright enemies. It used to irritate me when people treated me badly, but I've learnt that the best trick is to ignore them and move on! I know some people are jealous of what I've achieved and they think I'm lucky. But they haven't seen all the struggles I've been through. The people who matter know that I deserve any luck that has come my way.

I1: OK, great. Thanks. That's the end of the interview.

8 WELL-BEING

Lesson 8.1, Listening, Exercise B

8.1 **C = Cheryl J = Jake L = Luke**

L: Hey, Cheryl.

J: Hello, Cheryl. What you doing?

C: Oh, hey guys. Check out my brand new … smart watch! What do you reckon?

L: Cool. I've been meaning to get one of those. Is that switched on, Cheryl?

C: Erm … maybe.

J: Smart watch eh? Hmm … not a hundred per cent convinced about those. I mean if I want to check my email I can just look at my phone.

L: Yeah, yeah … but you can use it whenever you exercise to monitor the amount of activity you do.

J: Didn't know you were so big on fitness Cheryl.

C: Yeah, sure. I mean … I do like to keep fit … and … well, OK so … You'll never guess what … I've just been commissioned to write an article about wellness technology.

L: Amazing!

J: Cool. Congratulations. But what's wellness technology?

C: Good question. So wellness technology is … technology with which we can improve our health and well-being.

J: Did you just read that somewhere?

C: Might have done. But you get the idea. There are lots of other devices you can get to track things. Actually, you can monitor whatever you need to keep an eye on: your breathing, temperature, glucose levels in your blood, amount of sleep, pretty much everything!

J: Yeah. And it sounds a bit like information overload to me.

C: Well, yes and no. Sure more information doesn't necessarily mean better health. But I've just read several news stories about people whose lives may have been saved because their smart watch alerted them to a problem. For example, on this smart watch take this handy … heart rate tracker.

L: Eighty-five beats per minute. Isn't that quite high …

C: Not for me, Luke. No. And anyway I'm a bit stressed. I'm meeting the person writing the article with me for lunch today. I'm supposed to share my ideas. But I think I'm out of new ideas!

L: Well, what about the smart swimsuit? Have you heard of that?

C: Hmm … tell me more.

L: Hang on – here it is. It's a swimsuit with a tracking tag embedded, so you can log your time and how far you swim. It will start tracking all that whenever you put the swimsuit on.

J: I don't know. What happened to just going for a swim? People are obsessively tracking everything these days. Writing down everything they eat or do. It takes over your life – when really all you need to do is take some exercise and eat healthily.

L: But I don't think wellness technology is just about fitness fads. For example, monitoring devices can help show your doctor the big picture so he or she will be more likely to pick up on any problems. And it goes beyond just tracking. Like the smart pill bottle.

C: The smart pill what? Let me write this down.

L: It's a pill bottle for medication, like the Adhere Tech bottle. It glows blue when it's time to take your medication. And … if you forget … it starts flashing red. It can also text you or email you to remind you to take medication.

J: OK, maybe that could be quite useful for my grandpa.

L: There are a few health devices like that now. I was also reading about this thermometer. It's basically a thermometer which a smartphone can be attached to. Here it is. It says … this device has an automated diagnosis feature whereby it checks the symptoms of the person to whom it's attached against a database. I'll send you a link to the review. And look at th s – this could be a great quote for your article.

'As tech gets smarter and people get smarter about tech, this could be the decade in which we revolutionise healthcare.'

C: Yeah. Yeah. I think that would work as a strapline. Great! Thanks, guys. One last question though. Is this thing really switched on?

Lesson 8.2, Listening, Exercise B

8.3 **L = Laura B = Bill R = Rohan J = Julie**

L: Hello, everyone. This is *First Past the Post*, the sports performance podcast. My name is Laura Ford …

B: And I'm Bill Williams.

L: This week, we're talking about sports psychology. A lot of the big teams have sports psychologists these days. But what do they actually do? This week we set out to find out more.

B: First up, we spoke to Professor Rohan Kumar, a lecturer in sports psychology. Here's what we discussed …

L: So Rohan, could you explain what a sports psychologist does?

R: Certainly. Essentially, our job is to help athletes perform at the peak of their abilities. We do that by offering training and therapy. Training usually means things like encouraging positive thinking, whereas therapy could be supporting them with off-field issues – this is particularly important in the case of long-term injuries.

L: You mentioned working on positive thinking. How exactly does that work?

R: Well, athletes, even elite athletes, suffer from the same fear of failure that we all do. They have times when they doubt their abilities or get cold feet because they're anxious about competing. Our job is to help athletes cope with these feelings, so they can perform to the best of their abilities.

L: So what kind of training do you do with them?

R: Well, I said before that positive thinking is important – but that doesn't just mean encouraging people to imagine winning a game or winning a trophy. It's actually more about visualising your performance, thinking about the individual steps that you need to take, and imagining doing each one of those steps in exactly the right way. It's all about staying calm and focused, so they can give it their best shot.

L: So you encourage them to break things down into smaller goals?

R: That's right. It helps people focus by thinking about these smaller goals rather than getting distracted by the big picture. We also work on self-talk, which means trying to get control of that little voice inside your head that says you're not good enough or that you're having a bad day. We train athletes to use positive self-talk to build self-confidence and self-belief – and if it's a team game, to talk out loud and encourage those same feelings in the rest of the team.

L: That's been really helpful. Thank you for your time, Rohan.

R: You're very welcome.

Lesson 8.2, Listening, Exercise D

8.4 **B = Bill J = Julie L = Laura**

B: After Laura spoke to Professor Kumar, I spoke to Julie Matic, a sports psychologist working with a local football team. I should mention that Julie was speaking to me from a training session, so there's a bit of background noise during this interview.

B: Julie, thank you for taking the time to talk with me today.

J: No problem.

B: So, can you tell me a little about your role with the team there?

J: Well, before I started here, the team had been going through a bad period, so one of the first things I needed to do was to help the team get over their fear of failure. I've been helping them to think about failure in a more positive way, so they don't dwell on the fact that they failed, but they try to learn from that experience, so that failure becomes a positive thing. Nobody can win every game, so it's not a disaster to lose – as long as you just think about what you can do differently next time.

B: What about working with individual players? What kinds of things do you focus on?

J: Well, the most important thing is to get to know the individuals, and encourage the manager to do the same, so that we can work out the best way to get the most out of each person. When people think about coaching, most people have a stereotypical image of a coach shouting at the players, but that's very outdated because many players won't respond positively to that kind of coaching. Different players need different approaches – some people need a lot of guidance, some need a lot of praise, others need to feel trusted and important. It's important to talk to the players – to listen to them and find the right way to work with them.

L: Apologies again for the sound quality on that interview, but she said a lot of really interesting things. I completely agree that it's important to think about the right kind of coaching to suit individual players. I need someone to nag me and tell me to up my game, but I know that's not everyone's cup of tea.

B: Yeah, actually I find that kind of coaching ends up distracting me because I get so angry with the coach. It means I don't concentrate on the game and I end up playing even worse! I prefer a more supportive approach.

L: Yeah, I can imagine that! So we also interviewed …

9 BEHAVIOUR

Lesson 9.1, Vocabulary, Exercise B

9.1 **M = Man W = Woman A = American**

M: I could do with some new wheels but they'd set me back at least ten grand … and I'm completely skint.

A: Hey, can you lend me ten bucks? Ah, sweet. That's awesome, dude.

W: I don't mean to whinge, but the office do last night was a total shambles. I was so gutted!

M: This bloke offered me a brand new telly for fifty quid, so I'm like 'Sounds dodgy to me – it's probably nicked or something.'

A: I wanted to hang out with my buddies tonight but I'm totally beat, so I guess I'll just chill out and crash instead.

W: I'm well chuffed cos I got myself a new flat. So I'm sorted now.

Lesson 9.1, Listening, Exercise B

9.3 **L = Lisa G = Greg J = Jake H = Helen**

L: Er, hello.

H: Hey. Come on in. I'm Helen.

J: What's up? I'm Jake.

G: Good morning. How are you doing? I'm Greg.

L: Good, thanks. I'm Lisa. Are you all here for the psychology experiment too?

G: Yeah. The organisers offered us ten quid, so we signed up.

L: Yeah, same here.

J: I don't know what they're testing, though. Do you?

L: Something about perception skills and stuff like that. Are we supposed to wait for the experimenters?

H: Nah, there were two blokes here earlier, psychology professors or whatever, and they were like 'sorry but we've got to go and teach.' They left some questions in an envelope.

G: Total shambles! Shall we get cracking?

J: OK. Task 1: Which line is the same length as the one on the left? Easy. It's line B, innit?

H: Yeah, definitely B. It's obvious.

G: Yeah, it's line B. Lisa?

L: Er, yeah. Line B.

H: Hey, those doughnuts look kind of yummy. Do you think they're for us?

L: I suppose so. Look, there's a note. It says this plate's for the 12 o'clock group and this is for the 11.30 group – that's us.

G: Sorted! Mmm, yummy!

H: What's the next task? Let's see: AFC or PTU?

G: PTU, no question. What about you, Jake?

J: Definitely PTU.

H: Yeah, me too. Lisa?

L: Er, yeah, PTU, I suppose.

J: Great. Those doughnuts were well yummy. Shall we have some more?

L: Well, the others are supposed to be for the next group.

H: Yeah, but we could just eat them and hide the note!

J: Yeah, whatever.

G: Fine with me. Lisa?

L: Oh, go on then. I mean, they are yummy!

G: Sorted! Well done Lisa! You passed the test!

L: What are you on about?

H: Sorry, Lisa, but it wasn't about perception at all. It was about social pressure and conformity: how groups influence our behaviour, and so on.

L: How do you know? Aren't you participants like me?

J: Nah, we're the experimenters. We were only pretending. Sorry.

L: So what do you mean, I passed the test?

G: OK, so the first part was the lines. Did you really think it was line B?

L: Not really. It seemed obvious it was line A, but then you all seemed sort of convinced it was line B. I thought my eyes were playing tricks on me in some way!

H: Yeah, that happens to more or less everyone. Sometimes it's easier to follow the crowd, in a sense, than to trust your own eyes!

L: So it was line A after all?

H: Yeah, of course it was! OK, so the second test was AFC versus PTU. Why did you go for PTU, Lisa?

L: Cos you all chose it! I don't even know what PTU stands for. What is it?

J: PTU? Pretending to understand! Most people hate admitting they don't understand something, especially when everyone else is nodding their heads, or something like that, so you pretend. But maybe everyone else is pretending too! They're all kind of too embarrassed to admit they don't know what's going on!

L: So what's AFC?

J: Ask for clarification! Always ask, even if it makes you feel stupid!

G: Enjoy the doughnuts, Lisa?

L: Yeah, they were yummy.

G: Yummy? That's a strange word! Why do you say that?

L: Ach, you got me again! You all called them yummy, didn't you? I never say 'yummy'! Gutted!

G: Yeah, sorry. We wanted to influence your choice of words. We used loads of slang too, and stuff like that, to get you to conform to our style of speaking.

L: Ah, yeah. I always thought 'yummy' was uncool, but when you all started using it, I thought maybe it was cool again!

H: Nah, yummy is always a lame thing to say!

J: How did you feel about eating the other group's doughnuts, Lisa?

L: Not good. But you all convinced me it was fine. It was some kind of trick again, was it?

J: Yeah, sorry. That was an example of 'groupthink', where people make bad decisions as a group that they wouldn't make as individuals. That's why we agree to things we don't want to do. And it's why many business teams make such terrible decisions.

L: OK. And what was with that humming at the end?

H: Hah! That was the last task. We wanted to make you copy us. And it worked!

L: Yeah, I know. I felt kind of stupid cos I didn't know what was going on, so I just joined in. You must think I'm some sort of sheep, copying everything you did!

G: Chill out, Lisa. Most people are just as bad as you! Anyway, cheers for taking part. You were wicked! Want another doughnut?

Lesson 9.2, Listening, Exercise B

9.6 **P = Presenter M1 = Man 1 M2 = Man 2 W = Woman**

P: Hello and welcome to *Human Behaviour*. Today we're looking at one of the most famous experiments of all time.

In the 1940s, the leading behavioural psychologist, B F Skinner, conducted a remarkable experiment. Some hungry pigeons were placed in a cage with a mechanism that delivered food.

The twist in this particular experiment was that the pigeons' actions had no effect whatsoever on the mechanism, which simply delivered food at completely regular intervals, regardless of what the pigeons did. The pigeons, of course, didn't know this, so they kept pecking and pushing and so on in a desperate attempt to make the mechanism deliver food. Inevitably, there were occasions when food appeared immediately after the pigeon had performed a particular action. That was enough to convince the pigeon that it was that action that had caused the food to be delivered, so the pigeon kept repeating it again and again. And of course, every time the mechanism delivered another serving of food, the pigeon became more and more convinced that it could influence the mechanism with its actions.

According to Skinner's report, the pigeons swung and moved around a lot, making it look like a kind of bizarre pigeon dance. Surely humans wouldn't believe such actions could influence something beyond our control … or would we?

In fact, when the experiment was repeated on humans, who received points instead of food, the results were almost identical. By the end of one experiment, the participants were convinced that they'd got a point for a particular combination of shrugging, fidgeting and rocking back and forth. What never seemed to occur to them was that the points were simply awarded after completely random lengths of time. If they'd just sat there and waited, they'd still have won the points just the same, without making themselves look ridiculous in the process. But of course, it wouldn't have been so entertaining to watch.

Does anything like this happen in real life? Let's hear from a few people we interviewed on the street this morning to find out.

M1: I'm a big football fan. I try to watch all my team's matches on TV. In fact, pretty much whenever I miss a match, my team loses! So I make sure I'm sitting by the TV in good time for each match, wearing my lucky football shirt and scarf, to bring my team luck! And it definitely works – well, most of the time, at least.

W: It started when I was a youngster, and my aunt gave me a lucky hamster mascot before a big test. I forgot to take it with me for my next test, which was a disaster! So ever since then, I've always used mascots in exams.

M2: I always buy my lottery tickets at exactly 11.41 on a Thursday morning. I know it sounds crazy, but every time I've won any money on the lottery, it's after buying my ticket at that time. Unfortunately, it doesn't always work, for some reason, but it certainly seems to improve my chances of winning.

P: I'm sure it does. Anyway, join us again next week on *Human Behaviour* …

10 SOCIETY

Lesson 10.1, Listening, Exercise B

10.1 **D = Denise**

D: Walking along the streets of Beijing, you really get the sense of a city going through a rapid period of change. Huge skyscrapers dominate the skyline, while construction work continues all around. As the city evolves, its population has swelled to over 21 million, making Beijing one of the most populated cities in the world. And the more people there are, the more challenging it becomes to provide comfortable environments for people to live and work in.

Fortunately, researchers at the Well Living Lab on the northern outskirts of Beijing are conducting an extensive research project to identify ways that building design can make people healthier, happier and more productive. And if people feel better about their environment they have a higher inclination to interact positively with the people around them. Inside an unassuming office building, human guinea pigs are being carefully monitored inside a simulation of a typical office environment. I talked to environmental psychologist Wang Wei about how this kind of research can help with building design.

Lesson 10.1, Listening, Exercise C

10.2 **W = Wang D = Denise**

D: So, Wang Wei, what research is being done at the Well Living Lab here in Beijing?

W: They're looking at how small changes to the environment, such as changes to the lighting, air quality or noise levels affect people. They're observing people's emotional responses and using wearable technology to monitor people's physical reactions.

For example, recently they've been looking at what kind of light makes workers most productive. They experimented by using different kinds of light. They found that people strongly preferred daylight to electric light – and, as a matter of fact, other research has shown that people have a tendency to be less productive if their desk is more than 7.5 metres away from a window. They also found that certain kinds of blue lighting can have a positive effect on workers' moods.

D: What other things have psychologists learnt about office environments?

W: Some fascinating research has focused on shapes and lines. Apparently, people feel more comfortable in places with round shapes and curved lines. On the other hand, straight lines and sharp edges have been shown to create feelings of fear. Other research has looked at colours. Red walls have been shown to be better suited for tasks that require accuracy and attention to detail – perhaps because people associate the colour red with danger, so they're more alert. Conversely, blue walls suit creative tasks – in fact, people trying to be creative in rooms with blue walls had twice as many ideas as those working in rooms with red walls.

D: And what have we learnt about the design of the city?

W: People living in cities tend to have higher levels of stress, so unsurprisingly a lot of the research has looked at what can be done about this. One interesting study showed that people are more relaxed when they see lively and interesting shop facades, whereas plain, monotonous facades make people anxious and give them the urge to hurry past. Other studies have looked at how spaces can facilitate more communication – because cities can be very isolating places. Some ideas include arranging spaces that encourage interaction between strangers, such as providing more seating in communal spaces. It sounds simple, but many places have had this kind of seating removed in recent years and people didn't realise the impact this would have.

D: If you don't believe the importance of thinking about these details, you only need to look back at the story of the Pruitt-Igoe housing complex that was built in Missouri in the US in the 1950s. When it opened, the complex was lauded as magnificent architectural design. Yet, when people actually began to live there, several problems with how people interacted in the space became evident – for example, the wide spaces between the different apartment blocks in the complex meant people in different blocks had little chance to interact. This meant there was no sense of shared community between residents of different blocks, and as a result, the complex quickly became a hostile and unpleasant place to live in. The project's failings were a reminder for architects to think not just about the look of buildings, but also about how people would interact within the spaces they create.

Today, architects and designers are much more aware of the importance of psychology when designing buildings. Various studies, like the ones being carried out in Beijing, are looking at how places make people feel and act. This research is vital for creating the buildings of the future. With so many people living close together, the environment should encourage positive feelings.

Lesson 10.2, Listening, Exercise B

10.4 **R = Robin J = Joanna Mr E = Mr Evans**

J: A few weeks to go and then we're done with uni for good. Can't quite believe it.

R: Me neither. The end of an era. So … you going to work at your dad's company then?

J: Hmm … hope not. Not if I can help it, anyway. But yeah … may need to. Any idea what you're going to do?

R: Well, funny you should ask that. I've just been trying to sort out my CV and looking for some interesting stuff to apply to. The thing is I really want to do something to help people. But I haven't seen too much of that sort of thing.

J: Really? Oh OK, thought you were going to apply for something in business though, like one of those management trainee schemes.

R: I don't know. I don't think all that is really for me. I'd like to make some kind of a difference to the world. You know my cousin works for a charity, right?

J: Oh yeah?

R: Yeah, a clean water organisation. Anyway, we've been talking a lot recently about all the stuff she's doing and it kind of made me want do something similar too.

J: Oh, OK got you. But you wouldn't earn that much working for a charity. At least not at first. Any other ideas?

R: Well, yeah I thought about politics too.

J: Hmm. Don't know. I mean all they seem to do is argue with each other. Just don't know how much of a change you'll be making.

R: OK … and there's also social work. You know, looking out for children, vulnerable people …

J: Hmm OK…

R: I take it you're not convinced then?

J: I just think that looks like a tough job, coping with lots of difficult situations. I couldn't do it myself personally. I was thinking … what about teaching? You'd be a great teacher. You could train to be a teacher or just volunteer in your spare time.

R: Yeah … I guess.

J: Hey, there's Dr Evans. Isn't he the new career's advisor? Why don't you talk to him?

R: Good idea. Hang on sec … Excuse me, Dr Evans. Would you have a moment for a quick word at all?

Mr E: Oh hello Robin. Sure. How can I help?

R: I was wondering if you could offer me some advice. I've just been considering what to do after graduation.

Mr E: OK right. So what are you interested in doing?

R: Well I think … first and foremost I want to do a job which involves helping people, you know, that are less fortunate than myself. So I was quite keen on applying for a position with a charity.

Mr E: Aha. OK. So my first question then would be: what kind of charity do you have in mind?

R: So, ideally one that campaigns for clean water … or maybe disease prevention.

Mr E: So second question: what do you see yourself doing for them?

R: Well … I'd like to be assisting with making policy, I guess.

Mr E: OK let me just stop you there. Of course that is one area of charity work. But it's highly competitive. And you don't have experience or a specialist qualification. You're more likely to be involved in fundraising, persuading people to donate money, at least initially. And even then, it would definitely strengthen your application if you can show some commitment to their particular work.

R: Like volunteering perhaps. I was thinking about some kind of voluntary work.

Mr E: You should definitely do it.

R: Brilliant, thanks Mr Evans. I can look into it.

Mr E: But let me get to my final point. You should bear in mind, that working for a charity isn't the only way you can help people. If you're likely to be helping the organisation get money, you may actually be able to make more of a difference pursuing a career in business. Especially with your background. Then you can commit to donating a portion of your salary to your chosen charity.

R: Right … I hadn't thought of that before.

Mr E: Yes, there's a very, very interesting book about a Wall Street trader, called *The Most Good You Can Do.* If you haven't read it, you should do. The guy was a philosophy student, quite brilliant in fact. Just like you he was thinking how to make a difference. He decided that the way he could make the biggest impact was by working hard in finance and donating money to charity. He's been able to donate over $100,000 a year to his chosen charities – and as a result touched many people's lives.

R: Thank you, I'll look it up. And thanks for the advice Mr Evans, it's much appreciated. I definitely have a lot to think about.

Mr E: You're welcome.

J: So, come on then. What did he say?

R: Not what I expected. At all. He said it might be better to get a normal job, you know, an office job and that.

J: Told you so.

R: No, but then give the money to charity.

J: Oh. Great.

R: Yep, that's what he said. Apparently, there's a guy who does that and has given over a hundred grand a year away.

J: No way!

R: Yeah I know. Crazy, right?

J: Well, it's kind of good advice. The bit about an office job. I'd do that. I'm just not sure about the giving away part.

Macmillan Education
4 Crinan Street
London N1 9XW

A division of Macmillan Education Limited

Companies and representatives throughout the world

Language Hub Advanced Student's Book B ISBN 978-1-380-04661-1
Language Hub Advanced Student's Book B with Student's App
ISBN 978-1-380-04655-0

Written by Jeremy Day and Graham Skerritt

First published 2020

Designed by emc design ltd
Cover design by Restless
Cover illustration(s)/photograph(s) by Getty Images/Luís Henrique Boucault (bg), Plainpicture/Cavan Images
Picture research by Emily Taylor

Authentic video footage supplied by BBC Studios Distribution Limited
Café Hub videos produced by Sharp Focus

Authors' acknowledgements
Jeremy Day would like to thank the team at Macmillan Education for their support.
Graham Skerritt would like to thank the students who tried out activities and gave invaluable feedback. Thank you to the Macmillan Education Editorial team for your excellent comments and suggestions. And thank you to my family for your patience and support.

The authors and publishers would like to thank the following for permission to reproduce their photographs:

Alamy/Zoltan Gabor p65, Science History Images p69, David Wall pXX(t); **Getty Images** pp64, 77(3), 94–95, 106(b), 10'000 Hours p112, AFP/Adem Altan p109, AFP/Ronaldo Schemidt p118(tl), Ascent Xmedia pp74–75, Nathan Benn p61, Ira Block p67(tr), Nikolay Bogdev/EyeEm pXXI, Jon Cartwright pp104, 105(tr), Matteo Colombo pp82–83(background), Ian Cuming pp70–71(background), Markus Daniel p110(bl), Steve Debenport p66, Enrique Díaz/7cero pp88–89, Digital Vision p77(5), Erik Dreyer p97, Michael England p70(c), ER Productions Limited pXXVI, Clare Fieseler p115(bl), Goldfaery p87(tr), Grandriver p76(2), Hero Images pp91(b), 98, Hoozone p88(bl), Hoxton/Martin Barraud pp114–115(background), Imagemore p76(1), Image Source pp106–107(background), iStockphoto/Ellerslie77 p94(tr), Johner Images p85, Peetatham Kongkapech pp62–63, Littleting/Pradthana Jarusriboonchai p82, Ty Milford p79(b), Moodboard p105(tm), Morfous p78(bl), Aaron Oberlander pXXIII(br), Orchidpoet p110(tr), PeopleImages p88(tr), Busakorn Pongparnit pp118–119(background), Franz Pritz p73, Purestock/Punchstock p90, Gavin Quirke pXXIII, Ken Redding p77(4), RichVintage p100, Tim Robberts p105(tl), Alexis Rosenfeld pXXIV, Jenny E. Ross p67(br), Audrey Saracco/EyeEm pXXVII, Anup Shah p103, Jordan Siemens pp86–87, Skynesher pp80(b), 91(cl), SolStock pp116(cl), 117, Paul Souders pXXV, SpVVK p113, Stocktrek Images p79(tl), Thehague p111, Camille Tokerud p116(br), Topical Press Agency p62(tr), Universal History Archive p70(a), Vctor Vargas/EyeEm p118(tr), Vasantytf p87(cl), Westend61 p81, Tim Zurowski p102(tr); **Hero Images** p116(bl); **iStockphoto** 70(b); **Powerstock** p102(b), **Shutterstock**/Margouillat photo pp92–93; **Stockbyte** p80(stapler); **Thinkstock** pp80(pizza), 92(tr)

Commissioned photographs in the Café Hubs by Sharp Focus pp71, 83, 95, 107, 119

The author and publishers are grateful for permission to reprint the following copyright material: Extract from 'From Forest Bathing to 'Halotherapy': 5 Ridiculous Wellness Trends' by Loulla-Mae Eleftherious-Smith. Originally published in The Independent, 7 October 2016. © Independent Digital News and Media Limited 2019. Reprinted with permission of Independent Digital News and Media Limited, p87; Extract from 'Political activism is as strong as ever, but now it's digital – and passionate' by Ethan Zuckerman. Originally published in The Guardian, 15 October 2013. © 2019 Guardian News & Media Limited or its affiliated companies. All rights reserved. Reprinted with permission of Guardian News & Media Limited, p120.

Printed and bound in Mexico
by Compañía Editorial Ultra, S.A. de C.V.

2021 2020
04 03 02 01

Language Hub

ADVANCED
Workbook B
with Key + access to Audio

macmillan education

C1

Macmillan Education
4 Crinan Street
London N1 9XW
A division of Macmillan Education Limited

Companies and representatives throughout the world

Language Hub Advanced Workbook B with Key ISBN 978-1-380-04664-2
Language Hub Advanced Workbook B with Key + access to Audio
ISBN 978-1-380-04658-1

Written by Signature Manuscripts

Signature Manuscripts has asserted their right to be identified as the author of this work in accordance with the Copyright, Designs and Patents Act 1988.

First published 2020

Original design by emc design ltd
Page make-up by SPi Global
Cover design based on original design by Restless
Cover photographs by plainpicture/Cavan Images, Getty Images/Luís Henrique Boucault
Picture research by Emily Taylor

The authors and publishers would like to thank the following for permission to reproduce their photographs:

Alamy p67; **EyeEm**/Amit Goldstein p71(a); **Getty Images**/Benoitb p43(tr), Getty Images/Chris Bennett p56, Getty Images/Rimma Bondarenko p57(c), Getty Images/Caiaimage/Paul Bradbury p54, Getty Images/Caiaimage/Agnieszka Olek p41, Getty Images/Amos Chapple p39(tl), Getty Images/Cultura p50, Getty Images/Cultura/Frank and Helena p61, Getty Images/Adam Gault p45, Getty Images/Geber86 p59, Getty Images/Mike Harrington p52(mr), Getty Images/Hero Images pp42, 46(tr), Getty Images/Jon Hicks p71(c), Getty Images/Insights p43(tl), Getty Images/iStockphoto pp46(tl), 48, Getty Images/Istetiana p57(d), Getty Images/Jacobs Stock Photography Ltd p64, Getty Images/Johner RF p46(b), Getty Images/Kanawa_Studio p68, Getty Images/Aleksi Koskinen p70, Getty Images/Justin Lambert p60, Getty Images/Justin Lewis p51, Getty Images/Matthias Makarinus p40, Getty Images/OatmealStories p57(b), Getty Images/Kiszon Pascal pp63, 71(b), Getty Images/PeopleImages p55, Getty Images/PhotoDisc p58, Getty Images/Rawpixel p66(tr), Getty Images/SolStock p69, Getty Images/TommL p53, Getty Images/Claudia Totir p57(a), Getty Images/Vtwinpixel p52(tl), Getty Images/Westend61 p62, Getty Images/Zero Creatives p44; **Anna McNuff**/Peter Race p39(bl); **Shutterstock**/Vasyl Shulga p66(tl)

Printed and bound in Mexico
by Compañía Editorial Ultra, S.A. de C.V.

2021 2020
04 03 02 01

Contents

VOCABULARY
Journeys and adventures; Three-part phrasal verbs

A Complete the text with the words in the box.

beaten embarked globetrotters heart impenetrable long-haul provisions uncharted

Around the globe in 80 days

Around the globe in 80 days? Well the 19th-century journalist Nellie Bly did it in 72 days. But role models for intrepid female adventurers aren't confined to history books. The image of 19th-century explorers fighting their way through [1] ________ terrain and large expeditions into dangerous and [2] ________ territories is being replaced by solo modern-day adventurers and [3] ________.

Anna McNuff [4] ________ on a seven-month cycle ride into the [5] ________ of the USA. She crossed every state, travelling 11,000 miles on a pink bike. She had to deal with the various challenges, including weather (cold, wind, floods and blizzards) and wild animals. In 2015, she ditched the bike and ran about 1900 miles to complete the Te Araroa Trail in New Zealand. While water wasn't a problem, she sometimes had to carry essential [6] ________ (like chocolate!) to last for up to seven days.

While we can certainly learn from the spirit of past adventurers who endured difficult conditions to explore their world, we shouldn't forget modern-day female role models and the amazing adventures that are being had right now. And with the advent of more affordable [7] ________ flights, getting off the [8] ________ track is more possible than ever.

B Complete the sentences with one word in each gap.

1 I need a holiday to help me switch ________ from work for a while.

2 I'm playing tennis tomorrow morning at eight o'clock. Are you up ________ it?

3 Carol is always talking about tidying her desk, but she never seems to get ________ to it.

4 If you come up ________ any problems, just phone me.

5 When you look ________ on your schooldays, do you think of them as a happy time?

6 Nobody found ________ about the missing money until the thief had left the country.

7 The best way to brush ________ on your French is to spend some time in France.

8 The problem with having a mobile and a computer at home is that there's no getting away ________ work.

GRAMMAR
Past modals of speculation and deduction

A Choose the correct options to complete the sentences.

1 He *can't / mustn't* have been serious about leaving – he loves it here.
2 She *must / might* have mentioned it, but I really don't remember.
3 It's highly *likely / distinct* that the bad weather contributed to the accident.
4 Sandra *may have decided / may decided* to turn back because of the snow on the road.
5 Some people say the pyramids must *had / have* been built using very advanced technology.
6 There's a distinct *probability / possibility* that the explorer died of some kind of disease.
7 You *could / must* have seen that film – everyone knows it!
8 He *may well / well may* have phoned me – I've had my phone switched off all morning.

B Complete the second sentence so that it has a similar meaning to the first sentence. Use three words including the word given in bold.

1 There's a good chance he has decided not to come because of the weather.
WELL
He ________________ decided not to come because of the weather.
2 I think he probably changed his mind about applying for the job.
EXTREMELY
It's ________________ he changed his mind about applying for the job.
3 I'm sure they got out of the building.
LEFT
They ________________ the building safely.
4 It's possible that Andrea forgot where we live.
MIGHT
Andrea ________________ where we live.
5 It's very likely that he fell asleep.
DISTINCT
There's ________________ that he fell asleep.
6 I'm certain it wasn't me who phoned you. I would remember.
CAN'T
I would remember phoning you, so it ________________ me.

PRONUNCIATION
Showing your attitude

A Read the sentences aloud, paying attention to the way you pronounce the underlined phrases.

1 Well, in general, I agree with most of the changes to our contracts, but the question is, can we afford to live on the wages they're offering?
2 Allegedly, he got the job because his father is friends with the manager. The main thing is, he is pretty good at it, so that might just be a rumour.
3 Supposedly, the money's going to come from the sale of one of the smaller companies – the question is, which one?
4 On the whole, I think the project has been successful. Surely, the management must be pleased with it.

6.1 **B Listen to the sentences from Exercise A. Practise saying the sentences in the same way as the speakers do in the recording.**

GRAMMAR

-ing and infinitive forms

A Complete the text with the correct form of the verbs in brackets.

Finding sources you can trust

For the curious mind (and for those minds paid to be curious), the internet is an amazing tool. Researchers and journalists have access to stories across business, politics and humour. And the public has got used to [1]____________ (*read*) online. But in some cases, fake stories are circulated on purpose.

It's just so easy [2]____________ (*spread*) a story nowadays – whether it's true or false. Before the internet, most news came via newspapers which had a reputation [3]____________ (*maintain*), so they would at least take care not [4]____________ (*do*) too much that damaged their credibility. But now, with both the speed at which stories are being written and shared and the ease with which fake news can be spread online, we may have difficulty [5]____________ (*tell*) the difference between credible and questionable news.

B Match the beginnings of the sentences (1–6) to the endings (a–f).

1 When I have guests, I always worry that there's not enough food ____
2 I don't think you'll get into trouble for ____
3 Is this a good time ____
4 Have fun ____
5 There are lots of online resources ____
6 In your opinion, is there any point ____

a surfing, but don't take any risks.
b to help you.
c to go round.
d being five minutes late.
e to talk to you about my essay?
f waiting to see the manager today?

C Choose the option which is closest in meaning to the sentence.

1 They stopped to analyse the data.
 a They were analysing data, then stopped.
 b They were doing something else, then started analysing data.

2 She remembered to heat the liquid.
 a She remembered something she needed to do.
 b She had the memory of doing something.

VOCABULARY
Binomial expressions

A Complete the binomial expressions with the words in the box. There are three extra words that you do not need to use.

away by greet order quiet soul sound take tear there tidy

1 When we go to the country, we like to sit and enjoy the peace and ________.

2 ________ and large, my job gives me everything I need.

3 Every relationship needs a bit of give and ________.

4 The boss always comes early to meet and ________ people when there's an event.

5 That was far and ________ the best film I've ever seen!

6 The job of the police is to uphold law and ________.

7 Keeping the work area clean and ________ is a matter of safety, too.

8 There's a bit of wear and ________, but you'd expect that on a ten-year-old car.

B Complete the binomial expressions with two words in each gap.

1 We searched far ________ for the phone, but it was gone.

2 His is a real rags-________ story – they weren't rich as children.

3 When he plays football, he really puts his heart ________ into the game.

4 Time ________, they get the work wrong, even after I've shown them.

5 Frank had worked two shifts back ________ so he was exhausted.

6 It didn't happen straight away. Slowly ________, I got used to living here though.

7 We watched grandfather and grandson walking side ________ down the lane.

8 Why is she getting so upset? It's not a life-________ situation – she's just deciding which outfit to wear!

PRONUNCIATION
Pauses and pitch in presentations

A Read the beginning of a presentation and mark a (/) in red where you would take a pause. Also think about where you would step up to a higher pitch to start a new topic or step down to a lower pitch to end a topic.

I'd like to talk to you today about the bad side of staying informed. I don't mean for one minute to suggest that you should stay uninformed – it's good to keep up-to-date with what's happening – but too much news causes us stress, and that's official! Studies suggest that many of us check headlines on an hourly basis, and now experts are telling us that's not good for our state of mind, our sleep patterns or even our relationships. One of the biggest dangers is that the news, in order to hold our attention, has to be shocking. Now, I like to see an action or a horror film occasionally, but imagine that level of tension *all* the time. Our nerves just wouldn't take it. And yet that's just what happens when we are constantly plugged in to continuous news stories. The very least we should do is to make sure we don't watch the news just before going to bed. At least that might help us to sleep better at night, which in turn will help us cope with everything else.

6.2 **B Listen to someone reading the text from Exercise A. Does the speaker pause and change pitch in the same places as you? Now practise reading the presentation with the same pauses and pitch changes as the speaker in the recording.**

READING

A PREDICT Look at the pictures and the title of the article. What information will the article include? What questions will it answer?

B Read *Mungo Park: the last adventure*. Were your predictions in Exercise A correct?

C READ FOR DETAIL Read the article again and answer the questions.

1 Why was Mungo Park chosen to lead his first expedition to Africa?
2 Which two things caused him to abandon his first expedition?
3 What can we understand about Park's personality from his communication with home?
4 What happened to the people who went looking for Mungo Park?

D REFLECT Think about the answers to these questions.

1 What makes people undertake dangerous expeditions?
2 What motivates modern-day explorers to follow in the footsteps of older explorers?

Mungo Park: THE LAST ADVENTURE

MUNGO PARK.

Mungo Park was a young Scottish explorer who went in search of the Niger River in West Africa. After training to be a surgeon, he travelled to South-East Asia as a ship's medical officer. While in the region, he studied the plant and animal life of Sumatra and, on his return, described several new species of fish and plants that he had recorded. This gained him a certain amount of recognition and, when the African Association was looking for someone to head an expedition to explore the course of the Niger River, Park was an obvious choice.

His first African expedition therefore began in 1795 and Park followed the Gambia River for 200 miles (about 320 km), entering into unknown territory as he encountered the Senegal River. He was then taken prisoner for four months before escaping and eventually reaching his target, the Niger River. Lack of supplies meant that he was only able to follow it for 80 miles (about 128 km) and, on turning back, he became seriously ill. When he finally made it back to Britain in 1797, he wrote *Travels in the Interior Districts of Africa*, which was popular and helped to further his reputation.

In 1805, he was commissioned for a second expedition to chart the course of the Niger River. This expedition was dogged by misfortune from the start. Forty men set off from the Gambia in the rainy season – the worst time to do so. By the time they reached the Niger, only 11 men remained alive. However, Park made no mention of these tragic events in the letters which he sent home. He was determined to complete the expedition and set off from Bamako along the unmapped stretch of the Niger.

Eventually, a party was sent to find out what could have happened to Park and his men. Isaaco, a local guide, was hired to help them. Given that they had set out in the rainy season, might their canoes have been caught in rapids and overturned or broken against rocks and the men drowned? Had they run out of provisions? Despite being well-armed, could they have been attacked and overcome by a hostile tribe? Or could they have died of disease or been the prey of wild animals? Although death was the most likely outcome, and with no trace of Park, there were still many rumours back in Britain claiming that he had survived.

Isaaco managed to find a man named Amadi, one of Park's guides, who gave his account of events. They had been attacked several times by men in canoes and they had, as expected, encountered dangerous rapids, which they survived until they reached the rapids at Bussa where the river narrows. There, they were caught on a rock and attacked by hostile tribesmen who had been waiting in ambush. The odds against them were too high; the story goes that Park jumped into the river and it is assumed that he drowned. Amadi was taken prisoner.

In 1827, hopeful that his father might still be alive, Mungo Park's son, Thomas, set off to Africa in search of him. Within a month, however, all contact with him was lost. Stories circulated that he had died of fever but his body was never recovered. As recently as 2003, a man named Christian Velten set out on a six-month expedition following in the footsteps of Mungo Park. After a short time, contact with him was also lost.

Glossary

ambush (n) a surprise attack by people in a concealed place
be dogged by (v phr) to have problems/difficulties over a long period of time
rapids (n pl) a steep, rocky place in a river with a fast current

LISTENING

A PREDICT What logistical problems do you think 19th-century explorers faced? Think about:

- transport
- communication
- provisions
- technology.

6.3 **B LISTEN FOR MAIN IDEA** Listen to the first part of a podcast about two Antarctic expeditions and answer the questions.

1 What were the names of the two explorers?

____

2 What was their goal?

____

3 When did these events take place?

____

4 What was the result of the expeditions?

____

6.4 **C** Listen to the rest of the recording. Tick (✓) the topics mentioned.

- ☐ Communication
- ☐ Finances
- ☐ Friendship
- ☐ Food and nutrition
- ☐ Goals
- ☐ Historical background
- ☐ Mountaineering
- ☐ Route planning
- ☐ Transport

6.5 **D LISTEN TO MAKE NOTES** Listen to the whole podcast. Make notes on the following questions.

1 Why Antarctica?	
2 What was life like for the explorers?	
3 What equipment was needed?	
4 How did Scott and Amundsen's goals differ?	
5 What means of transport did Scott use?	
6 What was wrong with his choices?	
7 How did Amundsen plan his route?	
8 What was wrong with Scott's preparations?	

Glossary

depot (n) place where things are stored
hardship (n) situation in which life is very difficult
rations (n pl) restricted amounts of food for people such as soldiers

E REFLECT Does this story remind you of any other similar adventures you have read or heard about?

WRITING

A Look at the picture and the essay question below. How do you think the picture might be related to the content of this essay?

What are the benefits of discovering new species?

B Complete the essay by matching these missing topic sentences (1–5) to the paragraphs (a–e).

1. Penicillin was produced from a fungus.
2. If you thought there was nothing new under the sun, then think again.
3. Clearly, there is still much to learn about the surface of the planet we inhabit.
4. Each life form has a special role in the ecosystem.
5. 'Biomimicry' is the science of copying nature's adaptations and applying them to technology.

The benefits of discovering NEW SPECIES

a___ And new species may provide further breakthroughs in medicine. For example, extracts from a newly discovered plant, *Kindia gangan*, a member of the coffee family, suggest that it may have medical applications.

b___ The gecko's ability to stick to walls and ceilings, the silk with which spiders spin their webs and the way butterfly wings react to light have all been exploited in technological innovations. Discoveries of new species may well lead to other innovations in the future.

c___ Biologists estimate that the vast majority of life on Earth – between 3 and 100 million species – remains undiscovered. There are three enormous benefits to discovering new species: each new life form helps us understand more about biodiversity, may prove a valuable source of new medicines or could inspire new technology.

d___ The benefits of continuing to discover new plants, insects and micro-organisms are enormous. They will help us treat the planet with greater knowledge and respect, with more informed conservation strategies. They can provide us with new medicines, possibly even for diseases we think incurable. Also, the weird and wonderful adaptations plants and creatures make to survive in their environments provide the inspiration for technologies that benefit us all.

e___ Biodiversity is the way in which all these life forms function together to maintain a balance. As we discover new species, the better we understand how these systems work, which will help us implement more effective conservation strategies for threatened ecosystems such as coral reefs.

C STRUCTURING AN EXPOSITORY ESSAY Put the paragraphs (a–e) in the correct order (1–5).

1. introduction ___
2. first benefit ___
3. second benefit ___
4. third benefit ___
5. conclusion ___

WRITING PRACTICE

A PREPARE Read the essay question below. Use the questions 1–5 to write notes for the essay.

What are the benefits of foreign travel?

1. Have you ever travelled to another country? If not, would you like to?
2. What did/could you learn by visiting another country?
3. What did/could you learn about yourself?
4. Can travelling abroad teach you more about your own country?
5. Make a list of the benefits of travel.

B PLAN You are going to write an expository essay for the task in Exercise A.

- Organise your notes into an appropriate structure for an expository essay.
- Use a topic sentence to introduce each main paragraph.
- Finish with a conclusion that summarises the points you made in the main body of the essay in the same order.

C WRITE Write your essay in 220–260 words.

GRAMMAR
it clefting

A Write one word in each gap to complete the sentences.

1 It ______ you who caused the problem; it was me.
2 It was the long sea journey ______ put me off the idea.
3 The problem wasn't her lack of qualifications – ______ was her personality.
4 The money's OK, but ______ the hours that I don't like.
5 It was ______ visit my parents that I last went home.
6 It was my brother ______ persuaded me to go to university.
7 It was ______ I had to pay for something that I realised my wallet was missing.
8 It wasn't until we got home ______ we realised how close we had come to disaster.

B Rewrite the sentences using *it* clefting to draw attention to the underlined words or phrases.

1 I applied to run the race <u>to raise money for charity</u>.
______
2 <u>The physical challenge</u> isn't a problem for me; <u>the psychological challenge</u> is!
______
3 I've only noticed the pain in my legs <u>now</u>, <u>after I've been running for five days</u>.
______
4 <u>My sister</u> persuaded me to enter the race.
______
5 I didn't run <u>a marathon</u> – I ran <u>an ultramarathon</u>!
______

C Rewrite the sentences beginning with *It*. Sometimes more than one answer is possible.

1 They really wanted to see the landscape paintings.
______
2 He was to blame for breaking the window, not her.
______
3 The part Steven didn't understand was at the end.
______
4 I'm talking to you!
______
5 What bothers me is the cost.
______
6 Eliza said 'no' because she was scared.
______
7 You only really appreciate something when it's gone.
______
8 I didn't realise how dangerous it was until I got back.
______

D Complete the sentences so that they are true for you.

1 It wasn't only ______ it was ______.
2 It was my ______ who ______ me to ______.
3 It was because ______ that I ______.
4 It was to ______ that I ______ not to ______.

VOCABULARY
Feelings

A Chose the correct options to complete the text.

In touch with your FEELINGS?

A lot of the time, we do not have control over our emotions because they are instinctive reactions in response to a particular set of circumstances.

This is often useful – for example, when we are [1]***indifferent / disgusted*** by the sight of something, such as rotten food, it may well mean that we should stay away from it to be safe. Some people, however, sometimes try to stay in control of their emotions. They may want to appear tough or [2]***frustrated / resilient***. But sometimes these people can seem arrogant or [3]***superior / hysterical***.

However, there are times when we need to be a little [4]***humble / disgusted*** and accept that it is not always in our power to control how we feel. We should accept that it is natural to be [5]***devastated / humble*** when something awful happens.

But we should still strive to be [6]***grumpy / courageous*** even when we are frightened and to deal with things in a calm manner. At times like these, it really is possible to control our emotions.

B Complete the sentences with words from Exercise A. Sometimes more than one answer is possible.

1 Jack was very ________ and kept calm up until the last moment.
2 Emma is a very ________ person who never likes to talk about her achievements.
3 When we saw the extent of the damage, we were ________.
4 The BASE jumpers were left feeling ________ after their jump was cancelled three times due to high winds.
5 Carla seems almost ________ to fear – however terrifying the situation, she always looks the picture of calm.
6 Nigel thinks he's better than everyone and he always acts in a(n) ________ manner.
7 Stop being horrible to everyone! I think the reason you're so ________ this morning is that you went to bed so late last night.
8 Alex was ________ – he just kept screaming and crying.

PRONUNCIATION
Intonation in question tags

A Look at the question tags and draw arrows to show whether they should have rising (↗) or falling (↘) intonation.

1 It's ridiculous, isn't it? ___
2 Let's meet at the weekend, shall we? ___
3 We couldn't make it next weekend, could we? ___
4 Wow, that's good. You know what you're doing, don't you? ___
5 It's cold today, isn't it? ___
6 You couldn't help me out here, could you? ___

7.1 B Listen to the sentences from Exercise A and check your answers.

C Practise saying the sentences in the same way as the speakers do in the recording in Exercise B.

7.2 Extremes

Extreme jobs

VOCABULARY
Polysemy; Intensifiers

A Complete the text with the words in the box.

application competition conditions land pressure sick

A life in CYBERCRIME

When I left school, my number one priority was to [1] ________ a well-paid job. I didn't care what. All I knew was that I was [2] ________ of studying and I wanted to use my computer skills.

I knew there was a lot of [3] ________ in the job market, especially for IT jobs – I had heard crazy numbers, like 500 people applying for one job. I felt a great deal of [4] ________ on me to get a job and the longer I stayed unemployed, the greater it became.

Almost a decade later and I am still amazed that I am now a legal computer hacker. That's right, I work for a security company and use my computer skills to make companies safer against cybercrime.

A very impressive [5] ________ got me my first interview with my current employer and after two more I was finally successful!

There were a few strange [6] ________ in the contract, and I have to be very cautious about personal data and intellectual property, but the money is very good.

B Rearrange the letters to make intensifiers.

1. Paul was **miymelnse** ________ proud of his success in the competition.
2. It's **tuetyrl** ________ ridiculous to expect your parents to support you when you're in your 20s.
3. I'm not **lgtoeharte** ________ sure I trust him.
4. Jane was **ayntcoiebl** ________ different after her trip to India.
5. It's **yetlairvel** ________ easy to get a job with that company – they're desperate for staff.
6. Georgia did **krrebmyaal** ________ well in her exams.
7. You can't call it 'his version of the truth'; it was an **utrogiht** ________ lie.
8. Things changed **ciradlyal** ________ once the new management team took over.
9. It's **capryalctil** ________ impossible to get a transfer to another branch – they almost never allow it.
10. Yeah, I think Philip was **tsohemwa** ________ confused – he had a strange look on his face!

GRAMMAR
what clefting and *all* clefting

A Find and correct the mistakes in the sentences.

1 What that happened was I got confused.

______

2 Why crashed the computer I have no idea!

______

3 Pets are easy – they all need is food, water and some attention.

______

4 That Lara likes about summer is being able to relax on the balcony.

______

5 You all need is a snack and some good company!

______

6 What's that Simon can't stand about this job – the silly rules!

______

7 That we ended up doing was taking the train.

______

8 I didn't have my phone on me so what did I do was ask a colleague to borrow hers.

______

B Rewrite the sentences using the words in brackets.

1 In the end they turned back. (*what*)

______

2 We don't need anything except a map. (*all*)

______

3 I can't stand sleeping in a tent. (*what*)

______

4 Rex loves playing with his ball in the garden. (*what*)

______

5 They needed a drink of water. (*all*)

______

6 You need a holiday. (*what*)

______

7 Tanya wanted to be a ballerina more than anything. (*what*)

______

8 She's just asking for a short break. (*all*)

______

C Complete the second sentence so that it has a similar meaning to the first sentence. Write between two and five words, including the word given.

1 She loves basketball because she gets to meet up with her friends – that's what she loves most.

WHAT

______ basketball is that she gets to meet up with her friends.

2 She only wants a little bit of consideration, nothing else.

ALL

______ little bit of consideration, nothing else.

3 He didn't know what to do so he phoned his dad.

DID

He didn't know what to do so ______ his dad.

4 I like camping, except for the insects. I hate dealing with them.

STAND

______ camping is dealing with insects.

5 I've realised something about my job – it doesn't take a genius to do it!

WHAT

______ that it doesn't take a genius to do my job!

6 My sister doesn't remember much about her first school – just playing outside.

ALL

______ about her first school is playing outside.

PRONUNCIATION
any and *quite*

A Underline *quite* and *any* in these sentences when they are stressed.

1 The film was quite amazing, actually – we loved it!
2 I don't want any old doctor – I want the one I always see.
3 The questions they asked me were quite ridiculous!
4 Any questions you have will be answered at the end, OK?
5 Well, you don't tell your password to just anybody.
6 Let's go – anywhere's better than here!
7 The test was quite hard but he thinks he passed.
8 'Which film do you want to watch?'
'Oh, any one. You choose.'

7.2 **B Listen to the sentences from Exercise A.**

C Practise saying the sentences in the same way as the speakers do in the recording.

Surf's up

[1]_______ may look like fun in the sun, but for some surfing is a job, a full-time occupation. Also a passion. And there is money to be made – if you're good enough. I'll come back to that later. But before [2]_______ get on your board, and paddle out to where the waves break, you should be aware of some of the dangers involved in surfing – or just being in the sea.

Shark attacks are everyone's fear, surfer or not, but they are not as frequent a cause of injury or death as other factors; though [3]_______ do get a lot of media coverage. Waves are powerful forces of nature and a wipeout, or being thrown off your board, can cause serious injuries. Your board, too, becomes a danger in such incidents, as it is sent spinning into the air and you have no idea where it will land. You just hope it doesn't hit you, especially with the pointy end. Now you're struggling in rough water, there are riptides to worry about, which are often present at good surfing areas. [4]_______ takes us to the most obvious danger – drowning. So why take it up, let alone make it your profession?

The excitement, of course. Even with a small wave, say one metre high, you experience the awesome power of nature – and you're going with it. Riding [5]_______ taller than yourself, the experience is even greater. [6]_______ claim there's no better sensual experience in the world. There's nothing but the wave, your board and your body – all your senses fully engaged: the sound of the surf, the taste of salt, the colours and the sensation of speed. The slightest shift in weight will alter your trajectory in the direction you want to go, or send you crashing into the surf. And no two waves are ever the same. An extreme challenge, then, but one that brings great pleasure. Imagine what it would be like to catch a wave as tall as a tower block. For some, [7]_______ is their speciality; but I assume they must be inhumanly confident or mad!

For [8]_______ are just onlookers, the lifestyle, too, has its attractions. What could be better than a job that takes you all over the world to exotic places, spending your days on beaches? It sounds like a permanent holiday. But [9]_______ not all travel and parties. Like anything worth doing, it takes hard work, ambition and time. I mentioned earlier that there was money to be made, but it's not great. There's no real job security, like a salary, health insurance, pension or paid leave. Top surfers get money from winning competitions, and a lot of that goes on travelling to the next competition. It's a sport and like, say, tennis, those at the top get the big money, while the rest fight it out for smaller and smaller amounts. Apart from [10]_______, once a surfer has made a name for himself or herself, there's money to be made from sponsorship and endorsements.

READING

A PREDICT Look at the picture and think about these questions.

1 What are some of the dangers involved in surfing?
2 What is it about this sport that appeals to people?

B READ FOR GIST Read *Surf's up* and answer the questions.

1 What is the main danger for surfers?
2 What claim do surfers make about the appeal of their sport?
3 What impression do non-surfers have of the surfing life?
4 As a profession, does surfing pay well?

C Complete the article with the reference devices in the box.

it it's many one such incidents that (x2) those who which you

D READ FOR REFERENCES What do the reference devices in Exercise C refer to? Decide if they are anaphoric: referring back (A), cataphoric: referring forwards (C) or exophoric: referring outside the text (E).

1 ___ 3 ___ 5 ___ 7 ___ 9 ___
2 ___ 4 ___ 6 ___ 8 ___ 10 ___

Glossary

endorsement (n) support given by a well-known person to products as a form of advertising
riptide (n) a strong surface current from the shore out to sea
sponsorship (n) support from an organisation that promotes sporting or artistic activity
trajectory (n) path, direction of a moving object

E REFLECT Think about the answers to these questions.

1 Why do we sometimes like to be scared?
2 Would you like to earn your living from doing an extreme sport? Why/Why not?

LISTENING

A PREDICT What personal qualities do you think a performer would need to be a successful tightrope walker?

7.3 **B LISTEN FOR SPECIFIC INFORMATION** Listen to a programme about tightrope walking. Complete the texts with a word or short phrase in each gap.

Nik Wallenda

The famous tightrope walker comes from a family of [1] ______ performers going back generations. His great-grandfather's died in [2] ______ trying to walk between two buildings. His most famous stunt, walking across the Niagara Falls, attracted [3] ______ viewers.

Philippe Petit

A [4] ______ film about his achievement called *Man on Wire* was released in 2008. He found fame after walking a tightrope between two skyscrapers in [5] ______ City for a distance of [6] ______ metres. The event was organised [7] ______ because it was illegal. A [8] ______ were used to fire a guiding rope across the space.

7.3 **C LISTEN FOR CAUSATION** Listen again and choose the correct options (a, b or c) to answer the questions or complete the sentences.

1 What is the key factor behind Nik Wallenda's successful career as a tightrope walker?
  - **a** Pressure from his family
  - **b** The achievements of his great-grandfather
  - **c** His desire for publicity

2 He attracts audiences of millions because
  - **a** he walked across the Niagara Falls.
  - **b** they think he has a lot of charisma.
  - **c** he knows how to successfully exploit the media.

3 Many people became interested in Philippe Petit again because
  - **a** his exploits are illegal.
  - **b** his most famous walk involved New York's Twin Towers.
  - **c** of a film which featured his most famous achievement.

4 What was the immediate result of Philippe Petit's walk between the Twin Towers?
  - **a** The New York police arrested him.
  - **b** He became famous overnight.
  - **c** A film was made about his exploit.

Glossary

feat (n) an impressive and often dangerous act
heist (n) an organised robbery (of a bank, jewellery store, etc)

D REFLECT Think about the answers to these questions.

1 Do you think that the people you heard about in the recording are courageous or foolish?

2 Why do people enjoy watching such terrifying stunts?

Tree Surgeon – Scotland

The Forestry Commission is recruiting an arborist/tree surgeon. The job involves collecting data, assessing tree health and treatment, assessing hazards posed by trees, pruning and removing branches and planting and felling trees.

A qualification in Forest Management is not essential, but some experience in woodland ecology and conservation or arboriculture would be valuable. We are looking for an experienced climber skilled in the use and maintenance of power tools. The candidate must be prepared to work outdoors in all conditions, be able to work at height, remain calm in tense situations, follow instructions in detail and work well as a member of a team.

Applications to: Henry Swaffer,
Forestry Commission.

Dear Mr Swaffer,

I am writing to apply for the position of tree surgeon at the Forestry Commission.

You will see on my CV (attached) that I have a qualification in arboriculture and experience in woodland conservation as a volunteer for the Woodland Trust, where I [1]was in charge of a team [2]whose task was to collect data about the health and growth of trees. This work provided me with valuable insights into woodland preservation.

Later, I [3]became the manager of a small tree surgery company where I [4]had responsibility for the care and maintenance of woodland in the Bramlow area on behalf of the local council. Here my climbing skills and expertise in the use of power tools were put to good use. [5]I was also involved in the development of new methods of tree preservation, which the council subsequently adopted as policy. The job also allowed me to demonstrate my leadership qualities and ability to work with a team.

I look forward to the opportunity of an interview.

Best regards,

Anthony Waite

WRITING

A Look at the picture to the left. What skills, personal qualities and qualifications do you think are required to do this job?

B Read the job advert and answer the questions.

1 Which of the skills, qualities and qualifications that you noted down in Exercise A are mentioned?

2 Which are the most important for the job?

C **USING POWER VERBS** Read the cover letter. Rewrite the underlined sections using verbs to make the letter more powerful.

WRITING PRACTICE

A **PREPARE** Read the job advert and underline the key information regarding skills and qualifications required.

Lifeguard – Team Leader at Ocean Resorts

We are looking for a dynamic individual to join our team at Ocean Resorts. Your role will be to support, coach and guide team members in creating a safe and fun environment.

The candidate will have proven experience in busy sea- and poolside environments and have a current RLSS (Royal Life Saving Society) qualification. Excellent physical fitness is essential, as well as being a strong swimmer. A practical knowledge of first aid and a commitment to health and safety are also required. Flexibility in the role and the ability to take on extra responsibilities when required is a plus.

Applications to: Mr Kevin Scholes, Manager, Ocean Resorts.

B **PLAN** You are going to write a cover letter in response to the advert for a lifeguard.

- Use the information you underlined in Exercise A.
- Organise your notes into an appropriate form for a cover letter.
- Use power verbs to talk about your achievements.

C **WRITE** Write your letter in 120–200 words.

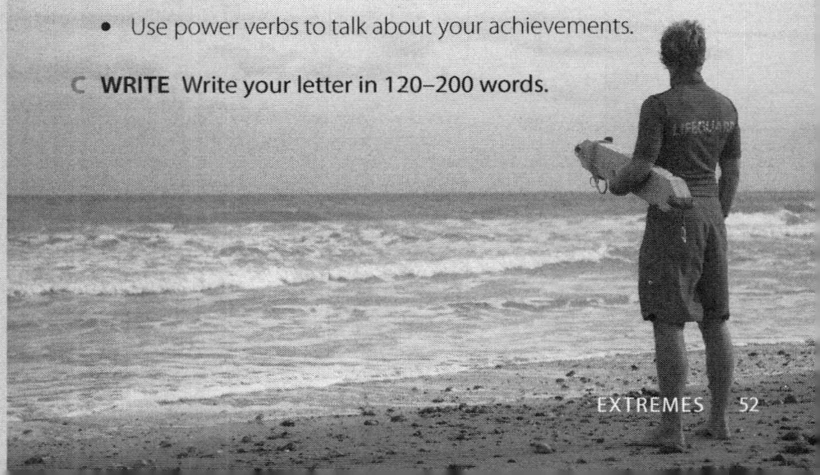

VOCABULARY
Health problems

A Complete the text below with the words in the box.

dislocate fractured pressure pulled
rash rate sore sprained

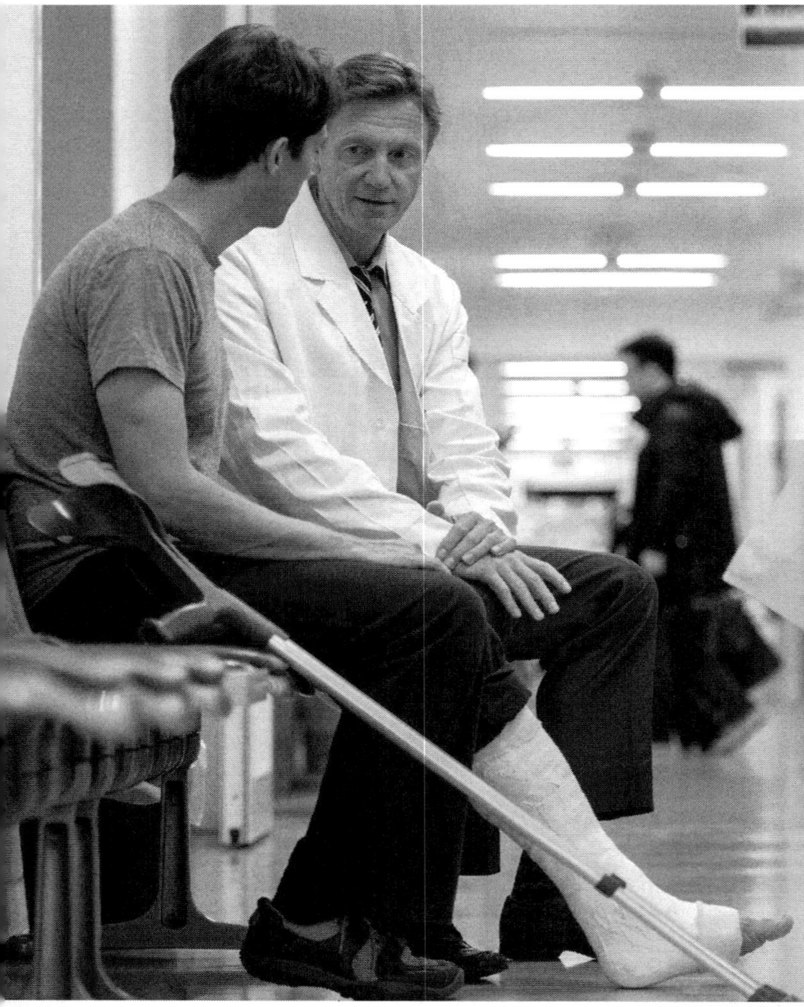

B The words in bold are in the wrong sentence. Replace with the correct word.

1 Geoff's leg's in plaster because he **inflamed** ________ it when he slipped on some ice.
2 I didn't warm up properly before the match and I **sore** ________ a muscle.
3 My knee is very **fractured** ________ – it has swelled up a lot so I'm putting ice on it.
4 A normal resting heart **blood** ________ is 60 to 100 beats per minute.
5 If I fall asleep in a chair, I often wake up with a **sprained** ________ back.
6 Kate's **pulled** ________ her ankle – she twisted it on the stairs but it's not too serious.
7 I've got a **rate** ________ on my skin and I don't know what's causing it.
8 The first thing the doctor did was to take my **rash** ________ pressure.

HEALTH CHAT

Post your questions or medical issue on the HealthChat Portal and a qualified doctor will respond within minutes. You can post in both the private and public chat forums.

Woke up with a [1] ________ throat a few days ago, and a strange itchy red [2] ________ on my arms, chest and legs. Am seeing the doctor tomorrow …
Jared | 3.44 pm

Went for a ride last Saturday and noticed that my heart [3] ________ was much faster than usual. Got it checked out and found I've got high blood [4] ________. My doctor thinks it might be stress-related.
Emily | 3.45 pm

Came off my mountain bike – again! – and [5] ________ my ankle. It was extremely painful, but could have been worse. The race medical team bandaged it up for me. Really glad it wasn't [6] ________ or broken!
Connor | 3.45 pm

Having [7] ________ a muscle in my leg about a month ago, I thought I was getting fit again – only to [8] ________ my shoulder this weekend. Really painful! And spent four hours in A&E!
Liz | 3.47 pm

GRAMMAR
Relative clauses with complex relative pronouns

A Complete the sentences with one preposition in each gap.

1 The police were keen to interview victims ________ whose houses the burglars had broken.
2 The treadmill ________ which I was most interested is no longer for sale.
3 The leaflet lists all the surfaces that the device can be attached ________.
4 He was very formal on the phone and said, '________ whom am I speaking?'
5 The thief stole a car, ________ which he made his getaway.
6 'I don't know who this parcel is for.' 'Well, who is it addressed ________?'
7 It's a wellness treatment ________ which I've read a lot recently.
8 There are six team members, ________ whom three are women.

B Rewrite the sentences using the word in brackets.

1 This is the person. Her fitness business is now worth millions. (*whose*)
This is ________.
2 I trust Jonah. I trust him more than anyone. (*person*)
Jonah is ________.
3 I need a strategy which makes it impossible for me to get a virus. (*whereby*)
I need a strategy ________.
4 Be careful you don't get a training injury. You might never recover from it. (*from*)
Be careful you don't get ________.
5 We are targeting people. Exercise is not a priority for them. (*whom*)
We are targeting ________.
6 The owner of the company is very satisfied. The profits all go into his pockets. (*into*)
The owner of the company, ________.

PRONUNCIATION
Building suspense

A Read the sentences aloud. Use intonation and pauses to build suspense.

1 My health app told me that yesterday I did 5000 steps!
2 Well, someone in this room has just passed their exams!
3 There's no more waiting – you get the results at the touch of a button.
4 I spent an hour shopping for spices and after all that, I didn't find the one I wanted.
5 It hasn't really sunk in yet but … I won first prize!
6 Do you want to hear the good news? Danny's coming out of hospital … tomorrow!

8.1 **B Listen to the sentences from Exercise A.**

C Practise saying the sentences in the same way as the speakers do in Exercise B.

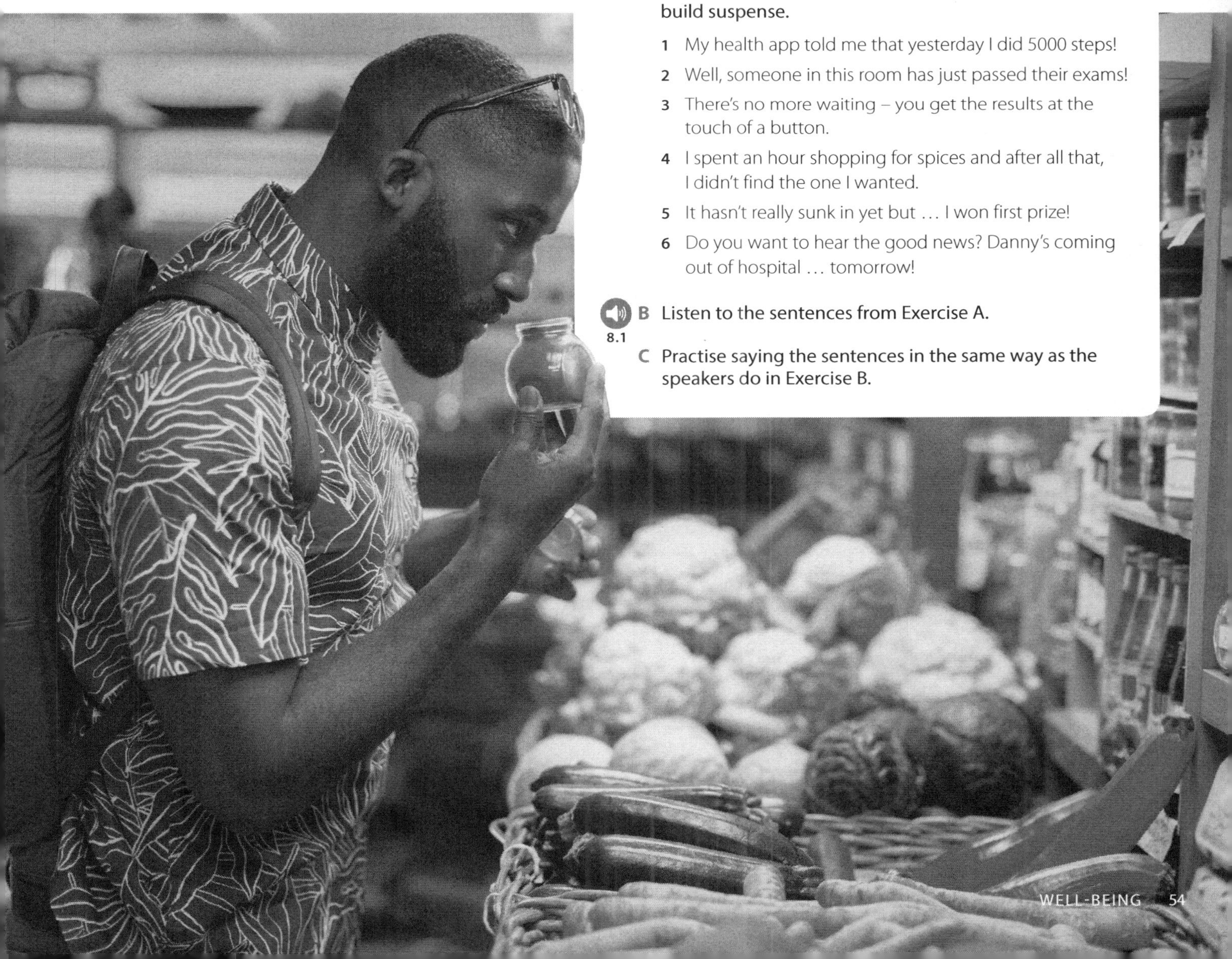

VOCABULARY
Idioms; Describing taste

A Choose the correct options to complete the text.

A TOUGH GAME

Only once had Roberto taken part in any kind of sporting competition, and that was in a tennis match. Someone persuaded him to play but his [1]***cup of tea / gut feeling*** was that he was making a terrible mistake!

A bigger mistake was watching his opponent play in a match before. That certainly [2]***made a meal of it / gave him food for thought*** because Roberto could see how good he was. Roberto very nearly [3]***got cold feet / kept an eye out***, but he decided to [4]***give it his best shot / take it with a pinch of salt***.

His opponent was really very good and Roberto was clearly [5]***out of his depth / head and shoulders below him***. Roberto thought about [6]***moving the goalposts / throwing in the towel***, but he stuck at it. In the end, Roberto lost of course, but he likes to think he put up a good fight!

B Complete the sentences with one word to describe taste in each gap. The first letter is given to help you.

1 I don't like **f**__________ drinks like lemonade or soda.
2 **C**__________ vegetables like carrots, which you can really bite into, are a good substitute for crisps.
3 I think the milk's gone **s**__________. Don't drink it.
4 Carol loves spicy food, but Mark prefers his to be **m**__________.
5 Jeanette always makes her food look really **a**__________.
6 Susan made a lovely smooth **c**__________ sauce to go with the mushrooms.
7 I like the **t**__________, slightly **a**__________ taste of grapefruit.
8 It's a terrible place. The meals they serve there are always **b**__________ and taste of nothing.
9 Their chips are usually covered in vinegar – far too **s**__________ for my taste.

PRONUNCIATION
Pronunciation of idioms

A Circle the words in the underlined idioms which are stressed. Then practise saying the sentences.

1 No, tennis isn't really my cup of tea.
2 I know it was a penalty, but he really made a meal of it, rolling all over the pitch like that!
3 Murphy didn't take part in the robbery – he was only there to keep an eye out for the police.
4 He exaggerates a lot, so you can take most of what he says with a pinch of salt.
5 Eva was the best student in our class – she was head and shoulders above the rest of us.
6 We knew where we were at the start of this project, but if the boss keeps moving the goalposts, we'll never get anywhere.

8.2 **B Listen to the sentences from Exercise A.**

C Practise saying the sentences in the same way as the speakers do in Exercise B.

GRAMMAR
Pronouns and determiners

A Choose the correct options to complete the sentences.

1 It would be better for all of us if we did *any* / *more* exercise.
2 There was a choice of two desserts, but I didn't fancy *either* / *neither*.
3 *Most people* / *The most people* feel better when they are fitter.
4 Do you want some coffee? I'll make you *some* / *some coffee.*
5 Some people like team sports, but *others people* / *others* prefer individual activities.
6 There were *a few* / *very few* members there, so they postponed the meeting until the following week.
7 One *of* / *from* the fitness programmes is bound to suit you.
8 There's *a little* / *little* point in worrying about it – we can't change anything now.

B Find and correct the mistakes in the sentences.

1 When you're doing a serious hike, you can't drink too much of water – in fact, most people don't drink enough.

....

2 There were two vegan options, but I didn't fancy both of them.

....

3 They who followed the diet reported an average loss of three kilos in the first week.

....

4 You have too much sugar and salt in your diet – it's best if you cut back on neither.

....

5 There are only few restaurants that serve good vegetarian food in this city.

....

6 You drink a lot of coffee, and I think you'd sleep better if you drank less of.

....

7 These are your books – my are still over there where I left them.

....

8 Jamie only needs six hours sleep a night, but I can never seem to get enough of.

....

a

b

FOOD, GLORIOUS FOOD

We are what we eat? Well I'm not sure what this received wisdom means if you're on a charcoal diet! With so much advice about food and eating available to us today, it can be hard to know what is good information and what can be downright harmful. With a growing global wellness industry keen to package and push us a never-ending stream of diets and food products, we decided to take a closer look at some of the diets out there at the moment.

Charcoal

Black cheese or black ice cream, anyone? Almost any foodstuff can be made black by adding activated charcoal. The thinking behind this is that charcoal is a porous form of carbon which supposedly absorbs harmful bacteria in the digestive system. While this may be true, critics of the diet argue that activated charcoal is so greedy it absorbs anything in your stomach, even the good stuff like food, vitamins and the medicines you might be taking. Not surprisingly, the fans of this diet don't accept this. I don't know about you, but, for me, variety of colour is a major 'ingredient' in the enjoyment of food. So that's one thing that would make it harder for me to follow this diet.

Ketogenic

Sounds rather scientific, doesn't it? The keto diet, as it is called, allegedly turns your body into a fat-burning machine by avoiding carbohydrates such as pasta. Admittedly, those who have tried it swear that it works and have lost weight and benefited from improved health associated with weight loss. Like most diets, though, this one also has its critics, who argue that any diet that excludes an entire food group from its regime is bound to have some side-effects, or not provide all the nutrition we need. But if losing weight is your goal, you could give it a go.

Cauliflower

Not just cauliflower, but cabbage, or any diet that claims sticking to any one foodstuff will bring rapid and amazing results. Cauliflower, it seems, can replace bread as a principal foodstuff! You can even get cauliflower pizza crust! There's no doubt that cauliflower is good for you; it is rich in anti-oxidants, is anti-inflammatory, is full of vitamin C and other vitamins and helps with digestion. It is also thought to improve both heart and brain health. But some dieticians and nutritionists advise that it should just be a part, along with other vegetables, of a well-balanced diet.

Vegan

Veganism seems to be very popular at the moment. Strict vegans will have nothing to do with any foodstuff that comes from animals. As well as meat and fish, they reject basic everyday foods such as milk, butter, eggs, even honey. Interestingly some vegans claim to enjoy better physical and mental health as a result – but critics might respond: well, they would, wouldn't they? Not all vegans do it for health reasons. They adopt veganism as a way of life, believing that modern farming methods are cruel to animals and harmful to the environment. It is an ethical diet, but opinions vary as to how filling or satisfying vegan meals are – gastronomically, that is.

READING

A SKIM Read *Food, glorious food* quickly. Match the diet plans to the pictures (a–d).

B READ FOR DETAIL Read the article again and answer the questions.

1 Which diet is said to be good for weight loss?
2 Which diet is said to be a larger lifestyle choice?
3 Which diet might have a negative effect on digestion?

C READ TO IDENTIFY OPINIONS Read the article again. Underline examples of the following.

1 Adverbs to show a positive attitude
2 Adverbs to show a negative attitude
3 Attitude to reported information
4 Use of colloquial asides, tag questions and rhetorical questions to comment on information

Glossary

gastronomist (n) person who studies the art of eating well
porous (adj) having a lot of very small holes so that air or water can pass through

D REFLECT Are any of the diets popular in your country?

c

d

LISTENING

A PREDICT You are going to listen to a radio interview about astronauts and well-being. What do you think might be some of the challenges of this kind of work?

8.3 **B LISTEN FOR GIST** Listen to the interview. Some parts are quite hard to hear because of interference on the line. Were any of your ideas from Exercise A mentioned?

8.3 **C LISTEN WITH NOISE** Listen to the interview again and choose the correct options (a or b).

1 Angela Schneider specialises in
   a research into weight loss and healthy eating.
   b nutrition and diet for astronauts.

2 What does Angela say about iron in the blood of a space traveller?
   a There's too much.
   b There's too little.

3 Astronauts are more likely
   a to break their bones when they come back.
   b to follow a strength training programme.

4 According to Angela, the food which astronauts eat today is
   a delicious.
   b unappetising.

8.3 **D LISTEN FOR DETAIL** Listen again. Make notes on what you hear in the table below.

1 **Key elements of an astronaut's diet**	
2 **Injuries that an astronaut could suffer after returning to Earth**	
3 **Measures to prevent injuries**	
4 **Amount of iron in an astronaut's blood**	
5 **Food items which appear on the menu**	

Glossary

collaborative (adj) involving people or groups working together
palatable (adj) tasting good enough to eat
supplement (n) a special food that you add to your regular diet

E REFLECT Think about the answers to these questions.

1 How important do you think space travel is for the future of the human race?
2 Would you change your diet for work?

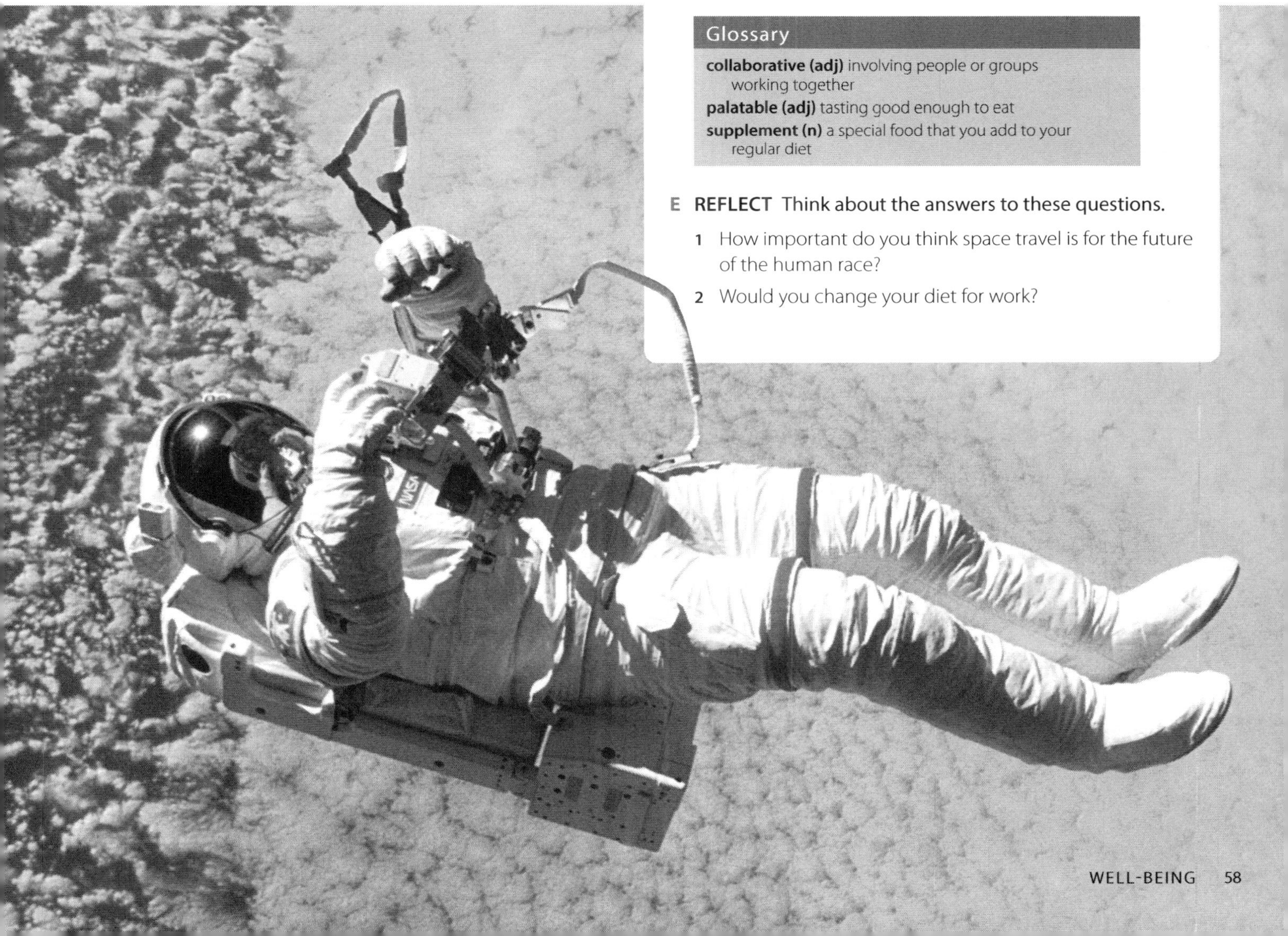

WRITING

A What physical and psychological effects might 'overtraining' have on an athlete?

B Read the first paragraph of *Time to slow down?* and complete the tasks.

1 Underline the keywords.

2 Which is the best one-sentence summary of the paragraph (a, b or c)? Give reasons for your choice.

a Consult a doctor before undertaking a training programme and devise your own programmes to avoid overtraining.

b Overtraining syndrome is the result of training too much and often leads to both physical and psychological symptoms.

c Too much training can push the body beyond its capacity to recover and both physiological and psychological symptoms may present themselves.

C PARAPHRASING Now read the second paragraph of the article and complete the tasks.

1 Underline the keywords and ideas.

2 What is the main focus of this paragraph?

3 Write a one- or two-sentence summary of this paragraph.

D Read the rest of the article and note down keywords and ideas.

WRITING PRACTICE

A PREPARE Read *Time to slow down?* again. Think about the answers to these questions and make notes.

1 What are the main points of each paragraph?

2 Which words (proper nouns, technical vocabulary) can you reuse in your summary?

3 Which parts of the text are unnecessary for your summary?

B PLAN You are going to write a summary of *Time to slow down?*

- Organise your notes from Writing Exercises B–D.
- Use your own words as much as possible. Check that you have not repeated unnecessary phrases or structures from the article.
- Make sure you have included all the key points.

C WRITE Write your summary in approximately 60 words.

TIME TO SLOW DOWN?

Consistency in strength, mobility and cardiovascular training is often held up as a key determiner for success and receiving the full health benefits of these types of exercise. But sometimes there is a fine line between consistency and what is known as 'overtraining syndrome'. Put simply, too much training can force the body beyond its capacity to recover. Those that push themselves hard in sports professionally or recreationally may be especially at risk. According to research by the *Journal of Athletic Training*, both physiological and psychological symptoms may present themselves when overtraining occurs.

Physiological symptoms

Various physical symptoms of overtraining include unexplained muscle and weight loss, an inability to build muscle among male athletes and excessive thirst. The cardiovascular system can be affected, with increased heart rate and a greater length of time to return to a normal heart rate, and both increased and decreased levels of blood pressure. Another common indicator is injury, which may occur as a result of the kind of loads used in training or because the body is unable to recover from training. Furthermore, there may be an increased risk of infections such as colds.

Psychological symptoms

It is not necessarily as easy to determine overtraining from psychological symptoms but if, for example, athletes find themselves generally run-down or mentally unprepared for training, this may be a warning sign. Sleep disturbance, tiredness and loss of energy all suggest potential overtraining. Emotional mood may also provide a clue, as mood swings and feelings of irritability and anger have been commonly observed. The self-confidence of an athlete may also decrease while levels of cortisol (stress hormones) might rise. Finally, it's sensible to keep an eye on the regularity of meals as loss of appetite has been noted as a symptom.

Prevention and treatment

The advice of medical professionals should be sought in cases of overtraining. Trainers and coaches also have a particularly important role to play in monitoring athletes for symptoms, as well as devising training programmes that prevent injury. Beyond recognising symptoms, action must be taken to tackle them, for example, through periods of rest or decreases in training intensity. It is possible to address psychological symptoms as well, by modifying programmes and sometimes allowing athletes more autonomy in the design of a programme.

9.1 Behaviour

Language and behaviour

VOCABULARY

Slang

A Choose the correct options to complete the sentences.

1 Mark was well ***awesome / chuffed / gutted*** when he got a place at university.

2 Jack's always ***whingeing / hanging out / chilling out*** about not having any money, but he doesn't go out and look for a job!

3 In the UK, we can refer informally to a male stranger as a ***buddy / cos / bloke***, but in the USA, he might be called a ***buck / dude / grand***.

4 €100 for a laptop? That sounds like a ***dodgy / crash / beat*** deal to me – are you sure it's not ***sweet / sorted / nicked***?

5 They offered to buy me a ***telly / shambles / grand***, but I was ***cos / do / like***, what do I want that for? I need some ***crash / wheels / bucks*** so I can get around!

B Read the extract from a story. Replace the words and phrases in italics with slang expressions from the box.

could do with	crashed	grand	quid	set her back	shambles	skint	sorted

1 ....
2 ....
3 ....
4 ....
5 ....
6 ....
7 ....
8 ....

Rose Robinson woke up and took a look around her flat. It was a [1]*mess*. She'd come home at who knows what time and [2]*fallen asleep* on the couch.

She knew she [3]*would benefit from* finding a new place, but she also knew that would [4]*cost* at least a [5]*thousand pounds* and she just didn't have that kind of money.

She looked in her pocket, 'Seven [6]*pounds*! I'm sick and tired of being [7]*without money*,' she muttered to herself, 'I need some money fast and then I'll be [8]*fine*!' Just then, a dangerous and life-changing plan started to form in her sleepy brain.

PRONUNCIATION

Pronouncing vague expressions

A Underline the vague expressions in the sentences. How would you pronounce them?

1 I feel kind of strange – like I've been here before or something.

2 We have to give a talk, or a speech, or something like that.

3 I have to do some jobs – shopping, cleaning and so on.

4 You know, I think that, in some way or another, he must be involved.

5 So, in a sense, this is the easiest job in the world!

6 What do you take me for – some sort of fool?

7 Don't give me excuses like you overslept or whatever.

8 My course covers health and safety issues, stuff like that.

9.1 **B** Listen to the sentences from Exercise A.

C Practise saying the sentences in the same way as the speakers do in Exercise B.

9.1 Behaviour

Language and behaviour

GRAMMAR
Noun phrases

A Underline two noun phrases in each sentence.

1 Those students who haven't completed the assignment should stay behind at the end of the lecture.
2 Both of the solutions he suggested sounded a little like a desperate attempt to please the boss.
3 He invested all the money he'd saved up into some crazy get-rich-quick scheme and lost everything.
4 The thing that annoys Pierre most is the way young people don't seem to care about language.
5 Three of the 20 people present were first-time attendees.
6 The idea that simply punishing children teaches them to behave has fallen out of favour with many modern educationalists.
7 Do you know a good place to eat that would suit a group of hungry teenagers?
8 Sometimes it seems to me that almost everyone I know is hooked on some computer game or other.

B Find and correct the mistakes in the sentences.

1 I spend all my free time almost doing sport.
______
2 The belief what you can change things is all you need in order to make a difference.
______
3 The person where I spoke to didn't seem to have a clue what was happening.
______
4 I need a place for staying for a few days.
______
5 Both of ideas seem a little hard to put into practice.
______
6 The woman who sitting next to Claire is Frances.
______
7 Very few of people in this country have travelled abroad.
______
8 The interviewer was impressed by the fact how I knew so much about their company.
______

C Complete each sentence with one word only.

1 Unfortunately ______ of the students failed yesterday's history exam – only a few passed.
2 ______ man sitting at the bus stop works in a science laboratory.
3 Out of all my colleagues, Daniel is the ______ I trust the most.
4 Few members ______ the community spoke out against the mayor.
5 Unlike ours, ______ study was well funded, so they could afford the best equipment.
6 The fact ______ I love communication affected my decision to study languages.

9.2 Behaviour

Animal behaviour

PRONUNCIATION
Intrusive stops

A Read the sentences aloud, paying attention to the way you pronounce the underlined sections.

1 A lot of youngsters enjoy going out to dance.
2 Hamsters build nests for warmth.
3 It must be nice being a prince, but your life would be pretty intense.
4 I did four lengths of the pool, but I didn't have the strength to do more.
5 Once you get into trouble for something, it can influence the way other people see you.

9.2 **B** Listen to the sentences from Exercise A.

C Practise saying the sentences in the same way as the speakers do in Exercise B.

VOCABULARY
Verb + object + infinitive; Gestures and body language

A Match the beginnings of the sentences (1–8) to the endings (a–h).

1 Listen! I think I can hear someone ____
2 A thoughtful family friend let me ____
3 The manager had us ____
4 I heard a dog ____
5 Not only must justice be done, but it must also be seen ____
6 I wonder if you could help me ____
7 I thought I could feel something ____
8 Were you made ____

a climbing up my leg.
b bark once, and then there was silence.
c coming. Don't make a sound.
d fill in this form. It looks difficult.
e to sign any documents when you started working there?
f drive her car to see if it suited me.
g to be done.
h wait for an hour before she spoke to us.

B Choose the correct options to complete the story.

When John caught up with Sharon, she was sitting on a rock, 1***gazing* / *crossing* / *bending*** out to sea. She held something in her hand that she was 2***folding* / *fidgeting* / *shaking*** with.

'Are you OK?' John said gently. She just 3***shrugged* / *smirked* / *grinned*** her shoulders.

Then she 4***glared* / *nodded* / *shook*** her head and said, 'No, I'm not OK!'

'Sharon, what's wrong?' John asked. She turned to look at him and 5***winked* / *blinked* / *wiggled*** her eyes a few times as the bright sun lit up her face.

She took the ring off her finger, stood up and 6***beckoned* / *stared* / *leaned*** him to follow her to the water's edge. She 7***bent* / *pointed* / *folded*** back across the beach and said 'That was where we met'. She threw the ring into the sea.

John 8***grinned* / *crossed* / *raised*** his eyebrows and stood open-mouthed, too shocked to react.

GRAMMAR
Participle clauses and verbless clauses

A Complete the second sentence so that it has a similar meaning to the first sentence. Write between two and five words, including the word given.

1 Because she got out of bed early, Nina had the view of the city all to herself.
UP
__________, Nina had the view of the city all to herself.

2 I didn't know anything about maths, but I still worked out the answer.
DESPITE
__________ anything about maths, I still worked out the answer.

3 If you do the job properly, it shouldn't take more than a day.
DONE
__________ shouldn't take more than a day.

4 As I am not practical, it made more sense after I had read the instructions.
READING
__________ instructions meant it made more sense.

5 He was not interested in any special offers because he had bought a new phone yesterday.
JUST
__________ phone yesterday, he was not interested in any special offers.

6 If you give them a positive environment, most children will learn quickly and easily.
RIGHT
__________ environment, most children will learn quickly and easily.

B Find and correct the mistakes with participle and verbless clauses.

1 They were feeling threatened, the animals instinctively hid behind the wall.
____

2 Had never been on a plane before, I was both excited and nervous.
____

3 If you successful in your application, you will be notified by email.
____

4 Grown up in the USA, Marvin has always spoken English well.
____

5 Been exhausted and short of money, Carrie cut short her trip to Bolivia.
____

6 Before started work in insurance, Lionel was a factory worker.
____

7 Despite I hadn't been there before, I soon found my way around.
____

8 While suffering badly from flu, a couple of close friends visited Angela every day.
____

C Choose the correct options (a, b or c) to complete the text.

Languages contain so much of a people's culture that it's a shame that more isn't done to preserve them. [1]__________, I find languages infinitely fascinating. I thought I might be able to help preserve African languages, [2]__________ much of my youth there.

Many of these languages, [3]__________ by just a handful of people, are dying. [4]__________ in funds to preserve them themselves, many tribes are destined to lose a valuable part of their heritage. So I applied to work with an association whose mission is to preserve the culture of several African tribes.

[5]__________ the head of the association, I felt inspired to get to work. However, we must often rely on the elders of a community, who, [6]__________ how to read or write, struggle with transcribing words and phrases. This presents further challenges with accurate translation.

	a	b	c
1	**a** A linguist	**b** Being a linguist	**c** To be a linguist
2	**a** while to spend	**b** spent	**c** having spent
3	**a** having spoken	**b** speaking	**c** spoken
4	**a** Lacked	**b** Lacking	**c** Being lacking
5	**a** After meeting	**b** Being met	**c** Despite meeting
6	**a** never teaching	**b** having never been taught	**c** having never taught

WORDS *have* POWER

In a well-documented experiment (Bargh, Chen and Burrows, 1996), students at New York University were given five words which they had to use in order to construct sentences of four words (i.e. they had to leave one word out). They did this 30 times. Of the 30 groups of words, 15 contained words related in some way either to rudeness (e.g. *disturb* or *annoyingly*) or politeness (e.g. *respect* or *patiently*). There was also a neutral set, containing words that were neither connected to rudeness nor politeness (e.g. *give* or *occasionally*). Students didn't know whether they had the 'rude set', the 'polite set' or the 'neutral set'. In fact, they thought the experiment was simply to test their speed in forming grammatically correct sentences.

Participants were told to come and find the experimenter when they were finished. What they didn't realise was that this was really the important part of the experiment, because the researchers had staged a delay, whereby the student was forced to wait while the experimenter was deeply involved in a conversation with another 'participant' (in reality, another researcher). Unknown to the student, a stopwatch had been activated the moment they stood up from the task with the sentences. The purpose of the experiment was to see how long the students would wait before interrupting.

READING

A PREDICT Do you think that words or names have the power to change people's behaviour? How?

B READ FOR GIST Read *Words have power* quickly. Were any of your ideas in Exercise A mentioned? Have you changed your opinion? Why/Why not?

C READ FOR DETAIL Read the article again. Are these sentences true (T) or false (F)? Correct the sentences that are false.

1. Students were asked to make 30 sentences of 4 words each. *T / F*
2. The experiment was to see how fast they could form sentences. *T / F*
3. Participants were timed to see how quickly they completed the task. *T / F*
4. Most of the participants waited ten minutes after the task. *T / F*
5. The last paragraph suggests that we purposely avoid basing major life choices on how similar things are to our own name. *T / F*

D READ FOR OUTCOMES Read the article again and make notes to answer the questions.

1. What was the purpose of the experiment?
2. What were the main results?
3. What conclusions were drawn?
4. What do you think about the results of the experiment?

Glossary

neutral (adj) neither one thing nor its opposite
stage (v) make someone believe that something is real

E REFLECT Think about the answers to these questions.

1. Do you think that names could influence people to choose different careers? Why/Why not?
2. Can you think of any other ways that words can influence social behaviour?

As expected, students who had been exposed to the 'rude' words interrupted the soonest, followed by the neutral group and, lastly, the students who had just processed 'polite' words.

John Bargh, who devised the experiment, admitted that we should not rush to the conclusion that exposure to rude or polite words makes us behave in that way. In fact, one of the problems with such a conclusion is that, in the experiment described above, 21 of the 34 participants did not interrupt at all in the 10 minutes that they were kept waiting. However, Bargh re-analysed the results and looked only at those who had interrupted. Of these, over 60 per cent had just processed the 'rude' words.

Is there more evidence to suggest that words play a more important role than we once thought? Pelham, Mirdenberg and Jones (2012) have suggested that our name – as one of the words that we learn first and hold dear – influences whether we like other people and things with similar names. In the most surprising results, it was shown that more people called Dennis had chosen dentistry as a profession. Similarly, more women called Laura, and more men called Lawrence, became lawyers. Similar links have been shown between a person's name and the place they choose to live, as well as their choice of a husband or wife.

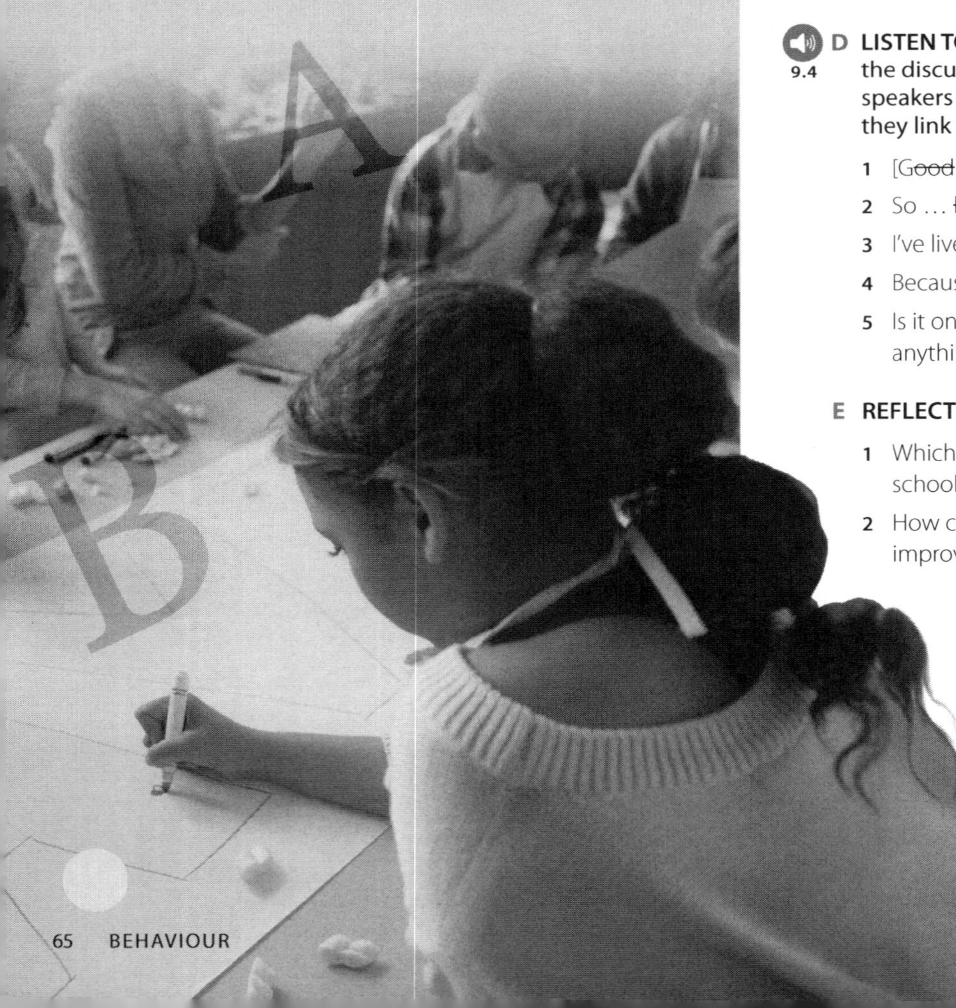

LISTENING

A PREDICT Tick (✓) the skills you think are important at school.

- passing exams ☐
- practical skills ☐
- developing your imagination ☐
- thinking independently ☐
- developing personal interests ☐
- artistic skills ☐
- physical exercise ☐

9.3 **B LISTEN FOR GIST** Listen to a conversation about education. Were any of your skills in Exercise A mentioned?

9.3 **C LISTEN FOR DETAIL** Listen again. Are these sentences true (T) or false (F)?

1. Cassie is new to the area. *T / F*
2. The Steiner education method places great emphasis on creativity. *T / F*
3. Rob and Cassie agree that passing exams is not a legitimate educational goal. *T / F*
4. Inspections at Rob and Sandy's school create tension. *T / F*
5. Steiner school courses are designed to meet the needs of individual students. *T / F*
6. The curriculum at the Steiner school is broadly similar to a mainstream school. *T / F*

9.4 **D LISTEN TO RAPID SPEECH** Listen to some extracts from the discussion. Cross out words and sounds that the speakers leave out. Put brackets [ ] round the phrases they link together. The first two have been done for you.

1. [G~~ood~~ ~~to~~ meet y~~ou~~].
2. So … ~~have~~ you just moved here, Cassie?
3. I've lived here for let me see … for four years.
4. Because it's you know … it's really unique and stuff.
5. Is it one of those places where you can, you know, do anything you want?

E REFLECT Think about the answers to these questions.

1. Which is the most important skill developed at school? Why?
2. How could secondary schools in your country be improved? Think of examples.

Write a conclusion to an academic report

WRITING

A PREDICT Look at the pictures. What do you think it feels like to be in one of these crowds? Do people behave differently when they are in a crowd? Why?

B Read the conclusion to an academic report and match the topics (a–d) to the paragraphs (1–4).

- a Areas that still need investigation ___
- b Summary of theories researched ___
- c Aims of research ___
- d What was learnt ___

C LINKING IN ACADEMIC WRITING Read the conclusion again and complete it with the linking words and phrases (a–e). Sometimes more than one option is possible.

- a However
- b On the other hand
- c Additionally
- d Nonetheless
- e Admittedly

D Underline two sentences where a colon is used to show that one idea explains another. Underline two sentences where a semi-colon is used to show that two related ideas are of equal importance.

WRITING PRACTICE

A PREPARE Choose a piece of academic research or use your imagination and make notes about the points you will make in your conclusion.

B PLAN You are going to write a conclusion to an academic report.

- Organise your notes from Exercise A into an appropriate structure for the conclusion to an academic report.
- Use linking words, colons and semi-colons to show the relationship between ideas.

C WRITE Write your conclusion in 200–300 words.

Conclusion

1 Our research set out to examine theories of crowd behaviour, beginning with classic contagion and convergence theories, which have been the basis of all subsequent theories. It became clear that most of the research so far stems from disciplines such as psychology and sociology; there has been little recent research into crowd behaviour at large outdoor events.

2 Contagion theory states that individuals are protected by their membership of the crowd and that individual responsibility is ignored: normal values and the ability to reason are abandoned. [1]___, ideas and emotions within the crowd become contagious and spread rapidly. [2]___, convergence theorists argue that individuals in a crowd do not lose personal identity: personal beliefs and values are communicated and crowd behaviour depends on shared feelings and beliefs. [3]___, some individuals may well exploit the anonymity of being in a crowd to take part in antisocial behaviours they normally would not.

3 It seems clear, then, that once individuals join a group they become part of a group personality. [4]___, our research revealed that there are many factors that can influence the behaviour of individuals in a crowd: crowd catalysts such as police presence, the space available, type of event and so on. We shall be conducting further research in this area.

4 While both theories form the basis of most research into crowd behaviour, they assume some kind of antisocial behaviour is the outcome. They fail to demonstrate why some crowds remain passive and why individuals in a crowd who hold similar beliefs behave differently; nor do they examine the difference between organised and spontaneous crowds. [5]___, we believe that these theories are still useful in understanding mass behaviour in general.

VOCABULARY
Culture and heritage; Nouns with *to*

A Complete the sentences with the words in the box.

architectural designated endangered funds habitats heritage preserve refurbish ruins settlement

1 Some areas near the city have been ________ national parks so they can't be built on.

2 Because their ________ are threatened, many species are ________.

3 The unique ________ qualities of these buildings make them an important part of our country's ________.

4 The ________ found by archaeologists are said to be part of a ________ going back thousands of years.

5 We would like to at least ________ these houses to stop the damage getting worse until there are enough ________ available to ________ them.

B Complete the article with one word in each gap. The first and last letters and the number of letters needed are given to help you.

Building a future

For anyone who has the [1]**u**________**e** (*4*) to go into city planning, we need you – but don't expect an easy ride. What you need more than anything is the [2]**d**________**e** (*6*) to create better living conditions for city dwellers. It will be your [3]**r**________**y** (*14*) to make sure that the future does not become a nightmare scenario. You will have an [4]**o**________**n** (*10*) to future generations and you should be ready to improve things.

Why is it so hard? Well, historically, we have seen a [5]**f**________**e** (*7*) to learn from the mistakes of the past. We have also seen a flat [6]**r**________**l** (*7*) to adopt green measures and sometimes a general reluctance to think more than a few years into the future. There is a problem in that people often have a [7]**t**________**y** (*8*) to only do things that will benefit them in the short term. Sometimes, these people need a [8]**r**________**r** (*8*) to focus on long-term solutions as well.

PRONUNCIATION
Introducing new information

A **Read the sentences aloud. Does the pitch go up or down on the underlined words?**

1 I enjoyed getting to see some of the sights. And I made some great friends on my travels.
2 There's no doubt that travel broadens the mind. On the other hand, you won't learn much about a culture if you stay in a resort and never go exploring.
3 Some older holidaymakers tend to be happy with relaxed beach holidays and a bit of light sightseeing, whereas younger tourists usually want a little bit more action.
4 You're going to Cyprus? I love Cyprus. As a matter of fact, I was born there!
5 I know a lot of people find travelling exciting, but for me it's always really stressful.
6 I know tourism brings money to companies, but at the same time, I wonder how much ordinary people benefit from it.
7 I love travelling overseas. And it's good for the economy of the countries you visit.
8 Tourism isn't always beneficial to countries in many ways. And in fact, some resorts are now looking for ways to discourage big numbers of people.

10.1 **B** **Listen to the sentences to check your answers to Exercise A.**

GRAMMAR
Discourse markers

A **Match numbers (1–10) to letters (a–j) to form full sentences.**

1 There are so many European countries, for instance, ____
2 I don't like travelling very much. As a matter of fact, ____
3 We spent most of our trip in Bolivia. Conversely, ____
4 They cut their holiday short owing to the fact ____
5 I'm happy to fly everywhere, whereas ____
6 He claims he doesn't travel, yet ____
7 Some cities suffer from a big problem, namely, ____
8 I think it's the best museum in the world, ____
9 We enjoyed the sights despite ____
10 My summer in Spain was very relaxing. Moreover, ____

a he went on three holidays last year!
b that they were running out of money.
c I hate it!
d it really helped me get to grips with the language.
e the fact that there were huge crowds.
f the best I've been to in any case.
g that there are too many tourists.
h Belgium, that I still haven't visited.
i we only had two days in Venezuela.
j my husband says it's better to travel slowly by boat or train.

B **Complete the second sentence so that it has a similar meaning to the first sentence. Write between two and five words, including the word given.**

1 Although it was a long journey there, we enjoyed the view of the mountain immensely.
DESPITE
We enjoyed ourselves immensely ______________________
a long journey.

2 We didn't go to Warsaw, but it didn't matter because I've been there before.
CASE
We didn't go to Warsaw, but in ______________________
been there before.

3 There are two countries I really want to visit, and they are Australia and China.
NAMELY
There are two countries I really want to visit, ______________________.

4 The bad weather prevented us from going to the national park.
OWING
We didn't go to the national park ______________________.

5 The return journey seemed very quick compared to the outward journey.
WHEREAS
The outward journey seemed to take a long time, ______________________
very quick.

6 To tell you the truth, I wouldn't mind if I never got on another plane in my life.
MATTER
______________________, I wouldn't mind if I never got on another plane in my life.

VOCABULARY
Word building

A Choose the correct options (a, b or c) to complete the sentences.

1 She loves her job – she's very ___ about it.
  - a passion
  - b passionate
  - c passionhood

2 Nobody knew the ___ of the mystery donor.
  - a identity
  - b identify
  - c identification

3 I grew up in quite a run-down ___.
  - a neighbourly
  - b neighbour
  - c neighbourhood

4 Clark wanted to enter ___ life as soon as possible after graduating.
  - a politics
  - b politician
  - c political

5 Some countries make you take a ___ test in order to adopt their nationality.
  - a citizenship
  - b citizen
  - c citizenry

6 It was totally ___ of you to mention her brother – you know they don't speak to each other.
  - a insensible
  - b senseless
  - c insensitive

7 Depositing huge sums of money in offshore accounts may be legal, but is it ___?
  - a ethics
  - b ethical
  - c ethic

8 Charles is responsible for internet ___ at his company.
  - a secure
  - b securely
  - c security

B Complete the text with words from the box with a correct suffix. Make any other necessary spelling changes.

apathy commune effect passion person persuade

To change the world quickly, you have to be [1] __________ about your beliefs, you need to have a(n) [2] __________ strategy and you need good [3] __________ skills – such as being extremely friendly, polite and, of course, [4] __________ – so that people will listen to you.

Sometimes, however, the best changes are the ones that take place little by little. If you can find a way to stop people from being [5] __________ and to make them care about their [6] __________, the results will slowly but surely become global.

GRAMMAR
Ellipsis and substitution

A Cross out any words that can be omitted.

1 Some people think we can change the world but I don't think we can change the world.

2 If you get the opportunity to go, you should take the opportunity to go.

3 A lot of people struggle with course fees and I wish they didn't struggle with course fees.

4 They should target governments and they should target large companies.

5 We're going to have food and we're going to have music.

6 You asked me if I thought we could make a difference and the answer is yes I do think we can make a difference.

7 I know a lot of people who are pessimistic about the future, but I'm not pessimistic about the future.

8 Are you joining us for pizza? Do you have any preference as to what we order?

B Complete the sentences with a phrase including *do*, *does*, *so* or *not*. Write one or two words in each gap.

1 I take a short holiday away from everything. I ________________ to clear my head when I'm stressed at work.

2 He said he can't come, but I'm hoping he'll change his mind. Let me know if ________________.

3 I might go to the shops later, so I'll let you know if ________________.

4 Johnny went white-water rafting. I could never ________________.

5 'Will you be finished before four?' 'I expect ________________.'

6 You might need to access the archives. In order to ________________, ask one of the technical support team.

7 'We might have to do this again.' 'I ________________ – it took us days.'

8 'I'm planning to spend all my money on a sports car!' 'Why on Earth would you ________________?'

PRONUNCIATION
Managing conversations

A Read the sentences aloud. Try to say the underlined words according to the instructions in brackets. Pay attention to whether your intonation rises or falls.

1

A: So then I plan to travel to Cambodia.

B: <u>Right</u>. (because you think the speaker has finished/you want to say something yourself)

2

A: The chairperson said there might be an opening for me.

B: <u>OK</u>. (showing excitement/enthusiasm)

3

A: There'd be a team of four initially, then six, then eight or more.

B: <u>OK</u>. (hesitant, needing clarification)

4

A: I think it's a great opportunity.

B: <u>Right</u>. (sarcastic, unenthusiastic)

5

A: I'm planning to apply for a job there.

B: <u>I see</u>! (genuinely interested)

B 10.2 Listen to the conversations from Exercise A. Do the speakers say the underlined words in the same way as you did?

READING

A READ FOR GIST Read three short newspaper articles. Which urban problem(s) do they discuss?

B SYNTHESISE INFORMATION Read the articles again. Complete the table using information from all three articles.

	Problems	Solutions	Criticism of solutions
UK			
Paris			
Freiburg			

Parking just got PRICIER in the UK

In another move to fight congestion and pollution in the UK's most gridlocked cities, councils may impose a workplace parking fee of up to £1000, to be paid for by employers rather than employees. Growing concerns about the effects of congestion and air pollution on residents' health, including asthma and bronchitis, have led to the move.

Some opponents of the scheme say they have seen no evidence that fewer people were driving to work and that it could lead to job losses. Also it would force more people into using an already overcrowded public transport system.

A spokesman for the Automobile Association (AA) said that instead of taxing businesses, who may be forced to leave the area or stop trading, we should be concentrating on getting people to switch to electric vehicles.

By law, all funds gained from such charges are to be invested in improving public transport and infrastructure.

Paris' TRAFFIC PROBLEMS

The authorities in Paris have tried almost everything to reduce congestion and the mayor wants to halve the number of cars entering the city by making life difficult for motorists.

With concerns raised about premature death due to air pollution, Paris has now made permanent a sticker scheme. All vehicles in Paris must display an anti-pollution sticker or face a fine of €68 for cars and €138 for lorries. The stickers cost €4.18. Yet a recent police check found that only 1 in 50 vehicles stopped had the sticker.

About 600,000 vehicles drive around the city each day and most come in from the suburbs. Concerns have been raised by those travelling from the suburbs who are not as well connected by the public transport system. One driver complained, 'We're being taxed off the roads. It's not our fault. They should get the car manufacturers to make cars that don't pollute.'

As green as it gets?

It is obviously easier to deal with urban problems in a small city with a population of fewer than half a million people, but maybe larger cities with traffic problems could take a leaf or two from Freiburg's book. For a start, the entire city centre was pedestrianised back in 1973, and the city authorities have developed an integrated system of 500 kilometres of bike routes, tramways and a public transport system that is efficient, comfortable and above all cheap. In fact, those who choose to live without a car at all are offered cheap housing and free public transport.

Preference is given to environmentally friendly modes of transport such as walking, cycling and public transport, and clever urban planning has made it a city of short distances where people's needs can be met within walking distance. All this has made Freiburg one of the greenest and most pollution-free cities in Europe.

Glossary

disincentive (n) a plan/action that makes you not want to do sth
gridlocked (adj) with so much traffic congestion that vehicles cannot move at all
take a leaf out of/from somebody's book (idiom) to copy somebody else's actions because they are successful

C REFLECT Is it worth owning a car in a big city?

LISTENING

A PREDICT Read the advert. Would you be interested in applying for this job? What skills would you need? What might be the challenges of this kind of work?

> **Research Assistant – Orkney Native Wildlife Project, North Coast of Scotland**
>
> We are looking for a research assistant with a background in science. You must be physically fit, capable of working outside in extreme weather and available to work flexible hours. Salary depending on experience. Accommodation provided.

10.3 **B LISTEN FOR MAIN IDEA** Listen to the conversation and answer the questions.

1 What are the woman and man waiting for?

____

2 What are they both a little worried about?

____

3 What are they both positive about?

____

10.4 **C LISTEN FOR SPECIFIC INFORMATION** Listen to Jonathan's interview and complete the application form with one or two words in each gap.

10.5 **D LISTEN TO REGISTER** Jonathan used different registers to speak to Antonia and, later, to Dr Ramsey. Listen to some extracts. In each case, decide how Jonathan could say the same thing in a different register.

1 ______________________________

2 ______________________________

3 ______________________________

4 ______________________________

10.6 **E** Now listen to how Jonathan says similar things in a different register and check your answers to Exercise D.

F REFLECT Think about the answers to these questions.

1 What are the most difficult things about living in an isolated place?

2 Do you often change register in your own language? Why?

Research Assistant – Orkney Native Wildlife Project

Name : Jonathan Wheeler

Qualification(s) : Degree in [1] ______________

Studied at : University of [2] ______________ Anglia

Relevant experience :

- [3] ______________ months working for Nature Trust on the Isle of Skye
- Field trip: Northumberland, studying [4] ______________ of various species of bird
- Field trip: Forest of Dean, studying breeding habits of native [5] ______________
- Practical skills: maintenance work – fixing fences and maintenance of [6] ______________

In the space provided, please state what appeals to you about the Orkney Native Wildlife Project:

I think it's essential that we [7] ______________ nature as much as we can and, for me, this is a great opportunity to study a relatively unspoilt area. I think that tourism and industry are [8] ______________ so much of nature. It's vital that we conduct [9] ______________ while we still can, in the hope that we can protect wildlife.

WRITING

A Read the title of the essay. What are some of the pros and cons of tourism?

B Read the whole essay and answer the questions.

1. What is the writer's opinion of tourism?
2. What arguments does the writer use to support their opinions?
3. Does the writer mention any positive aspects of mass tourism?

C USING COUNTER-ARGUMENTS AND REBUTTALS Read the essay again and answer the questions.

1. Which paragraph includes examples of counter-arguments (i.e. stating an opposing position) and rebuttals (i.e. stating why you believe an argument is incorrect)?
2. What is the counter-argument and what is the rebuttal? Does the rebuttal directly answer the counter-argument?
3. What phrases are used to introduce the counter-argument and rebuttal?

WRITING PRACTICE

A PREPARE Read this essay title and make notes on each of the points.

> Do shopping malls have a positive or negative impact on local communities?

- job opportunities
- prices
- convenience
- local businesses
- environmental impact

B PLAN You are going to write a persuasive essay in answer to the task above.

- Organise your notes from Exercise A into an appropriate structure for a persuasive essay.
- Use a counter-argument and rebuttal in the third or fourth paragraph.

C WRITE Write your essay in 220–260 words.

Does tourism have a POSITIVE OR NEGATIVE IMPACT?

1 Cheap air travel has opened up the world to more and more people and few countries are unaffected by mass tourism. Many argue that this is a good thing – that it promotes understanding of different cultures and makes international connections. However, I believe that in the long term, tourism has a negative impact, spoiling the very places it promotes.

2 First, there is the environmental damage mass tourism brings with it. Ugly hotels built near traditional architecture, increased traffic congestion bringing pollution, more litter and waste to dispose of; the list goes on. Even if tourists do behave responsibly, sheer numbers can cause problems, such as damage to ancient buildings and monuments.

3 Mass tourism can also damage the heart and soul of a tourist destination by making it just like any other holiday resort. Cultural history and heritage are reduced to a spectacle for visitors, and tourists often lack respect for local traditions and culture, ignoring local codes of behaviour and upsetting the local community. It leads, therefore, to the opposite of promoting understanding between cultures.

4 There is an argument that mass tourism has a beneficial impact because it brings in money and creates new jobs. Hotels, shops and restaurants all need staffing. While this is true up to a point, it should be remembered that many of these jobs are low-skilled and are often seasonal and insecure with no benefits such as pensions, sick pay or healthcare. Also, most of the tourism industry is owned by big foreign companies: they get the profits, while local businesses receive little benefit.

5 In conclusion, the long-term effects of mass tourism are largely negative. It can impact negatively on the environment, damage or destroy local cultures and traditions, the jobs it provides are insecure and short-lived, and local businesses suffer while the profits go to foreign corporations.

Irregular Verbs

Infinitive	Past simple	Past participle
be	was/were	been
become	became	become
begin	began	begun
break	broke	broken
bring	brought	brought
build	built	built
buy	bought	bought
can	could	(been able to)
catch	caught	caught
choose	chose	chosen
come	came	come
cost	cost	cost
cut	cut	cut
drink	drank	drunk
eat	ate	eaten
fall	fell	fallen
feel	felt	felt
find	found	found
forget	forgot	forgotten
get	got	got
give	gave	given
go	went	gone/been
grow	grew	grown
have	had	had
hear	heard	heard
hit	hit	hit
hold	held	held
hurt	hurt	hurt
keep	kept	kept
know	knew	known
leave	left	left
lend	lent	lent
let	let	let

Infinitive	Past simple	Past participle
lose	lost	lost
make	made	made
mean	meant	meant
meet	met	met
must	had to	(had to)
pay	paid	paid
put	put	put
read	read **/red/**	read **/red/**
ride	rode	ridden
run	ran	run
say	said	said
see	saw	seen
sell	sold	sold
send	sent	sent
set	set	set
shut	shut	shut
sing	sang	sung
sit	sat	sat
sleep	slept	slept
speak	spoke	spoken
spell	spelt/spelled	spelt/spelled
spend	spent	spent
stand	stood	stood
steal	stole	stolen
take	took	taken
teach	taught	taught
tell	told	told
think	thought	thought
throw	threw	thrown
understand	understood	understood
wear	wore	worn
win	won	won
write	wrote	written

PHONETIC SYMBOLS

Single vowels

/ɪ/	f**i**sh	/fɪʃ/
/iː/	b**ea**n	/biːn/
/ʊ/	f**oo**t	/fʊt/
/uː/	sh**oe**	/ʃuː/
/e/	**e**gg	/eg/
/ə/	moth**er**	/'mʌðə/
/ɜː/	w**or**d	/wɜːd/
/ɔː/	t**al**k	/tɔːk/
/æ/	b**a**ck	/bæk/
/ʌ/	b**u**s	/bʌs/
/ɑː/	**ar**m	/ɑːm/
/ɒ/	t**o**p	/tɒp/

Diphthongs

/ɪə/	**ear**	/ɪə/
/eɪ/	f**a**ce	/feɪs/
/ʊə/	t**ou**rist	/'tʊərɪst/
/ɔɪ/	b**oy**	/bɔɪ/
/əʊ/	n**o**se	/nəʊz/
/eə/	h**air**	/heə/
/aɪ/	**eye**	/aɪ/
/aʊ/	m**ou**th	/maʊθ/

Consonants

/p/	**p**en	/pen/	/s/	**s**nake	/sneɪk/
/b/	**b**ag	/bæg/	/z/	**z**oo	/zuː/
/t/	**t**ea	/tiː/	/ʃ/	**sh**op	/ʃɒp/
/d/	**d**og	/dɒg/	/ʒ/	televi**si**on	/'telɪvɪʒən/
/tʃ/	**ch**ip	/tʃɪp/	/m/	**m**ap	/mæp/
/dʒ/	**j**azz	/dʒæz/	/n/	**n**ame	/neɪm/
/k/	**c**ake	/keɪk/	/ŋ/	ri**ng**	/rɪŋ/
/g/	**g**irl	/gɜːl/	/h/	**h**ouse	/haʊs/
/f/	**f**ilm	/fɪlm/	/l/	**l**eg	/leg/
/v/	**v**erb	/vɜːb/	/r/	**r**oad	/rəʊd/
/θ/	**th**ing	/θɪŋ/	/w/	**w**ant	/wɒnt/
/ð/	**th**ese	/ðiːz/	/j/	**y**es	/jes/

UNIT 6

Lesson 6.4, Listening, Exercise B

6.3 Perhaps one of the most well-known figures in modern British history is the explorer, Robert Falcon Scott. Tragically, he is not famous for his achievement, but for his failure. Scott headed an expedition whose goal was to reach the South Pole before anyone else. On the 17th of January 1912, Scott, with four companions, finally reached the South Pole, only to discover that a Norwegian party, led by Roald Amundsen, had beaten them to it – by just 34 days. Scott and his men died on their return journey.

Lesson 6.4, Listening, Exercise C

6.4 From *the* mid-19th century, a number of expeditions had travelled to Antarctica to try and map its extent and find out more about the wildlife and plantlife of this unknown territory. The men who undertook these journeys suffered terrible hardship; illness, injury, hunger *and* cold were part of their everyday experience. Every single item which the explorers needed *had* to be transported by ship. Then the provisions had to be carried across *the* ice. These included tents, sleeping bags, building materials, food for men and animals, heating oil, bedding, clothing *and* scientific equipment.

Both Scott and Amundsen set out for *their* final trek to the South Pole within a few weeks of each other. Amundsen's journey *went* smoothly and his entire team returned safe and sound a month later. In contrast, as *we* have already learnt, Scott and his companions were beaten to their goal and ultimately lost their lives. *What* factors led to these *two* totally different results?

Amundsen's only goal was to reach the South Pole before anyone else. In contrast, Scott's expedition *was* meant to be a voyage of scientific discovery and he put together a large scientific team including a zoologist, meteorologist, geologists and biologists. Some experts believe *that* Amundsen's clear focus on a single goal was key to his success.

Scott planned to use a mixture of transport – motor sledges, pony and *dog* sledges and 'man-hauling', in other words, the men themselves pulling sledges. *The* first motor sledge broke down before they even set out, the second fell through the ice, and the third broke down shortly afterwards. The ponies were totally unsuited *to* the climate and the heavy work and they all died of cold and hunger. The dogs *were* better-suited to the conditions, but they were worked so hard, and fed so little, that they too died eventually. By contrast, Amundsen's expedition relied entirely *on the best Antarctic transportation at the time*: dog sledges. *He* hired experienced dog drivers and made sure his dogs were fed properly and only travelled for short distances every day.

Amundsen embarked *on* his final trek to the Pole from a point far nearer than Scott. Advance parties *marked* almost the entire length of the route with flags and frequent food depots which were clearly marked so that they could not be missed by the men in the mist and snow. Scott's *food* depots were located far less frequently. Scott's team frequently lost *their* way and often had difficulty locating these. *The* food which Scott provided was not adequate for his team's needs. Some of the group were *suffering* from 'scurvy', a condition caused by lack of vitamins which slowly but surely weakens physical strength. Amundsen had taken care to provide enough food, including *a* specially designed mixture which contained vitamins. He supplemented this diet with *fresh seal meat*.

While Scott's story has become a legend of British history, Amundsen's *clear* thinking, expert planning, training and experience meant that he succeeded in his expedition.

UNIT 7

Lesson 7.4, Listening, Exercise B

7.3 **C = Caroline T = Thomas**

C: Welcome to *Beyond Brave* with me Caroline Spencer. Today, Thomas Bennett is here to talk to us about tightrope walking. Why has it become such a popular topic recently?

T: Well, what has brought it to public attention is the exploits of contemporary performers such as Nik Wallenda and Philippe Petit.

C: Tell us something about these two extraordinary people.

T: You might say that Nik Wallenda has tightrope walking in his blood. He represents the latest generation of a family who have been circus performers since the 1700s. It was his great-grandfather, Karl Wallenda, who perfected circus acts including the human pyramid, as well as high-wire walking and cycling. He was killed attempting to walk between two skyscrapers in 1978. That's probably why Nik has devoted his life to tightrope walking. In 2011, he successfully completed the same walk in honour of his great-grandfather.

C: Incredible! I find him a very charismatic figure. But he also uses the power of the media to his advantage, doesn't he?

T: Oh yes. I think it's partly as a result of his relationship with TV networks that his exploits have reached such a wide audience. It's been estimated that 16 million people watched his walk across Niagara Falls on live television.

C: You mentioned another great tightrope artist, Philippe Petit, earlier? His accomplishments were made into a film, weren't they?

T: That's right. *Man on Wire* won the Oscar for best documentary in 2008.

C: It's quite an obscure thing to make a documentary about, isn't it?

T: Well, yes it is. And to be honest, if the movie hadn't been made, I don't think there would have been so much interest in the whole idea of tightrope walking. The film tells the story of Petit's 1974 high-wire walk between the Twin Towers of New York's World Trade Centre. His incredibly daring – and I might add illegal – achievement was the focus of the film.

C: What do you mean 'illegal'?

T: Well, because the stunt was so incredibly dangerous. I mean … the guy was going to walk across a wire just two and a half centimetres wide, across a distance of nearly 40 metres which was … wait for it … more than 400 metres above the ground. If anything had gone wrong, well – the consequences would have been utterly dreadful. And New York City didn't want to be associated with the possibly tragic result of such an event, so obviously they never gave Petit permission to carry out the stunt. So the preparations had to be done in secret – examining the site, installing the equipment, the timings, everything. It was a bit like one of those classic bank heists which you see in the movies! He and his team had to get up the two towers in secret, fire a guiding rope from one tower to the other with a bow and arrow …

C: A bow and arrow?!

T: That's right! And then Petit crossed – not just once, but four times – backwards and forwards across the wire while a crowd of thousands gathered below and watched in terrified astonishment. After he'd completed the feat, he was arrested by waiting police officers. The police released him pretty soon afterwards though.

C: And there's been a more recent film, hasn't there?

T: The 2015 movie *The Wire* is a biographical drama of the same story. It's thanks to this that younger people are taking a renewed interest.

UNIT 8

Lesson 8.4, Listening, Exercise B

8.3 **S = Scott A = Angela**

S: Today, we're going to be broadcasting live from a space training facility in Germany. With me is scientist and researcher, Angela Schneider.

A: Good morning, Scott. It's a pleasure to be able to talk to you and your listeners.

S: So what do you do exactly, Angela?

A: I'm a nutritionist by training and over the last few years, I've specialised in research into the effects of a zero-gravity environment on the human body. Good nutrition is critical for human health and of course this is true for those travelling in space, too. It's important that astronauts have a specially designed diet which gives them exactly the right number of calories which they need to do their work and the correct balance of vitamins and nutrients for optimum performance and well-being.

S: What problems do astronauts face in terms of their physical health?

A: Astronauts are known to lose bone density during any extended stay in space, and this means they are at an increased risk of bone fractures once they return to Earth, so we've been looking at ways of dealing with that problem. New diet programmes include vitamin D and calcium supplements. In addition, astronauts follow a programme of resistance training, which has been proved to be very effective in preventing bone density loss.

S: What other nutrients are important?

A: That's an interesting question, Scott. Another essential nutrient that we've been studying is iron. As I'm sure you and your listeners know, iron deficiency in the blood can lead to anaemia – where you don't have enough red blood cells. Some of the symptoms of anaemia are fatigue, dizziness and headaches. So we were focusing on making sure that our astronauts had enough iron in their diet, but we've come to the surprising conclusion that actually, they end up with an *excessive* amount of iron in their blood as a result of living in space for long periods of time. So we're looking to actually reduce the iron content in the foods which we provide for our crews.

S: So … less of the spinach eh?

A: That's right And as well as these vital scientific aspects, we have to make the food palatable for the men and women who are working in space. In the past, some astronauts have complained that the food – in the shape of bite-sized cubes, powders and freeze-dried foodstuffs – was unappetising and bland. Today, we offer foods which are cutting-edge in terms of the latest scientific research, but which are also … well, really tasty actually.

S: Can you give us some examples of what an astronaut might expect to find on the menu here?

A: Um … let me see. Duck breast with capers, lobster, chocolate cake …

S: No! Really?

A: Yes, really. We've teamed up with chefs to come up with really delicious dishes. We even have a 'special occasion' menu for birthdays or when there's a change of crew.

S: That's amazing! Well, Angela. It's been absolutely fascinating to talk to you. Thanks so much.

A: Thank *you*!

UNIT 9

Lesson 9.4, Listening, Exercise B

9.3 **R = Rob S = Sandy C = Cassie**

R: All right, Sandy? What's up?

S: Hi Rob. This is my friend Cassie.

R: Hi, Cassie Good to meet you. How are you doing?

C: Good, thanks.

R: So … you just moved here, Cassie?

C: No, actually. I've lived here for … let me see … for four years.

R: So how come you don't go to our school?

C: I go to a Steiner school.

S: How cool is that? Like – *so* awesome!

R: Um … well, I don't mean to be rude or anything, but … why's that 'awesome' exactly?

S: Cos it's you know … it's really *unique* and stuff. Go on Cassie. Tell Rob all about your school.

C: No, it's OK. You probably don't want to hear about it anyway.

R: Yes … no … I mean, course I want to hear about it.

C: Well, the … you know … philosophy behind the school is that education is about more than just passing exams and learning a load of stuff.

S: That's *so* true!

C: So the idea is that you develop as a, well, a whole person. The school is supposed to develop your artistic and practical skills as well as your intellectual ones. Probably *the* most important thing is imagination. You learn to be a responsible … human being.

R: Yeah, right!

S: Be quiet, Rob!

C: Yeah, sounds daft I know …

S: No, no. Not at all. Don't take any notice of Rob. *I* think it sounds fantastic. I mean … at our school there's a huge amount of pressure on us to revise and pass exams.

R: Hang on. You're right – there *is* a lot of pressure, but I mean – like – I'd be gutted if I didn't get the grades I want to go to uni. So, there *is* a reason behind the pressure.

S: Yeah, but it's too much. Even the teachers are under pressure. If we don't get good exam grades, then they get into a lot of trouble. These inspectors come round every term and check *everything*.

R: Anyway, tell us some more about *your* school. Is it one of those places where you can, you know, do anything you want? Muck about all day? Not go to lessons.

C: No, it's not like that at all. Maybe I'm not explaining it well. It's more to do with *who you are*. For instance, we're not in classes according to our age – everybody lumped in together just because their birthdays happen to be in the same year. We're grouped according to our interests and stage of development. Each person is treated differently and you can learn at your own pace and in a way that suits you.

S: Do you have assembly in the morning, like we do?

C: No, we start the day with group exercises, recitals and songs. It's supposed to put you in the mood to learn – forget any negative thoughts, get in the right space to really focus. Then we have a two-hour lesson which is always based on one topic. It's not like – first, maths, then geography, then English like most other schools.

R: So why's it called 'Steiner' anyway?

C: Rudolf Steiner was the founder of the whole … philosophy … the system. He was this Austrian bloke who lived in … I'm not sure … at the beginning of the 20th century anyway. Today, there are hundreds of Steiner schools all over the world.

S: I think you're so lucky, Cassie. I wish I could go to your school.

UNIT 10

Lesson 10.4, Listening, Exercise B
10.3 J = Jonathan A = Antonia

J: Hiya. Jonathan. How you doing?

A: All right? I'm Antonia. You here for the interview?

J: Yep. Been waiting long?

A: Nah – 'bout five minutes. There's tea and coffee here. D'you want something?

J: Yeah, I wouldn't mind a cuppa.

A: Sorted.

J: Cheers.

A: So … we're both up for the same job?

J: Yeah. You done anything like this before?

A: No. You?

J: Well, I've studied – conservation I mean, so I've done a lot of field trips and stuff. I spent last summer working on the Isle of Skye in Scotland. But the Orkneys …

A: What? I've never been to either. I guess you've got a better idea of what the job will involve – if you lived in Skye?

J: Well, it's a commitment. It's quite cut off. I know you can fly, but it's expensive and sometimes, the ferries don't run. That's my only hesitation … It's a bit of an isolated place to live all year round.

A: You can say that again. It bothers me a bit, too, if I'm honest. I heard they have a tendency to cancel flights and ferries because of bad weather. You know I, erm, I'm not sure how I feel about that.

J: Yeah. You're right. The job looks great though. Everything I love doing. But I have no desire to be stuck there!

A: Yes, what a great thing to spend your time doing. You know … looking on the bright side …

Lesson 10.4, Listening, Exercise C
10.4 D = Dr Ramsey J = Jonathan

D: Jonathan Wheeler?

J: Hello Dr Ramsey. How do you do?

D: Good morning, Jonathan. Would you like to come on through? Can I get you anything? Tea? Coffee?

J: A glass of water would be great, thank you.

D: Please have a seat. So … you've just graduated. Tell me more!

J: Yes, that's right. I have a degree in environmental science from the University of East Anglia and actually have practical experience from several field trips.

D: And I see that you worked with the Nature Trust on the Isle of Skye last year. So you've worked in Scotland before?

J: Yes, that's correct. I was there for two months. It was fascinating.

D: And your field trips … one was studying birds in Northumberland …

J: Yes, we studied their natural habitats.

D: And you also went to the Forest of Dean.

J: Yes … to study the breeding patterns of the deer that live there.

D: Well, that's all good experience. How did you find the physical side of things? The post requires you to be physically fit – out in all weathers – that kind of thing.

J: Oh, I like hard work. I've done a lot of fencing, maintaining paths … that kind of thing.

D: OK. And I see here at the bottom of your form that you're very much committed to the environment and nature – you want to preserve it, you say here.

J: Yes, I think a lot of things are endangering so much of the environment – for instance, things like tourism and industry – and it's happening very quickly. So, while there is still time, I think we should carry out research and … hopefully … we will protect the wildlife we have – keep it for future generations.

D: One last question. What attracted you to this job in particular?

J: I really feel that the job is an ideal opportunity for me and it involves everything that I enjoy doing.

6.1 Challenging journeys

VOCABULARY

A

1 uncharted
2 impenetrable
3 globetrotters
4 embarked
5 heart
6 provisions
7 long-haul
8 beaten

B

1 off
2 for
3 round
4 against
5 back
6 out
7 up
8 from

GRAMMAR

A

1 can't
2 might
3 likely
4 may have decided
5 have
6 possibility
7 must
8 may well

B

1 may well have
2 extremely probable/likely that
3 must have left
4 might have forgotten
5 a distinct possibility
6 can't have been

6.2 Inquisitive minds

GRAMMAR

A

1 reading
2 to spread
3 to maintain
4 to do
5 telling

B

1 c 2 d 3 e 4 a 5 b 6 f

C

1 b 2 a

VOCABULARY

A

1 quiet
2 By
3 take
4 greet
5 away
6 order
7 tidy
8 tear

B

1 and wide
2 to-riches
3 and soul
4 after time
5 to back
6 but surely
7 by side
8 or-/and-death

6.3 Reading

READING

C

1 Because of the success and recognition his trip to Sumatra had brought him
2 Being taken prisoner and lack of supplies (falling ill only happened after he had decided to turn back)
3 He was either very optimistic and determined or he wanted to hide his misfortunes.
4 They also disappeared.

6.4 Listening

LISTENING

B

Possible answers

1 (Robert Falcon) Scott and (Roald) Amundsen
2 to (be the first to) reach the South Pole
3 January 1912 and 1911: the speaker says that Amundsen reached the South Pole 34 days earlier
4 Amundsen reached the South Pole first; Scott and his men died on the return journey

C

Historical background
Goals
Route planning
Food and nutrition
Transport

D

Possible answers

1 to map the area and study it
2 It was very hard – illness, injury, hunger and cold.
3 tents, sleeping bags, building materials, food, fuel, bedding, clothing, scientific equipment
4 Scott – to study the area and to reach the South Pole; Amundsen – only to reach the South Pole
5 motor sledges, pony and dog sledges, man-hauling
6 the motor sledges didn't work, the ponies died, he didn't know how to handle the dogs
7 carefully, using flags and clearly marked food depots
8 he didn't allow enough calories per man; he didn't include any vitamins in the diet

6.5 Write an expository essay

WRITING

B

1 c 2 e 3 a 4 b 5 d

C

1 a 2 c 3 d 4 e 5 b

WRITING PRACTICE

C

Model answer

Travel broadens the mind, they say, and I believe this to be generally true. Some people are apprehensive about finding themselves in unfamiliar places, but life is supposed to be an adventure. Three of the many benefits of travel are learning about the world, reaching a better understanding of your own country and teaching you about yourself.

First, travel can teach you more about the world than any book, because you are experiencing the culture of another country first-hand. Engaging with the local people, you learn about their history and traditions, habits, food and even the way they think.

Second, it forces you to make comparisons – how your own culture differs from the one you are visiting. You will notice the cultural differences and see what makes your home country unique. In short, having travelled, you will see your own country with new eyes.

Finally, you can learn a lot about yourself by travelling. You will learn how you cope with unfamiliar situations, how you react to strange habits and customs. You will also learn about how much you are able to tolerate. Travelling will also test your language and social skills. You will return home a different person if you have fully immersed yourself in the experience of travelling.

In summary, travelling is a whole education in itself. The benefits gained from travel and experiencing other countries first-hand – greater knowledge of the world and how people do things differently (or the same), a new perspective on your own country and the self-knowledge gained – are immeasurable. In addition, you will have memories to treasure for a lifetime.

7.1 Beyond the limits

GRAMMAR

A

1 wasn't 2 that/which 3 it 4 it's 5 to 6 who/that 7 when 8 that/when

B

Possible answers

1 It was to raise money for charity that I applied to run the race.
2 It's the psychological not the physical challenge that's a problem for me!
3 It's only now that I've been running for five days that I've noticed the pain in my legs.
4 It was my sister who persuaded me to enter the race.
5 It wasn't a marathon that I ran – it was an ultramarathon!

C

Possible answers

1 It was the landscape paintings that they really wanted to see.
2 It was him who/that was to blame for breaking the window, not her.
3 It was the part at the end that Steven didn't understand.
4 It's you (that) I'm talking to!
5 It's the cost that bothers me.
6 It was because Eliza was scared that she said 'no'.
7 It's (only) when/after something's gone that you really appreciate it.
8 It was only when I got back that I realised how dangerous it was. / It wasn't until I got back that I realised how dangerous it was.

VOCABULARY

A

1 disgusted
2 resilient
3 superior
4 humble
5 devastated
6 courageous

B

1 courageous
2 humble
3 devastated
4 frustrated/grumpy
5 indifferent
6 superior
7 grumpy
8 hysterical

PRONUNCIATION

A

1 ↘ falling
2 ↗ rising
3 ↗ rising
4 ↘ falling
5 ↘ falling
6 ↗ rising

7.2 Extreme jobs

VOCABULARY

A

1 land 2 sick 3 competition 4 pressure 5 application 6 conditions

B

1 immensely
2 utterly
3 altogether
4 noticeably
5 relatively
6 remarkably
7 outright
8 radically
9 practically
10 somewhat

GRAMMAR

A

1 What ~~that~~ happened was I got confused.
2 Why ~~crashed~~ the computer **crashed** I have no idea!
3 Pets are easy – **all** they ~~all~~ need is food, water and some attention.
4 **What** ~~That~~ Lara likes about summer is being able to sleep on the balcony.
5 **All you** ~~You all~~ need is a snack and some good company.
6 **That's what** ~~What's that~~ Simon can't stand about this job – the silly rules!
7 **What** ~~That~~ we ended up doing was taking the train.
8 I didn't have my phone on me so what **I** did ~~I do~~ was ask a colleague to borrow hers.

B

1 What they did in the end was turn back.
2 All we need is a map.
3 What I can't stand is sleeping in a tent.
4 What Rex loves is playing with his ball in the garden.
5 All they needed was a drink of water.
6 What you need is a holiday.
7 What Tanya wanted more than anything was to be a ballerina.
8 All she's asking for is a short break.

C

1 What she loves most about
2 All (that) she wants is a
3 what he did was phone
4 What I can't stand about/stand when
5 What I've realised is
6 All my sister remembers

PRONUNCIATION

A

1 The film was quite amazing, actually – we loved it!
2 I don't want any old doctor – I want the one I always see.
3 The questions they asked me were quite ridiculous!
4 Any questions you have will be answered at the end, OK?
5 Well, you don't tell your password to just anybody.
6 Let's go – anywhere's better than here!
7 The test was quite hard but he thinks he passed.
8 'Which film do you want to watch?''Oh, any one. You choose.'

7.3 Reading

READING

B

Possible answers

1 drowning
2 It is the greatest sensual experience.
3 that it is a life spent travelling and having fun in exotic places
4 only if you are in the top rank and have sponsorships and endorsements

C

1 It
2 you
3 such incidents
4 Which
5 one
6 Many
7 that
8 those who
9 it's
10 that

D

1 surfing; C
2 the reader/people in general; E
3 shark attacks; A
4 dangers/riptides; A
5 a wave; A
6 surfers; E
7 surfing big waves/catching a wave as tall as a tower block; A
8 non-surfers/onlookers; E
9 the lifestyle; A
10 prize money; A

7.4 Listening

LISTENING

B

1 circus
2 1978
3 16 million
4 documentary
5 New York
6 40
7 in secret
8 bow and arrow

C

1 b
2 c
3 c
4 a

7.5 Write a cover letter

WRITING

B

2 climbing ability; skill in the use and maintenance of power tools; working at height; calmness in tense situations; ability to follow instructions and to work well with others

C

Possible answers

1 led/managed
2 tasked with collecting
3 managed
4 oversaw/coordinated/organised
5 I (also) developed

WRITING PRACTICE

C

Model answer

Dear Mr Scholes,

I am writing to apply for the post of Lifeguard Team Leader at Ocean Resorts.

You will see from my CV (attached) that I have four years' experience as a beach lifeguard in Australia, where I headed a team of 20 lifeguards and coordinated sea and air rescue services when necessary. I have rescued swimmers from shark attacks on several occasions, so am able to work under pressure. During that time, I trained as a paramedic and have a good knowledge of first aid.

I have a lifesaving qualification from Australia and since coming to this country have acquired an RLSS qualification. In fact, I achieved the highest grade of my intake. I have worked poolside at a spa here for three years, and my duties included liaising with customer care and sometimes helping with front-of-house duties. Although I am no longer part of the Australian 4x4 medley relay team, I have kept up my training regime and remain as strong a swimmer as ever.
I look forward to your response.

Best regards,
Bruce MacNamara

8.1 Health and wellness

VOCABULARY

A

1 sore
2 rash
3 rate
4 pressure
5 sprained
6 fractured
7 pulled
8 dislocate

B

1 fractured
2 pulled
3 inflamed
4 rate
5 sore
6 sprained
7 rash
8 blood

GRAMMAR

A

1 into
2 in
3 to
4 To/With
5 with/in
6 to
7 of/about
8 among/of

B

1 the person whose fitness business is now worth millions
2 the person (who) I trust more than anyone
3 whereby it is impossible for me to get a virus
4 a training injury from which you might never recover
5 people for whom exercise is not a priority
6 into whose pockets the profits all go, is very satisfied

8.2 Sport and wellness

VOCABULARY

A

1 gut feeling
2 gave him food for thought
3 got cold feet
4 give it his best shot
5 out of his depth
6 throwing in the towel

B

1 fizzy
2 Crunchy/Crisp
3 sour
4 mild
5 appetising
6 creamy/cheesy
7 tangy; acidic
8 bland
9 soggy

PRONUNCIATION

A

1 isn't really my cup of tea
2 made a meal of it
3 keep an eye out
4 with a pinch of salt
5 head and shoulders above
6 moving the goalposts

GRAMMAR

A

1 more
2 either
3 Most people
4 some
5 others
6 very few
7 of
8 little

B

1 When you're doing a serious hike, you can't drink too much ~~of~~ water – in fact, most people don't drink enough.
2 There were two vegan options, but I didn't fancy **either** ~~both~~ of them.
3 **Those** ~~They~~ who followed the diet reported an average loss of three kilos in the first week.
4 You have too much sugar and salt in your diet – it's best if you cut back on **both** ~~neither~~.
5 There are only **a** / ~~only~~ **very** few restaurants that serve good vegetarian food in this city.
6 You drink a lot of coffee, and I think you'd sleep better if you drank less ~~of~~.
7 These are your books – **mine** ~~my~~ are still over there where I left them.
8 Jamie only needs six hours sleep a night, but I can never seem to get enough ~~of~~.

8.3 Reading

READING

A

Charcoal – c
Ketogenic – a
Cauliflower – d
Vegan – b

B

1 the keto diet
2 the vegan diet
3 the charcoal diet

C

Possible answers

1 Interestingly; Admittedly
2 supposedly; allegedly
3 positive attitude: There's no doubt
neutral attitude: It is also thought to
sceptical attitude: it seems
4 colloquial asides: I don't know about you
tag questions: Sounds rather scientific, doesn't it?
rhetorical questions: Black cheese … anyone?

8.4 Listening

LISTENING

C

1 b 2 a 3 a 4 a

D

1 right amount of calories; vitamins; nutrients; vitamin D; supplements
2 bone fractures
3 resistance training
4 excessive
5 duck breast; capers; lobster; chocolate cake

8.5 Write a summary

WRITING

B

Possible answers

1 'overtraining syndrome'; symptoms; physiological; psychological
2 Summary a misses the point and is irrelevant.
Summary b is the best because it includes the key points, phrased clearly in the writer's own words and without changing the original meaning.
Summary c repeats language from the text almost word for word.

C

Possible answers

1 increased heart rate; weight loss; excessive thirst
2 the negative physical effects of overtraining
3 The physical symptoms of overtraining to look out for are loss of both weight and muscle, inability to put on muscle and constant thirst. Further symptoms include an increase in heart rate, fluctuations in blood pressure, injury and susceptibility to infections.

WRITING PRACTICE

C

Model answer

Physical symptoms of overtraining syndrome include loss of both weight and muscle, inability to put on muscle and constant thirst. Psychological symptoms include a lack of readiness for training, sleeping problems and tiredness, changes in mood and a loss of confidence. Overtraining syndrome can be treated by identifying symptoms, seeking medical help and adopting a varied training regime with periods of rest.

9.1 Language and behaviour

VOCABULARY

A

1 chuffed
2 whingeing
3 bloke; dude
4 dodgy; nicked
5 telly; like; wheels

B

1 shambles 2 crashed 3 could do with 4 set her back
5 grand 6 quid 7 skint 8 sorted

PRONUNCIATION

A

1 I feel kind of strange – like I've been here before or something.
2 We have to give a talk, or a speech, or something like that.
3 I have to do some jobs – shopping, cleaning and so on.
4 You know, I think that, in some way or another, he must be involved.
5 So, in a sense, this is the easiest job in the world!
6 What do you take me for – some sort of fool?
7 Don't give me excuses like you overslept or whatever.
8 My course covers health and safety issues, stuff like that.

GRAMMAR

A

1 Those students who haven't completed the assignment should stay behind at the end of the lecture.
2 Both of the solutions he suggested sounded a little like a desperate attempt to please the boss.
3 He invested all the money he'd saved up into some crazy get-rich-quick scheme and lost everything.
4 The thing that annoys Pierre most is the way young people don't seem to care about language.
5 Three of the 20 people present were first-time attendees.
6 The idea that simply punishing children teaches them to behave has fallen out of favour with many modern educationalists.
7 Do you know a good place to eat that would suit a group of hungry teenagers?
8 Sometimes it seems to me that almost everyone I know is hooked on some computer game or other.

B

1 I spend **almost** all my free time ~~almost~~ doing sport.
2 The belief **that** ~~what~~ you can change things is all you need in order to make a difference.
3 The person (**who/that**) ~~where~~ I spoke to didn't seem to have a clue what was happening.
4 I need a place **to stay** ~~for staying~~ for a few days.
5 Both ~~of~~ / of **the** ideas seem a little hard to put into practice.
6 The woman ~~who~~ / who **is** sitting next to Claire is Frances.
7 Very few ~~of~~ / of **the** people in this country have travelled abroad.
8 The interviewer was impressed by the fact (**that**) ~~how~~ I knew so much about their company.

C

1 most
2 The / That
3 one
4 of
5 their
6 that

9.2 Animal behaviour

VOCABULARY

A

1 c 2 f 3 h 4 b 5 g 6 d 7 a 8 e

B

1 gazing 2 fidgeting 3 shrugged 4 shook 5 blinked
6 beckoned 7 pointed 8 raised

GRAMMAR

A

1 Having got/woken up early
2 Despite not knowing
3 Done properly, the job
4 Not being practical, reading the
5 Having just bought a new
6 Given the right

B

1 ~~They were feeling~~ (**Feeling**) threatened, the animals instinctively hid behind the wall.
2 **Having** ~~Had~~ never / **Never having** ~~never~~ been on a plane before, I was both excited and nervous.
3 If ~~you~~ / you **are** successful in your application, you will be notified by email.
4 **Having grown** ~~Grown~~ up in the USA, Marvin has always spoken English well.
5 ~~Been~~ (**Being**) exhausted and short of money, Carrie cut short her trip to Bolivia.
6 Before **starting** ~~started~~ work in insurance, Lionel was a factory worker.
7 Despite **not/never having** ~~I hadn't~~ been there before, I soon found my way around.
8 While suffering badly from flu, **Angela was visited by** a couple of close friends ~~visited Angela~~ every day.

C

1 b 2 c 3 c 4 b 5 a 6 b

9.3 Reading

READING

C

1 T
2 F (They were told this, but the experiment was to see if their behaviour was influenced by the words they had processed.)
3 F (They were timed from the moment they finished the task to see how quickly they interrupted, if at all.)
4 T
5 F (The opposite appears to be true – we make major life choices based on similarities of the names of people and things to our own name.)

D

Possible answers

1 to see how long the students would wait before interrupting and to see if students who had been exposed to the 'rude' words interrupted sooner
2 As predicted, students who had been given the 'rude' words interrupted sooner than the others.
3 Bargh himself was reluctant to conclude that exposure to certain types of words makes us behave in that way (because it was a very small sample).

9.4 Listening

LISTENING

C

1 F ('I've lived here for … four years.')
2 T
3 F (Rob says, 'I'd be gutted if I didn't get the grades I want to go to uni. … there is a reason behind the pressure.')
4 T
5 T
6 F (The Steiner school has a *'holistic' approach to learning* and doesn't divide it into specific subject areas.)

D

3 I've lived here for [~~let me see~~] … ~~for~~ four years.
4 ~~Be~~cause it's [~~you~~ know] … it's really *unique* [~~and~~ stuff].
5 Is it [one ~~of~~] those places where ~~you~~ can, [~~you~~ know], do anything you want?

9.5 Write a conclusion to an academic report

WRITING

B

a 3 b 2 c 1 d 4

C

1 c 2 b 3 e 4 a/d 5 d/a

D

Colon (Students underline any two of the following)
'… individual responsibility is ignored: normal values and the ability to reason are abandoned.'
'… convergence theorists argue that individuals in a crowd do not lose personal identity: personal beliefs and values are communicated …'
'… our research revealed that … in a crowd: crowd catalysts such as police presence …'
Semi-colon
'… most of the research so far stems from disciplines such as psychology and sociology; there has been little recent research into crowd behaviour at large outdoor events.'
'They fail to demonstrate why some crowds … behave differently; nor do they examine the difference between …'

WRITING PRACTICE

C

Model answer

Our research attempted to answer the questions of whether the use of slang had increased among the general population in recent years. This proved difficult at first; there is no reliable source of data on the frequency of the use of slang words from before 1970 with which to compare our findings. Nonetheless, we are confident our results relatively accurately reflect the current situation.

There is no doubt that we have been exposed to more informal language and slang since the introduction of the internet and social media, on television and in films, too. However, our research shows that this is not reflected in the workplace: the average person is not using or exposed to slang more frequently in his/her professional life. In our most recent survey, a larger proportion of the subjects were women; previous surveys were heavily weighted in favour of men. It is clear from the results that women today on average use slang as much as, but not more than, men.

Our research also found that the most frequently used slang expressions have remained much the same for the past 20 years, with newer terms and expressions not yet replacing the older words and phrases in popularity. We suggest that such data be collected periodically to see how the use of individual slang terms changes over time.

In conclusion, our data do not show that the use of slang has increased.

10.1 Urban problems

VOCABULARY

A

1 designated
2 habitats; endangered
3 architectural; heritage
4 ruins; settlement
5 preserve; funds; refurbish

B

1 urge **2** desire **3** responsibility **4** obligation **5** failure **6** refusal **7** tendency **8** reminder

PRONUNCIATION

B

1 up
2 down
3 down
4 up
5 down
6 down
7 up
8 up

GRAMMAR

A

1 h **2** c **3** i **4** b **5** j **6** a **7** g **8** f **9** e **10** d

B

1 despite it being
2 any case, I have
3 namely Australia and China
4 owing to the bad weather
5 whereas the return journey seemed
6 As a matter of fact

10.2 How to change the world

VOCABULARY

A

1 b **2** a **3** c **4** c **5** a **6** c **7** b **8** c

B

1 passionate
2 effective
3 personal
4 persuasive
5 apathetic
6 community

GRAMMAR

A

1 Some people think we can change the world but I don't ~~think we can change the world~~.
2 If you get the opportunity to go, you should ~~take the opportunity to go~~.
3 A lot of people struggle with course fees and I wish they didn't ~~struggle with course fees~~.
4 They should target governments and ~~they should target~~ large companies.
5 We're going to have food and ~~we're going to have~~ music.
6 You asked me if I thought we could make a difference and the answer is yes ~~I do think we can make a difference~~.
7 I know a lot of people who are pessimistic about the future, but I'm not ~~pessimistic about the future~~.
8 ~~Are~~ you joining us for pizza? ~~Do you have~~ any preference ~~as to what we order~~?

B

1 do it / do so
2 he does
3 I do
4 do that/it
5 so
6 do so/that
7 hope not
8 do that

10.3 Reading

READING

A

traffic congestion and the related problem of air pollution

B

Possible answers

	Problems	Solutions	Criticism
UK	Health problems	Workplace parking fee improve public transport, electric cars	Job losses, strain on public transport
Paris	Premature deaths	Anti-pollution stickers, fines if no sticker, car manufacturers make non-polluting cars	Few people buy the stickers, people taxed off the road
Freiburg		Pedestrianised city centre, cheap and efficient public transport, prioritise walking, cycling and public transport, incentives for people who don't use cars, good urban planning	

10.4 Listening

LISTENING

B

Possible answers

1 a job interview
2 living in an isolated place
3 the job

C

1 environmental science
2 East
3 two
4 (natural) habitats
5 deer
6 paths
7 preserve
8 endangering
9 research

D

1 When speaking to Dr Ramsey, Jonathan says 'Hello Dr Ramsey. How do you do?'
2 When speaking to Dr Ramsey, Jonathan says 'A glass of water would be great, thank you.'
3 When speaking to Dr Ramsey, Jonathan says 'I have a degree in environmental science from the University of East Anglia and actually have practical experience from several field trips.'
4 When speaking to Dr Ramsey, Jonathan says 'I really feel that the job is an ideal opportunity for me and it involves everything that I enjoy doing.'

10.5 Write a persuasive essay

WRITING

B

Possible answers

1 Tourism has a largely negative impact.
2 environmental damage; disrespect for local cultures, traditions and behaviours; lack of benefit for local workers and business
3 Yes. Understanding different cultures; money and job creation

C

1 Paragraph 4
2 Counter-argument: that mass tourism brings economic benefits – more money and more jobs. Rebuttal: the jobs are seasonal, low-skilled and insecure; most of the money goes to large foreign companies, not the local economy.
Yes, the rebuttal directly answers the counter-argument.
3 Counter-argument: 'There is an argument that …'
Rebuttal: 'While this is true up to a point, …'

WRITING PRACTICE

C

Model answer

More and more shopping malls are being built in or near towns and cities all over the world. While some argue that they provide a more convenient and fun shopping 'experience', I would argue that they create a negative impact on local communities which outweighs their convenience.
Perhaps the greatest negative impact of shopping malls is felt by local businesses who, being unable to compete, can lose up to 90% of their business. The community as a whole loses out, because local businesses play an important role in creating community identity.

Shopping malls also have a huge carbon footprint; shopping centres in the UK are estimated to create 12 million tonnes of waste each year, including packaging and food waste. They also waste energy through excessive lighting, day and night, and heat loss through constantly opening doors.

Supporters of shopping mall developments claim that people benefit from the lower prices at malls, somewhere to park, the convenience of being able to do all their shopping under one roof and the fact that malls also provide all kinds of leisure activities, turning shopping into a fun day out for all the family. Yet the concentration of so much in one place brings its own problems, such as increased traffic, pollution, overcrowding and noise.

In summary, the negative effects of shopping malls on local communities outweigh any advantages. They destroy local businesses and community identity, create an enormous amount of waste and have a negative impact on the environment. These are all reasons enough, I believe, to encourage people to shop locally.

Notes

Notes

Notes